Ps 7951

BIRDS

OF THE
INDIAN SUBCONTINENT

For
**Nikhat, Samiha,
Raghu & Keya**

BIRDS

OF THE
INDIAN SUBCONTINENT

Bikram Grewal

LOCAL COLOUR

Published by Local Colour Limited
Unit 504, 5th floor, Westlands Centre, 20 Westlands Road
Quary Bay, Hong Kong

e-mail: ppro@netvigator.com

A CIP catalogue record for this book is available from the British
Library

Ditributed in the United Kingdom and Europe by Hi Marketing
38 carver Road, London SE24 9LT. Fax: (0171) 274-9160

Distributed in the United States by Seven Hills Book Distributors
Fax: (888) 777-7799

Project Editor: Ria Patel
Illustrations Editor: Ranjana Sengupta, Rajinder Bist
Design: Gulmohur Press
Map Artwork: Ajay Verma

Printed and bound in Hong Kong

Photo credits: Otto Pfister: pages vi-vii, viii-ix, x-xii, xiv, xx, xxvii,
xxix, xxx

ISBN : 962-8711-07-5

The author and the Publisher are constantly looking to improve the
book. Readers are requested to send their suggestions to:

Bikram Grewal
101/4, Kaushalya Park
Hauz Khas, New Delhi
India, 110 016
Email: biks@vsnl.com

ACKNOWLEDGEMENTS

The author and the Publishers would like to thank the following people for their help in making this book possible.

Rattan Singh, Bittu Sahgal, Kamal Sahai, Lt Gen. RK Gaur, Radhika Singh, Krupakar Senani, MK Kuppuraj, Dr. AG Urfi, Tania Sood, Joanna Van Gruisen, Ashok Dilwali, Rajinder Bist, Ganga Grewal, the late S Deb Roy, Ajay Verma, Tim and Carol Inskipp, Tara Sahgal, Geoff Cloke, Miel Sahgal, Richa Bhaskar, Steve Madge, Nigel Redman, MB Krishna, Navein OC, S Subramanya, JN Prasad, S Karthikeyan, Mohit Aggarwal, AV Manoj, E Hanumantha Rao, Thakur Dalip Singh, Dr Asad Rahmani, Gertrud Denzau, Hem Sagar Baral, Helmut Denzau, Otto Pfister, Sue Earle, Sanjeeva Pandey, Ranjana Sengupta, Deepshikha Singh, Sudhanshu Gupta, Ria Patel, Peter Morris, Tim Loseby, Goren Eckstrom, Simon Harrap, Per Alstrom, Indu Chandrashekar, Suresh Elamon, Manjunath Hedge, Krys Kazmierchek, Tikaram Giri and Alpana Khare.

Contents

INTRODUCTION

The Indian region is incredibly rich in birdlife. Over 1200 of the world's 8650 species of birds are found in the region. This number rises to over 2000 with subspecies included, which makes the Indian check list twice the size of those of Europe and North America. This abundance is due to the variety of habitats and climate. Altitude ranges from sea level to the peaks of the Himalaya, the world's highest mountain range; rainfall from its lowest in the Rajasthan desert to its highest in the north-eastern town of Cherrapunji in Meghalaya, one of the wettest places in the world. Unlike more temperate zones, the climate of large areas of the Indian region encourages continuous plant growth and insect activity—abundant sources of avian nourishment throughout the year.

The peoples of the region have lived for thousands of years in close contact with its rich natural life. The earliest Hindu religious work, the *Rig Veda*, refers to some 20 species of birds, but its anonymous compilers must have been familiar with many more. Legends and myths grew around certain familiar species. The Brahminy Duck, for example, became the symbol of fidelity; the pairs mating for life, separating from one another at night to feed but keeping in contact by calls, and then reuniting at dawn. The *chataka*, either the Hawk Cuckoo or the Pied Crested Cuckoo, was said to drink only rainwater, no matter how thirsty it was. The Sanskrit poet Kalidasa, frequently uses bird imagery in his plays and poetry. His *Meghdoot* is a sensuous poem about a lover exiled from his beloved in the monsoon, traditionally the season for passion and romance among humans, and in fact the time when large water birds like storks, cormorants, egrets and cranes breed. Addressing a storm cloud the lover says,

> hen-cranes will know the time ripe for mating
> and rejoice when they note in the sky
> your eye-delighting presence; rest assured
> they will attend on you in patterned flight.

Jewelled peacock, in the Golden Temple treasury, Amritsar

Blue-throated Barbet credited to Mansur, c. 1615

Not only poets, rulers too, expressed interest in ornithology. The great Mughals maintained royal menageries and revelled in hunting on a grand scale. But they were also meticulous in their observations of wildlife. In the 16th century, Babar, the first Mughal Emperor, observed his first Pied Myna.

> When I threw a bridge over the Ganges and crossed it, driving the enemy before me, I saw in Lucknow, Oudh and these countries a species of *sharak* which has a white breast and a piebald head with a black back. I had never seen it before. This species probably does not learn to speak at all.

Babar's keen interest in nature was inherited by his son Humayun, who even when fleeing India after being defeated by an Afghan invader, stopped to have a painting made of a bird of a type he had never seen before which happened to fly into his tent. The Emperor Jehangir noted with amazement the devotion of a Sarus Crane to its dead mate. The bird refused to leave the bones of its spouse, and when, weak and dying, it was lifted from the remains, worms and maggots were found to have dug into its breast.

The Mughal empire began to disintegrate at the beginning of the 18th century, and the spread of British power gave enormous scope to officers in the police, civil, forest and armed services to observe the region's plentiful bird life. As British power grew, there were increasing numbers of such officers, whose jobs required much less crippling paperwork than those of their successors today. The result was the pioneering work of Brian Hodgson, TC Jerdon and Edward Blyth, often called the founders of Indian ornithology. Jerdon's *Birds of India*, published in 1862, was based on the work of all three men, assisted by a loyal group of field workers.

The next major advance in ornithological knowledge came with the arrival of Allan O Hume—perhaps more widely known as a founder of the Indian National Congress. For over a decade he and his team collected birds for study over most of the Indian region. Hume also collected, edited and published eleven volumes of bird observations between 1872 and 1888. These volumes, collectively known as *Stray Feathers*, are valuable reference works even today.

A year after the last *Stray Feathers* was published, WT Blandford and Eugene W Oates produced the first volume of *Fauna of British India*. Three more volumes were published in the following nine years. These were the most significant reference works on Indian ornithology for at least twenty years. They included detailed observations from parts of the Indian region uncovered by previous work.

The next major work was by EC Stuart Baker, an Indian police officer for nearly twenty years, whose energetic enthusiasm for ornithology played an important role in popularising this branch of natural history study in India. In 1898 he joined the Bombay Natural History Society (BNHS), which had been gaining members and authority steadily since it was founded in 1883. Some of Baker's classic early work appeared first in the journal of the BNHS, including *Game Birds of India*. But Baker's most notable works are the eight bird volumes of the second edition of *Fauna of British India*, published between 1922 and 1930, and the *Nidification of Birds of the Indian Empire*, published between 1932 and 1935.

Brahminy Duck

Indian Postal Stamps, 1975

The 20th century saw an increasing number of talented and dedicated ornithologists in India—but the most celebrated and long lasting ornithological partnership was between Salim Ali and Dillon Ripley. Salim Ali's interest in birds resulted from a boyhood visit to the office of the Bombay Natural History Society with the corpse of a strange bird which he had shot. As he himself recalls.

This must have been somewhere in 1908, and my first contact with the BNHS which was to become such an important element in the shaping of my life and career. All my nervousness vanished completely in the face of the charming kindliness...of Mr Millard [the Honorary Secretary]. I then realized that perhaps ALL white men were not the dogs our youthful fancy had painted them...I fumbled out my credentials and the little paper packet containing the mystery bird. He identified it at a glance as a Yellow-throated Sparrow, and bid me follow him to the reference cabinets...He patiently opened drawer after drawer for me to see the hundreds of different birds found in the Indian Empire, and I believe it was at this moment that my curiosity about birds really clicked.

The Yellow-throated Sparrow showed Salim Ali his way forward in life and in 1944 he met a young US army man in transit through Bombay, who was to be his colleague, fellow-ornithologist and explorer. Dillon Ripley and Salim Ali planned ornithological field-trips for the post-war years, the first to be achieved being a journey to the Mishmi Hills in the extreme north-east of Assam. It was on this trip that they conceived the idea of their *Handbook of the Birds* of India and Pakistan. The first step towards compiling a handbook was an up-to-date check list, provided by Ripley's *A Synopsis of the Birds of India and Pakistan* published by the BNHS in 1961. The first volume of the *Handbook* was published in 1968, and the tenth and last in 1974, four days after Salim Ali's 78th birthday.

The *Handbook*, listing 2060 birds, remains the standard and most exhaustive work on Indian birds as such. What this guide aims to provide for the first time is a valuable aid to field identification through photographic illustrations of a large number of the region's birds.

Oriental and Subregions

In the 19th century, PL Sclater studied the world's birds and divided the planet into six bio-geographic realms. This was later slightly modified to apply to all animals. The Oriental realm covers South and South East Asia, the Himalaya separating it from the Palearctic to the north. Leaf birds are found exclusively in this region and broadbills nearly so. In general the region's birds have closest affinities with those of tropical Africa.

The Indian subregion has further been divided into seven different areas, in which different types of birds are found.

Western Himalaya

The northernmost of these areas is the **Himalaya**, which form an arc some 2500 km long and 150 to 400 km broad across the top of the sub-continent. The Himalayan mountains form roughly three parts, the foothills or Sivaliks to the south, the Himachal, or lower mountains, and the Himadri or high Himalaya to the north. The Ladakh plateau, with an average elevation of 5300 m, occupies a large portion of the Indian state of Jammu and Kashmir and consists of steppe country with mountain lakes where birds like the Bar-headed Goose and Brown-headed Gull breed in summer. The state of Himachal Pradesh, and the Kumaon and Garhwal regions of the state of Uttar Pradesh lie to the west of Nepal, which falls almost entirely within the central Himalaya. Further east the rainfall increases giving the Eastern Himalaya of Bhutan and Sikkim a very different range of species from those in the west.

Bank Myna community

The **north-west** covers the bulk of Pakistan, the flat plains of the Indian Punjab and the semi-arid and arid plains of Rajasthan in the west. The Punjab (divided now between India and Pakistan) is watered by the five rivers, after which it takes its name, and efficient farming on fertile soil means that it produces an immense surplus of wheat and rice. Further west, wherever irrigation has been possible the desert has bloomed. Mountains of red chillies, for example, can been seen drying next to the fields around Jodhpur, while there are verdant paddy fields in areas irrigated by the great River Indus in Pakistan's Sindh province. Areas without irrigation have to rely on the perennially deficient rainfall, but local grasses have adapted to this, and after a monsoon shower even the desert sprouts rich pasture. Much of the area is in fact thorn scrub rather than true desert. Among the numerous desert birds found in this area are many which are related to species further west. The shifting sands of the desert join ultimately with the Rann of Kutch, a large salt waste which runs into the sea, and are bordered to the south-east by the Aravallis, India's most ancient mountains.

North India comprises the Gangetic plain, enriched by thousands of years of alluvial deposits brought by the River Ganga and her tributaries from the Himalaya. The Gangetic plain is densely populated and highly fertile. This region extends up to an altitude of 1000 m in the north, which also means it includes the low foothills of the Himalaya, and the terai of India and Nepal, once a marshy area covered with dense forest. Much of the terai area has been cleared for farming but some of the forests which still exist reveal the fantastic variety of birdlife which these forests must once have supported.

Peninsular India, bordered on the north-west by the Aravallis and the north by the Vindhya mountains, on the west by the Arabian Sea and the east by the Bay of Bengal, makes up the largest physiographic division of India. The central plateaus of this area, which is also known as the Deccan, rise to over 1000 m in the south, but hardly exceed 500 m in the north. The peninsula has some wonderful

Mixed colony

landscapes, hills and huge boulders littering the countryside, and large areas of forest. Great rivers like the Narmada rise in the heart of the peninsula and flow into the sea. The steep escarpments of the Western Ghats, the mountains which stand between the plateau and the low-lying coastal strip, catch the full force of the monsoon.

The **south-west** region lies within the peninsula, but due to the particularly humid climate and the height of the hills here, its birds, like spiderhunters and laughing thrushes bear strong affinities with those found in the north-east and Burma. The highest of the hills here are the Nilgiris or Blue Mountains, much of whose characteristic downland and shola forest is now under eucalyptus, tea and other plantation crops. Tea is also the main crop of the Annamalai or Elephant Mountains of Kerala, while cardamom and other spices are grown lower down. Perhaps the most ornithologically fascinating part of this area are the forests of the Wynad, where Kerala, Karnataka and Tamil Nadu meet.

The **north-east** and **Bangladesh** region consists of the delta of the Ganga and Brahmaputra, with its tidal estuaries, sandbanks, mud-flats, mangrove swamps and islands. Further upstream are lands drained, and occasionally

Central Indian grasslands

flooded, by these great rivers and their tributaries. The north-east region also extends northwards to include all the forest regions of the states of Arunachal Pradesh, Mizoram, Meghalaya and Nagaland, as well as the Kingdom of Bhutan. As you progress eastwards, the birdlife has increasingly strong affinities with the Indo-Chinese subregion.

Sri Lanka is a remarkable area for birdlife. Although far from large, the country has a wide range of climate and habitat which supports some 400 species and subspecies of birds, including 21 species like the Ceylon Blue Magpie found nowhere else. Many of the island's birds are identical to those found in India, although for some reason vultures have not been able to cross the Palk Strait. Sri Lanka can be divided into three zones, the dry plains of the north, the mountainous central region and the humid wet zone around the capital Colombo. The most useful detailed work exclusively dealing with Sri Lankan ornithology is GM Henry's *A Guide to the Birds of Ceylon*.

Godwits, west coast of India

Habitat

While many common species are spread over large areas of the Oriental realm, others are limited not just to a region but also to habitat. Some birds of the conifer forests of the hills will be found only there, while grassland birds may be restricted to that habitat.

Indian Whiskered Tern

As the subcontinent has a very dense human population, birds which get on well with man flourish. These are not limited to house sparrows, crows and house martins. Indian culture has traditionally respected all forms of life and protected birds before sanctuaries and parks were ever thought of. India's only resident crane, the Sarus, is left unharmed no matter how much of a farmer's pea crop it consumes. The Peacock has in areas a semi-sacred status, which is why it is found in large numbers undisturbed. The Red Junglefowl has a long history of association with man and is the ancestor of the domestic chicken.

City gardens are homes for many species, including tailorbirds, sunbirds, white-eyes, babblers and the ubiquitous myna. Other birds take advantage of cultivation techniques; especially pond herons, who often take up position in paddy fields practising what villagers call *bagla bhakti*—supreme hypocrisy, sitting like a holy man lost in meditation, but in fact just waiting to stab something in the back. Dabchicks or Little Grebes also take up residence in village ponds, while garbage is in great demand by vultures and the pariah kites which along with pariah dogs haunt the rubbish heaps of the sub-continent.

Shallow lagoons, inland jheels or shallow lakes, and rivers are rich habitats for water birds from pelicans, storks, cranes, egrets and cormorants to the jacanas and gallinules among the lotuses, and the waders picking their way along the water's edge probing for food. Huge numbers of migratory waterfowl also congregate at jheels during the winter months. Other birds, like bitterns, conceal themselves among reed beds. Numerous birds of prey can be found near water. The attractive Brahminy Kite is particularly adaptable. It can be seen from the lakes of north India to the sea coasts of the south.

Many birds of the coast are distinctive. Typical is the Indian Reef Heron, seldom found far inland, which feeds on molluscs and crustaceans.

In the more arid inland areas are found larks, chats, sandgrouse and the rare Great Indian Bustard, a stunning bird seen in small flocks which fly into land like great avian aircraft. Desert birds tend to be sandy in colouration, which helps to camouflage them.

Forest birds are more difficult to spot especially when they are concealed in the tree canopy. However, they can often be seen in clearings flying from tree to tree or on the edge of forests where the sun can penetrate and there is a great deal of insect activity. Often assorted species form hunting parties and move together through the forest. So in one place you can see woodpeckers, warblers, tits and tree creepers. Often birds can be located and identified through their calls. Here it is also worth noting that Oriental forests are home to many more birds than those nearer either pole. A tropical forest can hold more than 200 bird species at more than 5000 pairs per km, but a northern forest may hold less than 20 species at 200 individuals per km.

Adaptation

The most outstanding way that birds have adapted is, of course, the conversion of their upper limbs into wings, the growth of feathers and the ability to fly. Plumage is further adapted depending on habitat and habits. The feathers of cormorants and snakebirds get drenched to allow them to swim under water, but other birds effectively coat their feathers with oil from oil glands to waterproof them. Plumage and body shape are adapted for specialised flight. Owl feathers are so formed as to give silent flight. Built especially for speed is the Peregrine Falcon, which swoops on its prey from a great height.

Colouring is also an important adaptation. Camouflage is seen for example in sandgrouse, snipe, bitterns, owls and nightjars.

Teeth would weigh down the head of any bird wanting to fly efficiently, and so over the past 100 million years birds have lost them and instead developed gizzards. The gizzard is situated near a bird's centre of gravity. Birds gulp food down into their crop from where it is ground down in the muscular gizzard with the aid of grit and small stones the birds swallow. The ability to disgorge indigestible bones, fur, insect shells or large seeds in the form of pellets is another form of adaptation.

Narcondam Hornbills

Shaheen Falcon

Birds have developed specialised bills and feet for feeding. The most generalised bill perhaps belongs to the omnivorous crow. It is straight, pointed and roughly triangular in section. Birds like herons and kingfishers have more dagger-like bills, suitable for catching fish and frogs. Not all kingfishers need water for their fishing. One of the secrets of the White-breasted Kingfisher's ubiquity is that it can live on insects, lizards and other small terrestrial animals. Other accomplished fish-catchers like cormorants have 'tooth-edged' bills with which they can grip fish.

Dabbling ducks have widened bills with laminations on the edges of the upper and lower mandibles. This adaptation is especially necessary for plankton-sieving shovellers, and the larger spoonbills and flamingos. Shore birds have thin, elongated bills for probing the mud in search for small animals.

Flowering silk-cotton

Birds of prey have developed deeper, shorter and downcurved bills for tearing and piercing flesh. But for them perhaps the most important piece of hunting equipment is their feet. They rely on the strength of their talons to kill.

Most species of birds are animal-eating, but most animals eaten are small invertebrates, in particular insects. Birds like swallows, martins and nightjars catch insects on the wing with wide gapes that scoop in their victims. Many other insects are caught on the plants on which they themselves feed. Small insectivorous birds like warblers have fine pointed beaks for collecting them. Woodpeckers, on the other hand, have strong, dagger-shaped bills, for chiselling wood and prising insects from crevices and beneath bark.

Flowering plants also support a great number of birds, and just as birds have adapted to feeding on flowers, trees and plants too have adapted themselves to being fed on. In 1932 Salim Ali wrote on *Flower-Birds and Bird-Flowers*. He listed as characteristics of the bird-flower that pollenisation is possible only through birds, that they have bright and conspicuous colours (red being a bird's favourite) and no scent (as birds have a very poorly developed sense of smell), but they do have an abundant supply of nectar. Typical bird-flowers of this sort can be seen on the spectacular silk-cotton tree *bombax malabaricum*, which is covered with waxy red or orange blooms around mid-February. Typical newer-birds

Dr. Salim Ali

are sunbirds, which have long, downcurved bills for drinking nectar.

A much larger number of bird species feeds on the fruit and seeds of plants and trees. Finches have stout beaks built for seed crushing, while barbets and fruit-eating thrushes both have large gapes for swallowing berries whole.

Habits–Feeding and Breeding

Breeding is related very much to food supply. As large areas of the Oriental region provide more abundant food to more birds for a longer period than in more temperate zones, this means the breeding period can be longer.

Large birds of prey breed between October and March, while large water birds like storks, cormorants, egrets and ibis, nest in colonies during the monsoon. This is also the period when munias and weaver birds breed. The peak breeding season for other common birds is February to May, although hill birds nest even later.

During the breeding season, males of many species produce long and complicated sounds called birdsong. Songs must be differentiated from the calls that birds of both sexes make throughout the year which are much simpler and used in a variety of circumstances, for example to express alarm, to threaten, to beg for food and so on. It should also be distinguished from the mechanical noises birds make, clattering of the bill or clapping of the wings, for similar reasons.

Once you are familiar with the song of a particular species, it is possible to identify it immediately by its voice. Not surprisingly, birds too use song to identify themselves to one another and to attract mates. In species which aggressively defend a territory, it is still debatable how much song is used simply to attract females, and to what degree it serves to demarcate the male's domain. The matter is complicated further by the fact that females are probably most attracted by the male with the largest territory. The size of territory varies enormously. In species which breed in colonies, it extends just a few feet around the nest.

If song is important in finding a mate, so are courtship displays. The peacock is blessed with a powerful though unmellifluous voice, but makes up for this by the male's unmatched courtship display. The peacock stamps and

Weaver-bird nest

turns with his tail outspread before a number of females. Even birds which pair for life are known to display. In the breeding season, Sarus Cranes frequently break into a striking dance, spreading their wings, lowering their heads and leaping into the air, trumpeting loudly all the while. Other birds indulge in less spectacular rituals, like making gifts of food to one another

Courtship culminates in mating, with the male mounting the female. The male's testes are internal and make up only a tiny fraction of the bird's bodyweight, as little as 0.005 per cent outside the breeding season. During the breeding season the testes increase up to a thousand fold in weight. In most birds there is a small erectile phallus, but this is well developed and protrusible in only a few species like ducks and geese. The female's ovaries are also contained in her body cavity, and fertilisation of an egg generally takes place once it leaves the ovary and passes down towards the shell gland where the outer layer of the egg becomes calcified to form the shell. Most females can store live sperm in their body and so fertilisation can take place some time after mating.

Darter

Victorian painting of eggs

Eggs are laid in the nest the pair has previously prepared. These vary from rough scrapes in the ground, as with plovers, to the holes in river banks tunnelled by kingfishers, the large untidy nests of vultures, and the elaborate nests of weaver birds often seen suspended in groups of ten or more from palms and other trees. The male weaver bird is a master of the nest-building art. Each male of a colony laboriously tears off strips of grass or leaves and proceeds to construct a retort-shaped nest, complete with entrance tunnel and egg chamber. When the nests are well under construction, the hen-birds arrive and set up house in whichever nest takes their fancy. When the nest is complete and the eggs laid, the male takes off to build another nest and attract another female.

Hornbills nest in holes in trees and are unique in imprisoning the female within the nest behind a mud wall, leaving open a gap just large enough for the male to pass her food. Not all birds form pairs. Some babblers breed communally with different females laying eggs in the same nest.

Eggs also vary in size, colour, shape and number. Those which require camouflage are well-mottled, although most are pigmented. Cuckoos parasitic on others' nests lay eggs which resemble those of the host species. In the case of Hawk Cuckoos and Pied Crested Cuckoos, these are babblers.

Hatchlings require different amounts of care from their parents. Songbird chicks, for example, are born naked, while gamebirds are born with feathers and are soon running after their parents. Most young birds have characteristic begging behaviour, and in many species parents have been observed to give them a diet richer in protein than their own normal diet, to promote their offspring's growth.

As the young gain their full plumage, the adults generally begin to moult. Feathers are shed and re-grown in a distinct pattern, generally beginning with the first flight feathers and ending with the replacement of the last. Moulting is necessary as feathers do wear out. Species which have distinct breeding and non-breeding plumage moult twice a year, while in larger birds, such as eagles, a moult may take two to three years to complete. In short individual birds shed feathers according to their needs. Migratory birds, for example, never moult at the time of migration.

Migration

Many species migrate locally or over long distances to avoid adverse climatic conditions and in search of food. Hundreds of thousands of waterfowl migrate each winter to India from central and northern Asia, covering huge distances. Smaller winter migrants include wagtails, warblers and bluethroats. The huge number of wintering birds also accounts for the large numbers of wintering ornithologists and bird enthusiasts who visit the subcontinent over these months.

Summer visitors are much fewer. The multi-coloured Indian Pitta is one such bird well worth searching out. It winters in south India and Sri Lanka, and visits the deciduous forest and scrubland of the Himalayan foothills and the north-west around May, staying until it has bred.

Scientists have still to discover exactly how birds navigate during migration, although it is clear that they have a number of means to do so. Apart from sighting landmarks, it has been proved that birds make use of an internal magnetic compass and of the position of the sun and stars. It is also thought that sound and smell may play a role. The Siberian Crane is one bird which finds its way every year from Siberia to the same square kilometre of wetland in the Keoladeo Ghana National Park at Bharatpur in Rajasthan.

Black-necked Cranes

Classification

As with other animals birds are classified into orders, families, genera and species. Each genus consists of a number of species which are obviously closely related. The first of a bird's two or three Latin names is that of its genus, and the second describes the species, while a third is used for subspecies. A species is a population of birds with a distinct identity which does not interbreed with other bird populations. Where there is a constant variation in a species, it is called a subspecies. Each bird of this region has been numbered by Dillon Ripley in his synopsis.

Bird-watching

Bird-watching is a way not only of learning about birds, but a channel for study of the natural world as a whole. The immense variety of birdlife in the Oriental region, and the large size and colourful plumage of many species makes it an especially attractive occupation. As you observe bird behaviour you cannot fail to notice how the changing seasons affect plant and insect life too.

Demoiselle Cranes

Bird-watching is also simple for the beginner to take up as it requires no special equipment, although binoculars are a great help in identification.

To see birds most easily you should be quiet, careful and inconspicuous. It is best to wear subdued colours, to walk slowly and make use of cover such as banks, trees and bushes. It is often a good idea to take up position on the edge of a forest clearing or near a fruiting tree and let the birds come to you. Lakes and jheels are also good locations for observation. Carry a notebook so that you can jot down details of any bird you can't immediately identify and then check your descriptions against those in a guide.

This guide in particular is designed as an aid to field identification and aims to help everyone from the newest of enthusiasts to the habitual bird-watcher. We have drawn on the vast reserve of subcontinental scholarship already in existence, notably the works of Salim Ali, Dillon Ripley, as well as many others.

Himalayan Pied Kingfisher

While Dillon Ripley's system of classification has been followed in earlier editions, this edition follows the taxonomic sequences based on DNA-D NA hybridization studies established by C.G. Sibley and B.L. Monroe Jr in 1990. We begin each bird description with, first, the common English name, followed by the scientific name in italics. This is followed by the size, indicating the approximate length of the bird from the tip of its bill to the end of its tail. Then follows a description of the bird's plumage, listed separately by gender when required and indications of seasonal variations of plumage, if any. After this, we have noted characteristic forms of behaviour that might help toward identification of the bird. Finally, we list the bird's food, voice, range and habitat.

Common names of birds are often revised and some birds have more than one name. In such cases we have followed the listings in *An Annotated Checklist of the Birds of the Oriental Region* (Tim Inskipp, Nigel Lindsey and William Duckworth, Oriental Book Club, 1996). In cases where there are alternative names, the common Indian name follows in parenthesis.

Finally, this edition carries, for the first time, maps showing the range of every bird's habitat; we have also included a systematic index of families and species and a comprehensive bibliography of works on the subject.

Jerdon's Courser

Vanishing Birds

One of the most significant and exciting achievements of Indian ornithology in recent years was the rediscovery of Jerdon's Courser in 1986. In *The Handbook of the Birds of India*, Salim Ali said that the last 'authentic record was in 1900, since when thorough search by competent ornithologists has failed to rediscover it'. **Jerdon's** or **Double-banded Courser** *Rhinoptilus (Cursorius) biturquatus* was first recorded by Dr TC Jerdon, an Indian Army Medical Officer, in 1848. Blandford recorded it in 1867 and 1871 and the last record was by Howard Campbell in 1900. Always a rare bird, these few sightings were restricted to the Penner and Godavari river valleys of Andhra Pradesh, to the north-west of Madras. Despite surveys by outstanding ornithologists such as Whistler and Kinnear in 1929 and 1931, by Salim Ali in 1932 and post-war surveys by the Bombay Natural History Society (BNHS) along the Godavari river, no birds were sighted. Salim Ali, however, was not convinced.

In 1985, under a joint Government of India and US Government sponsored Endangered Species Project carried out by the BNHS, Bharat Bhushan, a young BNHS scientist, surveyed the dry scrub covered hill country where Jerdon first recorded the bird. In January 1986, the species was rediscovered.

Jerdon's Courser is a nocturnal and crepuscular species found in open patches within scrub, bordering the dry deciduous forest of the region. Bharat Bhushan has identified six sites in the Lankamalai hills and suitable habitat in two valleys is restricted to about 2000 sq km. The timing of the rediscovery was providential as a month later it was realised that an irrigation scheme to take water from the large Nagarjunasagar lake to Madras would destroy the area. A large channel would have been built through the exact discovery site. Fortunately, BNHS lobbyed hard and with support from the Andhra Pradesh Forest Department, the State Government was able to realign the proposed canal.

Since the rediscovery, the area has been gazetted as the Sri Lankamalleswara Wildlife Sanctuary covering 464 sq km. The sanctuary has an interesting policy of employing local tribes as protectors of the area. To the south the 353 sq km Sri Venkateswara National Park has been gazetted in the Palakonda forest area, while to the east there is a proposal to declare another 1300 sq km of the Velikonda forests as a wildlife sanctuary. All these areas are potential habitat for the courser but are also home to many other species including the Golden Gecko that was also rediscovered in the 1980s, the dwarf palm and the red sandalwood tree *Perocarpus marsupium*.

The **Forest Spotted Owlet** *Athene blewitti,* one of India's most elusive birds, has recently been rediscovered. A British-American team of ornithologists came upon a specimen in the Dhule region of Madhya Pradesh in 1998. Col. Richard Meinertzhagen's claim to have sighted the

Forest Spotted Owlet

bird in Gujarat in 1914, was later discredited and there have been no definite sightings of the bird for 113 years. The British-American team speculate that the Owlet's sighting on the low foothills might be a response to the rapid destruction of plains forest and that its continued existence might still be in jeopardy.

Two other bird species that have not been recorded for the last 70 years are the **Pink-headed Duck** *Rhodonessa caryophyllacea* and the **Himalayan Mountain Quail** *Ophrysia superciliosa*. Despite rumours as late as the 1960s, it seems the last Pink-headed Duck has been extinct in the wild since about 1926. Originally thinly distributed through the wetlands, swamps and wilderness areas that formed around the confluence of the Ganga and Brahmaputra rivers in the vast plains of Bengal and what is now Bangladesh. The reed beds along the river banks have long since been cleared by the burgeoning human population and the isolated enclosed waters that were home to the ducks have mostly disappeared. Little is known about the Pink-headed Duck and only a few skins exist in museum collections around the world. Local sportsmen hunted and shot the bird, but it was never popular eating. In the early years of this century a few birds would be regularly found in the markets of Calcutta but as these became less frequent naturalists began to become concerned. In 1924 an expedition searched various areas of Bengal but failed to see a single specimen. A few reports in the last 50 years may have confused this species with the **Red-crested Pochard** *Rhodonessa*

Pink-headed Duck

rufina with which it has a superficial resemblance. The Pink-headed Duck has, as its name suggests, a bright pink head and neck with a dull brown body except for a pink speculum. It is probable that the last living specimen died around 1935 in a private collection in England.

Even less is known about the Himalayan Mountain Quail which was first reported in 1846 and has not been seen since 1876. Always a difficult

Himalayan Mountain Quail

bird to flush, Salim Ali believed a small population may have escaped detection in what remains of the forested mountain areas of the western Himalaya. The few specimens that were collected during the last century were found between 1500 and 1850 metres in the hills around Mussoorie in Uttar Pradesh. The last specimen was collected near Nainital, a little further east. Judging by their thick, soft plumage it has been suggested that they spent the summers at much higher altitudes and only spent the winters in the Himalayan foothills.

The rediscovery of Jerdon's Courser in 1986 and of the Forest Owlet in 1998 vindicated Salim Ali's belief that the bird may have survived the enormous pressures placed on India's wilderness. He also hoped the Mountain Quail might be 'rediscovered' but despite efforts over the last 10 years no reports have been received. It is, however, still possible that the thick mountain forests of Bhutan and Arunachal Pradesh in the eastern Himalaya may offer a new species or subspecies to the ornithologist at the beginning of the 21st century. It is also possible that the little known areas of the eastern ghats where the Courser was found, may also yield a new bird to science.

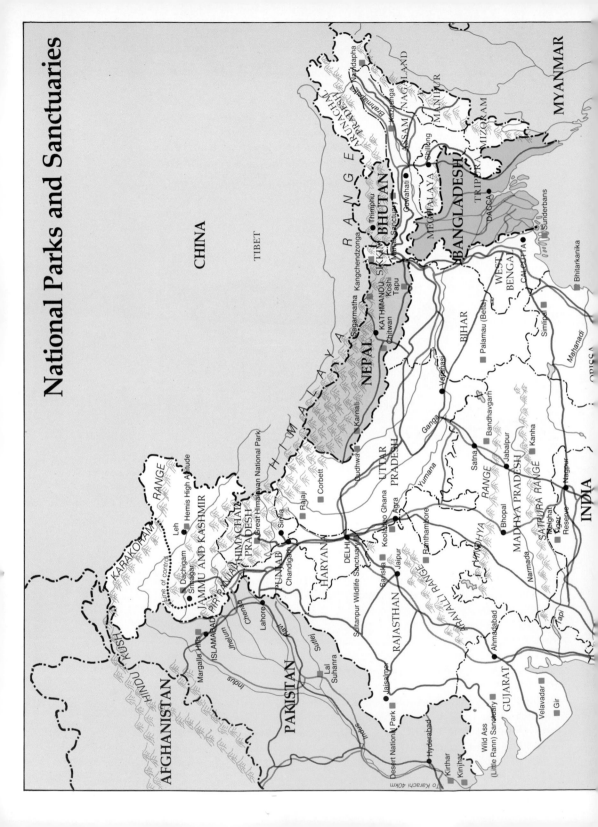

National Parks and Sanctuaries

Bay of Bengal

ANDAMAN AND
NICOBAR ISLANDS
(INDIA)

ARABIAN SEA

WESTERN GHATS

BOMBAY

Godavari

Hyderabad

ANDHRA
PRADESH

Krishna

EASTERN

Nagarjunasagar
Srisailam

Madras

Cauvery

Bangalore

KARNATAKA

Bandipur
Mudumalai

TAMIL NADU

Nagarhole

Eravikulam
Anamadi

KERALA

Cochin

Periyar
(Thekkady)

Trivandrum

LAKSHADWEEP
(INDIA)

Wilpattu

SRI
LANKA

Gal
Oya

Kandy

Lahugala

Kumana

Yala

COLOMBO

INDIAN

OCEAN

Legend

Roads

Railways

● Towns

■ National Parks and Sanctuaries

N

0   100   200   300   400   500   Kilometres

The external boundary of India, as depicted here may not be authentic or exact.

© The Guidebook Company Ltd

Rare Albino Kingfisher (Alcedo athis) Bharatpur 1992

SNOW PARTRIDGE

Lerwa lerwa 38cm. Sexes alike. Barred black and white above; deep chestnut below; broad white streaks on abdomen, flanks; chestnut undertail; streaked black and tipped white. Social; coveys of 5 to 20 on alpine pastures and amidst bushes; very tame where not harassed; easy to shoot; numbers decreasing. **Food:** seeds, vegetable shoots, lichens, moss. **Voice:** loud call, like that of Grey Partridge. **Range:** resident, the Himalaya, 2500-5000m. **Habitat:** alpine meadows, scrubby hillsides, rhododendron and fern undergrowth.

Snow Partridge

HIMALAYAN SNOWCOCK

Tetraogallus himalayensis 72cm. Sexes alike. Overall plumage grey, white, black and chestnut; streaked and blotched; white throat bordered by broken chestnut collar; dark grey below breast; white under tail-coverts; trailing edge of wings transparent white in overhead flight, against bright sky. Small parties of 3 to 10 birds, rummage the hillsides, scratching and digging furiously; mostly fly downhill; run up when alarmed; colouration hides the birds well in preferred haunts. **Food:** grass shoots, tubers, bulbous roots, swallows grit. **Voice:** noisy; cock utters loud whistle of several notes. **Range:** resident; the Himalaya; Kashmir to Kumaon and W Nepal; 3800–5500m in summer; low to about 2200m in winter. **Habitat:** alpine meadows, rocky country above tree-line.

Himalayan Snowcock

CHUKAR

Alectoris chukar 38cm. Sexes alike. Ashy-pink-brown partridge; chestnut in outer tail; prominent, broad black and buff bars on flanks; black stripe across forehead continues through and behind the eyes to form a necklace on upper breast; white cheeks, chin, throat. Female lacks spur on tarsus; also slightly smaller. Gregarious; coveys amidst cultivated areas, scrub and rocky country; collects at water; strong but short flight, flying much faster downhill. **Food:** grain, bulbous roots, grass shoots, wheat, barley; also insects. **Voice:** cock utters a loud chuckle, of up to a dozen notes. **Range:** resident; W Himalaya to C Nepal; about 1200–5000m. **Habitat:** scrub and rock-covered hills; cultivation.

Chukar

Black Francolin

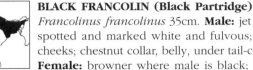

BLACK FRANCOLIN (Black Partridge)

Francolinus francolinus 35cm. **Male:** jet black, spotted and marked white and fulvous; white cheeks; chestnut collar, belly, under tail-coverts. **Female:** browner where male is black; rufous nuchal patch; no white cheeks or chestnut collar. Solitary or small parties in high grass and edge of canals; emerges in the open early mornings; sometimes cocks tail. **Food:** grain, seeds, tubers, fallen berries, insects. **Voice:** loud three to six note crow of the cock, frequently uttered, unmistakable once heard. **Range:** resident; N India, along foothills; south to N Gujarat and C Madhya Pradesh; an eastern race occurs east of Nepal in Duars; to about 2000m. **Habitat:** high grass, cultivation; prefers wetter areas along canals and rivers.

Painted Francolin

PAINTED FRANCOLIN (Painted Partridge)

Francolinus pictus 30cm. **Male:** blackish-brown above, profusely marked with white; dull-chestnut face, supercilium; chestnut throat; black below, thickly spotted white; rufous on abdomen-centre, vent. **Female:** similar to male but throat usually dirty white. Calls diagnostic. Pairs or adults with young; great skulkers, extremely secretive and not easily flushed; may roost in trees. **Food:** grain, grass and other seeds, fallen fruit, insects. **Voice:** noisy when breeding (SW monsoon); high-pitched, harsh grating four or five-noted *khik...kheek.kheek.khheeki* call, quite similar to that of Black Partridge; may call every 20-30 seconds, for up to 40 minutes; often in duet. **Range:** most of India, south of range of Black Partridge, south of line from C Gujarat, N Madhya Pradesh, S Uttar Pradesh. **Habitat:** grassland, scrub, cultivation.

Grey Francolin

GREY FRANCOLIN (Grey Partridge)

Francolinus pondicerianus 35cm. Sexes alike. Grey-brown and rufous above, barred and blotched; buffy-rufous below; narrow cross-bars on throat, upper breast; fine black markings on abdomen, flanks; black loop around throat encloses bright rufous-yellow throat; female smaller, with indistinct spur. Small parties, digging and moving amidst scrub and grass; seen on country roads, dust bathing or feeding; quick to take to cover on being alarmed, scattering over the area. **Food:** cereal grains, seeds, fallen berries, insects. **Voice:** loud, high-pitched two to three notes *pat..ee..la*; noisy. **Range:** resident; all India, south of Himalayan foothills. **Habitat:** open scrub, grass, cultivation.

COMMON QUAIL

Coturnix coturnix 20cm. **Male:** pale brown above, boldly streaked and marked; blackish chin, stripe down throat centre and narrow stripe curving to ear-coverts; rufous-buff breast with white shaft streaks; whitish abdomen. **Female:** buffy throat; breast heavily streaked with black. Pairs and small parties on ground; often huge numbers at favoured feeding sites; commoner in winter when numbers augmented; well known Indian bird, both for table as also for fighting and betting. **Food:** seeds, grain, insects. **Voice:** fluid whistling *wet..me..lips* of male is common and familiar call. **Range:** resident; local migrant; breeds in Kashmir to about 2500m and parts of N and NE India; common in winter over the country. **Habitat:** cultivation, standing crop, grasslands.

Common Quail

BLUE-BREASTED QUAIL

Coturnix chinensis 15cm. **Male:** slaty-blue forehead, supercilium, sides of neck, lower breast and flanks; grey-brown above, streaked and mottled; striking black and white on throat and upper breast; chestnut abdomen. **Female:** brownish, streaked and mottled; black-barred breast, flanks. Small parties in wet grasslands and scrub; drops into undergrowth soon after being flushed. The **Rain Quail** or **Black-breasted** *C coromandelica* has bold black streaks on flanks. **Food:** grass seeds, millets, small insects. **Voice:** soft double-note whistle *tiu..tiu...* **Range:** resident; some local movements; roughly east and south of a line Bombay to Shimla; commoner in the eastern parts. **Habitat:** wet grassland, scrub, agriculture, tea gardens.

Blue-breasted Quail

JUNGLE BUSH QUAIL

Perdicula asiatica 18cm. **Male:** brownish, streaked and mottled; dark buff and chestnut about face; bright chestnut chin, throat; whitish below with close black barrings. **Female:** like male above, pale pinkish-rufous wash on underbody; chestnut throat. Small parties in dense grass and undergrowth; have well laid favoured paths; explodes with a tremendous *whirr* when almost trodden upon. **Food:** grass seeds, grain, small insects. **Voice:** trilling, musical call, *tirri..tirri...* often longdrawn and loud; other calls when breeding. **Range:** resident; all India, to about 1200m in the outer Himalaya. **Habitat:** dense grass, scrub, edge of forest.

Jungle Bush Quail

Peter Morris

Hill Partridge

HILL PARTRIDGE

Arborophila torqueola 28cm. **Male:** chestnut cap, nape; black eyebrows, lores; rufous-buff ear-coverts; olive-brown above, streaked and mottled with black and chestnut; black throat and neck streaked white; prominent white band between breast and foreneck. **Female:** buff-rufous throat, sides of neck; black streaks on sides of head, neck. Small parties on forest floors; roosts up in trees at night, several huddled together. **Food:** seeds, insects, berries. **Voice:** mournful whistle *po..eer... po..eer...*, the second syllable slightly longer. **Range:** the Himalaya, east of Garhwal; 1000-4000m. **Habitat:** dense jungle undergrowth in hill country.

Suresh Elamon

Red Spurfowl

RED SPURFOWL

Galloperdix spadicea 35cm. A long-tailed game bird. **Male:** dark brown crown; brick-red naked patch around eye; reddish brown plumage, underparts scalloped with grey-brown. **Female:** sandy-rufous above, narrowly barred. Reddish legs with two to four sharp spurs in male, one or two spurs in female. Solitary or in pairs amongst dense cover in broken, hilly country; feeds in forest clearings and forest roads; runs fast on ground; roosts in trees at night. **Food:** grain, seeds, berries, insects. **Voice:** loud cackling notes; calls when flushed. **Range:** from Uttar Pradesh terai south across Gangetic plains through the peninsula. **Habitat:** scrub in forested, broken hilly country.

Gertrud Denzau

Painted Spurfowl

PAINTED SPURFOWL

Galloperdix lunulata 32cm. **Male:** metallic green-black crown has faint white streakings; black sides of head, neck, with white spots; chestnut above, with white eye-spots; metallic bronze-green in wings and tail. **Female:** plain rufous-brown; no white spots in plumage; chestnut about face, cheeks; dark crown. Pairs or small parties in undergrowth; very shy and usually difficult to spot. **Food:** seeds, berries, insects. **Voice:** loud calls reported by males. **Range:** south of a line from Gwalior to Bengal; absent in Gujarat and Konkan; commoner in central and eastern peninsula. **Habitat:** dense thorn and bamboo jungle in broken hilly, rocky country.

BLOOD PHEASANT

Ithaginis cruentus 45cm. **Male:** bright red and black about face; greyish above, streaked; yellow mop-like crest; apple-green below, thickly streaked yellow; crimson on upper breast, wings and tail. **Female:** rich rufous-brown overall, finely marked; scarlet around eyes. Gregarious; strong runner; flies rarely; feeds in open clearings; extremely tame in certain areas and hence easily shot. **Food:** shoots of ferns and pines, moss, lichens. **Voice:** long-drawn squeal. **Range:** bird of high elevation in the Himalaya, east of C Nepal; 3200-4300m. **Habitat:** steep hill forest, ringal bamboo, rhododendron and juniper scrub; prefers snow-covered areas.

Blood Pheasant

WESTERN TRAGOPAN

Tragopan melanocephalus 70cm. **Male:** crimson and black plumage, profusely spotted white: red-tipped crest, red face patch; deep blue throat featherless; reddish on upper breast. **Female:** grey-brown plumage; rufous on head, neck; black and white streaks and spots on upperbody. Solitary or in pairs; very shy and elusive; occasionally emerges to feed in the open, around melting snow patches, along with other pheasants. **Food:** fresh leaves, ringal bamboo shoots, seeds, berries; also insects. **Voice:** rather goat-like *waa...waa...wan...* call notes; unmistakable once heard. **Range:** west Himalaya, from W Pakistan, through Kashmir to Garhwal; rather uncommon and little known over its entire range. **Habitat:** dense forest undergrowth; ringal bamboo.

Western Tragopan

KOKLASS PHEASANT

Pucrasia macrolopha **Male:** 60cm; silvery grey above, streaked black; metallic green head, horns; long, brown occipital crest; pointed chestnut-brown tail; deep chestnut below. **Female:** 55cm; black and brown plumage, mottled and streaked: buffy-chestnut crown, with short crest. Pairs or small parties; keeps to steep slopes, where difficult to flush; emerges in clearings in early mornings; flies up at great speed when flushed, before plunging down. **Food:** tubers, shoots, leaves, seeds, insects. **Voice:** call is the best identification; loud *khok..kok.. kok..kokha...* with various tones; vocal around dawn and dusk, but intermittently through the day when breeding (April-June); interesting display of courting male. **Range:** the Himalaya; S Kashmir to CE Nepal; 1500–4000m, descending lower in winter. **Habitat:** steep forested hills, nullahs.

Koklass Pheasant

HIMALAYAN MONAL

Lophophorus impejanus 70cm. **Male:** mix of glossy, metallic purple, blue and bronze-green above; prominent crest of iridescent green feathers; white lower back and rump; chestnut wings, distinctive in flight; short rufous tail; velvety black underparts. **Female:** mottled and streaked brown; white throat; short crest. Solitary or small parties; actively digs for food, often in deep snow; feeds in cultivation; wild, ringing cries distinctive in flight. **Food:** tubers, shoots, berries, insects, flower seeds. **Voice:** wild whistling call, *coooor..lew*, much like a Curlew's. **Range:** Himalaya, west to east; 2300–5000m. **Habitat:** high forest, glades, snow patches.

Red Junglefowl

RED JUNGLEFOWL

Gallus gallus 65cm. Both sexes resemble domestic bantam breeds. **Male:** glistening red-orange above, yellow about the neck; metallic black tail with long, drooping central feathers distinctive. **Female:** 42cm; bright chestnut forehead, supercilia continuing to foreneck; reddish-brown plumage, vermiculated with fine black and buff. Small parties, often several hens accompanying a cock; shy and skulking; emerges in clearings and on forest roads; flies up noisily when flushed. **Food:** grain, crops, tubers, insects. **Voice:** characteristic crow of male, shriller version of domestic; other cackling sounds. **Range:** outer Himalaya, east of Kashmir; E and C India, south to Narmada river. **Habitat:** mixed forest and cultivation.

Grey Junglefowl

GREY JUNGLEFOWL

Gallus sonneratii **Male:** 80cm. **Br Male:** darkish-grey plumage, with white feather-shafts; blackish crown, neck, with white and yellow shaft-streaks and spots; rather waxy sickle-shaped arching tail distinctive. **Female:** 46cm; brownish overall, lightly streaked white above; white chin, throat; white underbody with bold markings on breast. Solitary, pairs or small coveys; rather shy and skulking; emerges in clearings and on forest roads to glean in early mornings and late evenings; roosts in trees and bamboo clumps. **Food:** seeds, tubers, crop shoots, insects, bamboo and *karvi* seeds. **Voice:** loud crow of male distinctive, *kuk..kuk..kkura.kuk...*; noisy in early mornings, but intermittently calls during day; rather vocal when breeding. **Range:** peninsula and S India, south of a line from Mt Abu to C Madhya Pradesh, E Maharashtra and NW Andhra Pradesh, its range coinciding with the teak country. **Habitat:** mixed deciduous forest; also forest clearings, abandoned tea and coffee estates and other overgrown sites.

Joanna Van Gruisen

E. Hanumantha Rao

Himalayan Monal

KALIJ PHEASANT
Lophura leucomelanos 65cm. **Male:** black above, with steel-blue gloss; glossy tail, ending in sickle-like feathers; whitish edges to rump feathers; bare, scarlet around eyes; long, hairy white crest; brownish-grey underbody; lanceolate breast feathers. **Female:** reddish-brown, scalloped paler; brown crest and bare scarlet patch around eye; brown tail, smaller than male's. Several races over the Himalaya and NE India, the males varying in colour from glossy black to black and grey/white; crest black in other races. Pairs or small gatherings; spends day on ground, gleaning on forest roads and clearings during early mornings and late afternoons; good flier; roosts in trees at night. **Food:** seeds, insects, small lizards, fruit; human excreta around habitation. **Voice:** loud crowing by male; chuckling calls on disturbance. **Range:** the Himalaya, NE hill regions; foothills country to about 3500m. **Habitat:** forest undergrowth, clearings, terraced cultivation, vicinity of hillside habitation.

Kalij Pheasant

Cheer Pheasant

CHEER PHEASANT

Catreus wallichii. **Male:** 100cm; pale buff above, close-barred black; dark brown head, long backward crest; bright red, naked orbital patch; buffy-white below; black on abdomen. **Female:** 70cm paler orbital patch; more chestnut below. Small coveys in undergrowth and grass; very shy and skulking; hurtles downhill when flushed. **Food:** seeds, roots, tubers, insects. **Voice:** noisy before dawn and at dusk; loud, distinct call, sounding *chir..pir...chir..pir*; also some cackling calls. **Range:** the Himalaya between NW Pakistan and C Nepal; 1200–3500m. **Habitat:** grass covered steep, rocky hillsides with scattered tree cover.

Indian Peafowl

INDIAN PEAFOWL

Pavo cristatus. **Male:** 110cm (including full tail or train 2.25m). Glistening blue neck and breast; wire-like crest and very long tail distinctive. **Female:** 85cm; lacks blue neck, breast; browner plumage; lacks the long train. Familiar bird of India; solitary or in small parties, several females with one or more males; wary in the forested parts, rather tame and confiding in many parts of W and C India around human habitation; ever-alert, gifted with keen eyesight and hearing. **Food:** seeds, berries, shoots and tubers, insects, lizards, small snakes, worms. **Voice:** loud *may-yow* calls at dawn and dusk; also loud nasal calls and cackles; very noisy during the rains, when breeding. **Range:** all India, from about 2000m in Himalaya. **Habitat:** forest, neighbourhood of villages and cultivated country.

Lesser Whistling-Duck

LESSER WHISTLING-DUCK (Teal)

Dendrocygna javanica 42cm. Sexes alike. Rufescent-brown plumage; browner head; chestnut upper rail-coverts; in flight, chestnut upper tail-coverts, upper wing-coverts and blackish flight feathers distinctive. Young birds are dull coloured. The **Fulvous Whistling-duck** *D bicolor* (50cm) is larger, and has white upper tail-coverts. Small flocks on edges of jheels and village ponds, especially where there is ample vegetation, reeds; mostly nocturnal feeder; flight slow, often accompanied by whistling calls. **Food:** tender shoots, grain, aquatic weeds, small fish, worms, frogs. **Voice:** shrill, musical whistle frequently in night. **Range:** resident, but moves locally; all India south of Himalaya. **Habitat:** vegetation and reed covered jheels, village ponds.

GREYLAG GOOSE

Anser anser 80cm. Sexes alike. Grey-brown plumage; pink bill, legs and feet white upper tail-coverts, lower belly and tip to dark tail; in flight, pale leading edge of wings and white upper tail-coverts distinctive. Gregarious and wary; flocks on jheels and winter cultivation; rests for most of day and feeds during night, in water and in agricultural land, especially freshly sown fields. **Food:** grass, shoots of winter crops like gram and wheat; aquatic tubers; recorded eating *singhara* (water-chestnut) in Kashmir. **Voice:** domestic goose-like single note honk, often uttered several times, loud and ringing; typical geese gaggles when feeding. **Range:** winter visitor; early-October to mid-March; commoner in N India, across the Gangetic plain to Assam, Orissa; south to N Gujarat; Madhya Pradesh; rarer south. **Habitat:** jheels, winter cultivation.

Greylag Goose

BAR-HEADED GOOSE

Anser indicus 75cm. Sexes alike. Two blackish strips on back of white head; white stripes down necksides; dark-brown neck; very pale-grey plumage; yellow bill, legs; black bill-tip; in flight, the pale coloured body, white head and dark wing tips distinctive. Gregarious, sometimes seen along with Greylags; rests during day on jheel banks and sandbars in rivers; crepuscular and nocturnal; causes damage to winter crops. **Food:** tender shoots of gram, tubers, paddy. **Voice:** nasal, quite musical honking. **Range:** breeds only in Ladakh within Indian limits; winter visitor, commoner from Kashmir, south to C India and east across Gangetic plains to Assam; less common south of Deccan. **Habitat:** rivers, large jheels.

Bar-Headed Goose

RUDDY SHELDUCK or RUDDY SHELDRAKE

Tadorna ferruginea 65cm. Whitish-buff head; orange-brown plumage; in flight, orangish body, white wing-coverts, green speculum and blackish flight feathers distinctive; black tail and ring around neck (breeding). Female has a whiter head and lacks neck ring. Young birds look like female and have some grey in wings. Pairs or small parties, rather wary; rests during day on river banks, sandbars, edges of jheels; prefers clear, open water. **Food:** grain, shoots, insects, molluscs; reportedly also carrion. **Voice:** loud goose-like honking, on ground and in flight. **Range:** breeds in Ladakh; winter visitor; all India, less common in south. **Habitat:** rivers with sandbars, large, open jheels.

Ruddy Shelduck

Comb Duck

COMB DUCK (Nakta)

Sarkidiornis melanotos 75cm. **Male:** white head, neck, speckled black; fleshy knob (comb) on top of beak; black back has purple-green gloss; greyish lower-back; white lower-neck collar and underbody; short black bars extend on sides of upper breast and flanks. **Female:** duller, smaller; lacks comb. Small parties, either on water or in bees over water; nests in tree-cavities; feeds on surface and in cultivation; can also dive. **Food:** shoots and seeds of water plants, grain, aquatic insects, worms, frogs. **Voice:** loud goose-like honk when breeding. **Range:** almost all India; mostly resident but moves considerably with onset of monsoons; uncommon in extreme S and NW India. **Habitat:** jheels and marshes with surrounding tree-cover.

Cotton Pygmy-Goose

COTTON PYGMY-GOOSE (Cotton Teal)

Nettapus coromandelianus 32cm. **Br Male:** white head, neck; blackish, green-glossed crown, back, neck-collar; white below; white wing-bar. **Female:** dull-brown above; indistinct white wing-bar; dark stripe through eyes; white below, mottled brown. **Non-br Male:** like female, but darker above; distinct wing-bar. Flocks, feeds either by themselves or along with other ducks; mostly feeds on surface, but can also dive; a familiar waterfowl on village tanks and ponds, rather confiding where not persecuted; strong flier, usually flying low. **Food:** shoots of aquatic plants, grain, insects, crustacea. **Voice:** cackling call in flight. **Range:** almost all India; not common, possibly absent over the arid NW regions. **Habitat:** ponds and tanks, preferably those covered with reeds and vegetation.

Gadwall

GADWALL

Anas strepera 50cm. White wing-speculum and chestnut wing-patch diagnostic. **Male:** dark grey, with brown head; white belly; heavily speckled breast. **Female:** plumage mottled brown; the Mallard female is larger, lacks white belly and has metallic white-bordered purple speculum; Pintail female also has white belly but pointed tail and more slender neck distinctive. **Winter Male:** like female but not so heavily mottled, especially above. Small flocks, sometimes with other ducks; surface-feeder; much sought-after table-bird. **Food:** chiefly vegetarian—tubers, shoots of aquatic plants, grain, seeds. **Voice:** single-noted, low call of malt; loud quacking of female. **Range:** winter visitor, quite abundant; all India, but decreasing in numbers towards S India. **Habitat:** jheels, marshes.

E. Hanumantha Rao

Mallard

MALLARD

Anas platyrhynchos 60cm. Broad purple speculum, bordered on each side by white bars, orangish legs, distinctive in flight. **Male:** glossy green head; narrow white collar. **Female (and eclipse male):** mottled brown; brownish bill; indistinct dark stripe through eye. Sociable and gregarious; crepuscular and nocturnal; feeds on marshy ground and in shallow water, up-ending when raking the bottom ooze: can rise vertically from water. **Food:** seeds, shoots of grasses and aquatic plants; also, tadpoles, fish spawn, worms. **Voice:** loud, wheezy *yheeep* of drake; female quacks loud, loudest when alarmed. **Range:** very small numbers breed in some of Kashmir's lakes; winter visitor to N and C India; rare in Deccan and further south. **Habitat:** reed-covered jheels.

Spot-Billed Duck

SPOT-BILLED DUCK

Anas poecilorhyncha 60cm. Sexes alike. Blackish-brown plumage, feathers edged paler; almost white head, neck; black cap, dark, broad eyestripe; green speculum bordered above with white; black bill tipped yellow; coral-red legs, feet. Pairs or small parties walking on marshy land, wet cultivation, or up-ending in shallow water; usually does not associate with other ducks; much prized table-bird; when injured, can dive and remain underwater, holding onto submerged vegetation with only bill exposed. **Food:** wild grain, seeds, shoots of aquatic plants; occasionally water insects, worms, water-snails; causes damage to paddy. **Voice:** loud duck-like quack. **Range:** resident; all India, to about 1800m in Kashmir; local migrant in some areas. **Habitat:** reed and vegetation-covered jheels, shallow ponds.

Northern Pintail

NORTHERN PINTAIL

Anas acuta 60cm. A slender duck with pointed tail. **Male:** greyish above; choco-brown head, upper neck: thin white stripe up neckside; bronze-green speculum. **Female:** mottled buff-brown; pointed tail lacks longer tailpins; whitish belly. Non-breeding male like female, but mantle greyish. In flight pointed tail between feet distinctive. Highly gregarious; extremely common on vegetation-covered jheels; males often in separate flocks, especially on arrival in winter grounds; crepuscular and nocturnal; characteristic hissing swish of wings as flock flies over. **Food:** shoots, seeds of aquatic plants, rice (wild and cultivated); also water insects and molluscs. **Range:** winter visitor; all India. **Habitat:** vegetation-covered jheels, lagoons.

Common Teal

COMMON TEAL

Anas crecca 32cm. **Male:** greyish with chestnut head with broad metal green band from eye to nape with yellow white border. Black, green and buff wing speculum. **Female:** mottled in dark and light brown, pale belly and black and green wing speculum. Commonest migratory duck, much sought by sportsmen. Swift flier and difficult to circumvent. **Food:** tender shoots and grains, mostly vegetarian. **Voice:** *krit..krit..*also wheezy quack. **Range:** all India in winter. **Habitat:** jheels, marshes, village ponds.

Yellow-Legged Buttonquail

YELLOW-LEGGED BUTTONQUAIL

Turnix tanki 15cm. A three-toed ground bird, resembling a true quail. Female slightly bigger. Yellow legs and beak in both sexes. **Male:** blackish crown has rufous and buff; pale stripe through centre of crown; white chin, throat; buffy under parts, with dark spots on sides of breast. **Female:** like male; prominent rufous-orange nuchal collar. Single or in pairs, rarely gathers into coveys; confirmed skulker, difficult to see; moves amidst dense, damp herbage. **Food:** seeds, insects, tender shoots. **Voice:** female has a loud drumming call. **Range:** all India, from about 1200m in the Himalaya. **Habitat:** damp grasslands, scrub, cultivation.

BARRED BUTTONQUAIL
(Common Bustardquail)

Turnix suscitator 15cm. Sexes alike. Female slightly larger. Distinctive white eye; dark brown crown; black speck on white sides of head; back speckled with white, black and brown. Pale buff on wing shoulders seen in flight diagnostic. **Food:** seeds, grains and small insects. **Voice:** females a loud drumming during breeding. **Range:** India, south of the Himalaya. **Habitat:** grass, scrub near cultivation, open forests.

Barred Buttonquail

YELLOW-RUMPED HONEYGUIDE

Indicator xanthonotus 15cm. Sexes alike. Olive-brown plumage; bright orangish-yellow forehead. cheeks and rump (lower back) diagnostic, seen also when bird is perched, with wings drooping slightly; finchlike beak; overall appearance sparrow-like. Solitary or in small scattered parties; keep to cliffs and rock faces around honeybee colonies: show marked preference for colonies where there is a mix of live and abandoned combs; clings on bee-combs or on rocks to feed on white upper wax of the combs; sometimes dive deep into forested valley; can be rather territorial and aggressive at feeding sites; no indication of guiding humans or any other mammal to honeycomb sites. **Food:** mostly beeswax; also bees and other insects. **Voice:** sharp *cheep...* call note, mostly uttered on wing, and rarely on perch. **Range:** Himalaya, from Pakistan to Bhutan, and possibly further east; optimum range 1400 to 2000m, but found over 3000m in Bhutan; overlooked species, little known. **Habitat:** rock faces and cliffs in forests; in some areas above tree-line.

Speckled Piculet

SPECKLED PICULET

Picumnus innominatus 10cm. Sexes alike. Olive-green above (male has some orange and black on forecrown); two white stripes on sides of head, the upper one longer; dark-olive band through eyes, moustachial stripe; creamy-white below, boldly spotted with black. Usually pairs; moves around thin branches, or clings upside-down; taps with beak, probes crevices; typical woodpecker behaviour; associates in mixed hunting bands; unobtrusive, hence often overlooked; perches across branch. **Food:** chiefly ants and termites. **Voice:** sharp, rapid *tsip..tsip...*; also a loud drumming sound. **Range:** Himalaya, west to east, foothills to at least 2500m. The slightly duller southern race *malayorum* has a wide distribution over the E Ghats and the W Ghats, south of Goa; also Nilgiris, Palanis and associated mountain-ranges. **Habitat:** mixed forests, with a fondness for bamboo jungle.

BROWN-CAPPED PYGMY WOODPECKER

Dendrocopos nanus Small woodpecker 13cm. **Male:** barred brown and white above; paler crown with short, scarlet streak (occipital); prominent white band from just above eyes extends to neck; pale dirty-brown-white below, streaked black. **Female:** like male but lacks the scarlet streaks on sides of crown. The male **Grey-Capped Pygmy** *D canicapillus* (14cm)

Krupakar Senani

of the Himalaya has short scarlet occipital crest; black upper back and white-barred lower back, rump. Mostly in pairs; often a part of mixed-bird parties in forest; seen more on smaller trees, branches and twigs, close to ground and also high in canopy; quite active. **Food:** small insects, grubs, obtained from crevices and under bark; also small berries. **Voice:** faint but shrill squeak, sounds like *clicck..rrr;* also drums, especially when breeding during March-May. **Range:** almost all over country, including some of the drier regions of N India. **Habitat**: light forests, cultivation, bamboos, orchards; also vicinity of habitation.

Brown-Capped Pygmy Woodpecker

YELLOW-CROWNED WOODPECKER (Yellow-Fronted Pied)

Dendrocopos mahrattensis 18cm. **Male:** brownish-black above, spotted all over with white; golden-brown forehead, crown; small scarlet crest; pale fulvous below throat, streaked brown; scarlet patch in centre of abdomen distinctive. **Female:** lacks scarlet crest. Solitary or pairs, sometimes small bands of up to 6 birds, occasionally along with mixed hunting parties; moves in jerks along tree stems and branches; hunts in typical woodpecker manner; rather confiding in some areas; birds keep in touch with faint creaking sounds. **Food:** chiefly insects; also figs, other fruits and flower nectar. **Voice:** soft but sharp *clic..click..clickurr...;* drums when breeding. **Range:** common and widespread; almost all India, from Himalayan foothills south; uncommon in NE regions. **Habitat:** open forests, scrub, cultivation, vicinity of habitation, gardens.

Yellow-Crowned Woodpecker

HIMALAYAN WOODPECKER

Dendrocopos himalayensis 25cm. **Male:** black back, upperbody; white shoulder-patch; white spots and barrings on wings; crimson crown, crest; white lores, cheeks, ear-coverts; broad black moustachial stripe; yellowish-brown underbody, darker on breast; crimson under-tail. **Female:** black crown, crest. Mostly in pairs, moving about in forest; jerkily moves up and around tree-stems or clings on undersides of branches; like other woodpeckers often moves a few steps back, as if to re-examine; sometimes seen in mixed hunting parties of Himalayan birds. **Food:** mostly insects hunted from under the bark and moss; seeds of conifers; nuts and acorns. **Voice:** fairly loud calls, uttered in night and occasionally when clinging onto stem; drums often between February and June. **Range:** Himalaya, from Kashmir to West Nepal; 1500-3200m. **Habitat**: Himalayan forests.

Himalayan Woodpecker

Rufous Woodpecker

RUFOUS WOODPECKER

Celeus brachyurus 25cm. Sexes alike. Chestnut-brown plumage; fine black crossbars on upper-body, including wings and tail; paler edges to throat feathers; crimson patch under eye in male, absent in female. Usually in pairs; sometimes four or five scattered birds close by; mostly seen around ball-shaped nests of tree ants; clings to outside of nests and digs for ants, plumage often smeared with gummy substance. **Food:** chiefly tree ants and their pupae; occasionally figs, other fruit; seen to suck sap from near base of banana leaves. **Voice:** rather vocal between January-April; loud, high-pitched three or four notes *ke..ke..kr.ke...*, like common myna's; drums when breeding. **Range:** all India, south of outer Himalaya, found up to 1500m. **Habitat:** mixed forests.

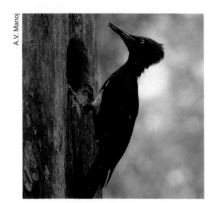

White-Bellied Woodpecker

WHITE-BELLIED WOODPECKER
(Indian Great Black)

Dryocopus javensis 48cm. **Male:** black head, upperbody, breast; white rump and underparts below breast; bright crimson crown (including forehead), crest and cheeks. **Female:** crimson restricted to nape. Pairs, sometimes four or five birds in tall forest; move up along tree stems, jerkily and slowly, inspecting bark-crevices for lurking insects; strong, lazy flight; chuckling note in flight. **Food:** chiefly termites, ants and wood-boring beetle larvae. **Voice:** loud, metallic *chiank* note, often while clinging onto tree stems; loud drumming sound during December-March. **Range:** forested areas of W Ghats, south of Tapti river; present range reduced due to habitat destruction and the bird perhaps no longer exists in the northern parts of W Ghats; also Bastar and perhaps across C Indian hills. **Habitat:** tall evergreen forests.

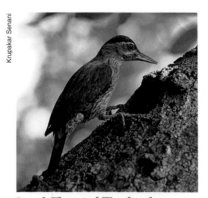

Streak-Throated Woodpecker

STREAK-THROATED WOODPECKER
(Little Scaly-Bellied Green)

Picus xanthopygaeus 30cm. **Male:** grass-green above; crimson crown, crest; orange and black on nape; white supercilium and malar stripe; yellow rump; bold, black scaly streaks on whitish underbody, with tawny-green wash on breast; throat greyer, also streaked. **Female:** black crown, crest. Solitary or in pairs; works up along tree stems; moves either straight up or in spirals; taps with beak for insects hiding in bark; also settles on ground. **Food:** mostly insects: ants, termites, wood-boring beetle larvae; also figs. Voice: occasional faint *pick...* mostly silent; also drums on branches. **Range:** almost all India found up to 1500m in outer Himalaya. **Habitat:** mixed forests, plantations.

GREY-HEADED WOODPECKER
(Black-Naped Green)

Picus canus 32cm. **Male:** darkish green above; crimson forehead; black hindcrown, faint crest and nape; dark sides of head and black malar stripe; yellow rump, white-barred dark wings and blackish tail; unmarked dull greyish-olive underbody diagnostic. **Female:** black from forehead to nape; no crimson. Solitary or in pairs; typical woodpecker, moving on tree stems and larger branches, hunting out insects from under bark; descends on ground, hopping awkwardly; also digs into termite mounds. **Food:** termites, ants, wood-boring beetle and their larvae; also feeds on flower nectar and fruits. **Voice:** loud chattering alarm; common call is a high-pitched *keek...keek..* of four or five notes; drums often between March and early June. **Range:** Himalaya from the lower foothills country to about 2700m. **Habitat:** forests, both deciduous and temperate.

Grey-Headed Woodpecker

BLACK-RUMPED FLAMEBACK
(Lesser Golden-Backed Woodpecker)

Dinopium benghalense 30cm. **Male:** shining golden-yellow and black above; crimson crown, crest; black throat, sides of head, with fine white streaks; white underbody, streaked black, boldly on breast. **Female:** black crown spotted with white; crimson crest. Usually pairs, sometimes half a dozen together; widespread and common; moves jerkily up and around tree stems or clings on underside of branches; taps out insects; often associates in mixed hunting parties; may descend to ground, picking off ants and other insects. **Food:** chiefly ants, termites; caterpillars and centipedes on ground; also figs, berries. **Voice:** noisy; loud, high-pitched cackle, like a laugh; drums often. **Range:** all India, from about 1800m in outer Himalaya; also found in drier areas of NW India. **Habitat:** forests, both dry and mixed deciduous; orchards; gardens; also neighbourhood of villages and other habitation.

Black-Rumped Flameback

Greater Flameback

Heart-Spotted Woodpecker

Great Barbet

GREATER FLAMEBACK
(Larger Golden-Backed Woodpecker)

Chrysocolaptes lucidus 32cm. **Male:** crimson crown, crest; golden-olive above; white and black sides of face, throat; whitish-buff below, profusely spotted black on foreneck and speckled over rest of underbody; extensive crimson rump, black tail and flight-feathers distinctive. **Female:** white-spotted black crown, crest. The **Himalayan Flameback** *Dinopium shorii* is very similar, but slightly smaller size, black nape, three toes and two narrow stripes down throat centre can help make the distinction. **The Common Flameback** *D javanense* (28cm) is also confusingly similar, but has single black malar stripe. Pairs or small bands; arboreal, moves jerkily up along tree-stems. **Food:** insects; possibly nectar. **Voice:** noisy; loud, grating scream; calls mostly in flight; loud drumming. **Range:** Garhwal to NE; parts of E Ghats, SE Madhya Pradesh; W Ghats, Kerala to Tapti river; plains to about 1500m. **Habitat:** forests.

HEART-SPOTTED WOODPECKER

Hemicircus canente 16cm. **Male:** black forehead (speckled white), crown and crest; black back; broad, pale-buff wing-patch (inner secondaries and wing-coverts) with heart-shaped spots; black night-feathers; whitish-buff, olive and black below. **Female:** extensive buff-white on forehead, otherwise like male. Pairs or small parties; active and arboreal; perches across branch and calls often as it flies from one tree to another. **Food:** insects, mostly ants and termites. **Voice:** quite vocal, especially in flight; a somewhat harsh *chur..* note; other sharp clicking and squeaky notes. **Range:** W Ghats from Kerala north to Tapti river; east across Satpuras to SE Madhya Pradesh, Orissa, NE states. **Habitat:** forests.

GREAT BARBET (Great Hill)

Megalaima virens 33cm. Sexes alike. Bluish-black head, throat; maroon-brown back; yellowish hind-collar; green on lower back, tail; brown upper breast; pale yellow below, with thick, greenish-blue streaks; red under-tail coverts distinctive. Large, yellowish beak. Either solitary or small bands; arboreal, but comes into low-fruiting bushes; difficult to spot and mostly heard. **Food:** fruit, flower petals. **Voice:** very noisy; a loud *pi..you* or *pi..oo,* uttered continuously for several minutes; often joined by the rather similar but more nasal calls of the **Golden-throated Barbet** *M franklinii* (2.7cm), of the E Himalaya. **Range:** Himalaya, 800-3200m. **Habitat:** forests, orchards.

BROWN-HEADED BARBET (Green)

Megalaima zeylanica 28cm. Sexes alike. Grass-green plumage; brownish head, neck, upper back, streaked white; bare orange patch around eyes. The **White-Cheeked Barbet** *M viridis* (23cm) of S India, has a white cheek stripe. Solitary or in pairs; occasionally small parties; strictly arboreal; keeps to fruiting trees, often with other frugivorous birds; difficult to spot in the canopy; noisy in hot season; strong, undulating flight. **Food:** chiefly fruits; also flower nectar, petals, insects and small lizards. **Voice:** noisy; its *kutroo...kutroo...* or *pukrook....pukrook* calls one of the most familiar sounds of the Indian forests; calls often begin with a guttural *kurrrr*. **Range:** most of India south of the Himalayan foothills (Himachal to Nepal). **Habitat:** forests, groves; also city gardens.

Brown-Headed Barbet

BLUE-THROATED BARBET

Megalaima asiatica 23cm. Sexes alike. Grass-green plumage; black, crimson, yellow and blue about head; blue chin and throat diagnostic; crimson spots on sides of throat. Solitary or in pairs; sometimes small parties on fruiting trees, along with other fruit-eating birds; strictly arboreal, keeps to canopy of tall trees; difficult to spot but loud, monotonous calls an indicator of its presence. **Food:** chiefly fruits; also insects. **Voice:** calls similar to that of Large Green Barbet of the plains; on careful hearing, sounds somewhat softer and there is a short note between the two longer ones; can be interpreted as *kutt.oo.ruk...* **Range:** the Himalaya east from Pakistan and Kashmir; found up to about 2250m; also found in Bengal. **Habitat:** forests, groves.

Blue-Throated Barbet

COPPERSMITH BARBET (Crimson-Breasted)

Megalaima haemacephala 17cm. Sexes alike. Grass-green plumage; yellow throat, crimson breast and forehead; dumpy appearance. The **Crimson-Fronted Barbet** *M rubricapilla* of the W Ghats, south of Goa, has crimson chin, throat, foreneck and upper breast. Solitary, in pairs or small parties; strictly arboreal; feeds on fruiting trees, often with other birds; visits flowering *Erythrina, Bombax* trees for flower nectar; often spends early morning sunning on bare branches. **Food:** chiefly fruits and berries; sometimes catches insects. **Voice:** noisy between December and end-April; monotonous *tuk..tuk...* calls one of the best known bird calls of India, likened to a coppersmith working on his metal. **Range:** all India, from about 1800m in outer Himalaya. **Habitat:** light forests, groves, city gardens, roadside trees.

Coppersmith Barbet

Indian Grey Hornbill

Oriental Pied Hornbill

Great Hornbill

INDIAN GREY HORNBILL

Ocyceros birostris 60cm. Grey-brown plumage; large, curved beak with casque diagnostic; long, graduated tail, tipped black-and-white. Casque smaller in female. The **Malabar Grey Hornbill** *O griseus* (58cm), restricted to the W Ghats, south of Khandala, lacks casque on beak; dark tail tipped white, except on central feathers. Pairs or small parties; sometimes large gatherings; mostly arboreal, but descends to pick fallen fruit or a lizard; feeds along with frugivorous birds on fruiting trees; noisy, undulating flight. **Food:** fruit, lizards, insects, rodents. **Voice:** noisy; normal call a shrill squealing note; also other squeals and screams. **Range:** almost throughout India, from about 1500m in Himalaya; absent in arid NW regions and the heavy rainfall areas of southern W Ghats. **Habitat:** forests, orchards, tree-covered avenues, vicinity of habitation.

ORIENTAL PIED HORNBILL (Indian Pied)

Anthracoceros albirostris 88cm. Sexes alike. Female slightly smaller. Black above; white face-patch, wing-tips (seen in flight), tips to outer tail-feathers; black throat, breast; white below. Black and yellow beak with large casque. The **Malabar Pied Hornbill** *A coronatus* (92cm) is very similar, except for completely white outer tail feathers. Small parties, occasionally collecting into several dozen birds on favourite fruiting trees; associates with other birds; arboreal but often feeds on ground, hopping about. **Food:** fruit, lizards, snakes, young birds, insects. **Voice:** loud cackles and screams; also a rapid *pak..pak..pak.* **Range:** Haryana and Kumaon to exteme NE; E Ghats, south to Bastar and N Andhra Pradesh. The Malabar Pied is absent in NE regions, but is found over the W Ghats south of Ratnagiri. **Habitat:** forests, orchards, groves.

GREAT HORNBILL (Great Pied)

Buceros bicornis 130cm. Sexes alike. Black face, back and underbody; two white bars on black wings; white neck, lower abdomen and tail; broad black tail band; huge black and yellow beak with enormous concave-topped casque distinctive. Female slightly smaller. Pairs or small parties; occasionally large flocks; mostly arboreal, feeding on fruiting trees, plucking fruit with tip of bill, tossing it up, catching it in the throat and swallowing it; may settle on ground to pick fallen fruit; noisy flight, audible from over a kilometre, even when flying very high, caused by drone of air rushing through base of outer quills of wing feathers; flight alternation of flapping and gliding, less undulating than in other hornbills. **Food:** fruits, lizards, rodents, snakes. **Voice:** loud and deep barking calls; loud *tokk* at feeding sites, audible for considerable distance. **Range:** lower Himalaya east of Kumaon, up to about 1800m; another population exists in W Ghats, south of Khandala. **Habitat:** forests.

COMMON HOOPOE

Upupa epops 31cm including beak. Sexes alike. Fawn coloured plumage; black and white markings on wings, back and tail; black and white-tipped crest; longish, gently curved beak. Solitary or in scattered pairs; small loose flocks in winter; probes ground with long beak, sometimes feeding along with other birds; flits among tree branches; crest often fanned open; becomes rather aggressive with onset of breeding season. **Food:** insects caught on ground or pulled from underground. **Voice:** pleasant, mellow *hoo..po..po..*, sometimes only first two notes; calls have a slightly ventriloquistic quality; calls frequently when breeding. **Range:** all India, from about 5500m in Himalaya; several races; spreads considerably in winter. **Habitat:** meadows, open country, garden lawns, open light forests.

Common Hoopoe

MALABAR TROGON

Harpactes fasciatus 30cm. **Male:** sooty-black head, neck, breast; yellow-brown back; black wings narrowly barred white; rich crimson underbody, white breast gorget. **Female:** duller overall; lacks black on head, breast; orange-brown underbody. Long, squarish tail diagnostic. Solitary or in pairs; strictly arboreal; difficult to see because duller back mostly turned towards observer or intruder; hunts flycatcher-style or flits amongst taller branches; flicks tail and bends body when disturbed. **Food:** chiefly insects; also fruits. **Voice:** diagnostic, often a giveaway to bird's presence in a forest; three to eight noted, somewhat whistling *cue..cue..* calls. **Range:** forested areas of Peninsular India; Satpuras range, W Ghats, east to Orissa and parts of E Ghats. **Habitat:** forest.

Malabar Trogon

Indian Roller

Common Kingfisher

Oriental Dwarf Kingfisher

INDIAN ROLLER

Coracias benghalensis 31cm. Sexes alike. Pale greenish-brown above; rufous-brown breast; deep blue tail has light blue sub-terminal band; in flight, bright Oxford-blue wings and tail, with Cambridge-blue bands distinctive. Solitary or in pairs; perches on overhead wires, bare branches, earthen mounds, small bushtops; either glides and drops on prey or pounces suddenly; batters prey against perch before swallowing. **Food:** mostly insects; catches small lizards, frogs, small rodents and snakes. **Voice:** usually silent; occasionally harsh *khak..kak.. kak..* notes; exuberant screeching notes and shrieks during courtship display, diving, tumbling and screaming wildly. **Range:** almost all India, south of outer Himalaya, where found up to about 1500m. **Habitat:** open country, light forests.

COMMON KINGFISHER

Alcedo atthis 18cm. Sexes alike. Bright blue above, greenish on wings; top of head finely-banded black and blue; ferruginous cheeks, ear-coverts and white patch on sides of neck, white chin and throat and deep ferruginous underbody distinctive; coral-red legs and blackish beak. Solitary or in scattered pairs; never found away from water; perches on pole or overhanging branch; flies low over water, a brilliant blue streak, uttering its shrill notes; sometimes tame and confiding; dives for fish from perch; occasionally hovers over water before diving. **Food:** fish; occasionally tadpoles and aquatic insects. **Voice:** shrill *chichee chichee*. **Range:** all India, south of 2000m in Himalaya; various races differ in shades of blue-green upperbody. **Habitat:** streams, lakes, canals; also coastal areas.

ORIENTAL DWARF KINGFISHER (Three-Toed)

Ceyx erithacus 13cm. Sexes alike. Brownish-chestnut crown; iridescent purple back, rump; deep purplish-blue of closed wings often hides the back; deep-blue and white spots on neck-sides and short, chestnut tail; orangish-yellow underbody and large, bright coral-red beak striking. Solitary or in pairs; a tiny forest bird, usually overlooked when perched on stumps or tangled roots along nullahs and mud walls, often by a forest path or road. **Food:** small fish, insects. **Voice:** sharp squeaky *chicheee* or *chcheee..* call. **Range:** apparently disjunct. From Garhwal east through NE states; W Ghats south from around Bombay; Nilgiris. Appears in many areas only with the onset of SW monsoons. **Habitat:** forest streams, nullahs.

STORK-BILLED KINGFISHER
Halcyon capensis 38cm. Sexes alike. Solitary, more heard than seen. Does not normally hover. Enormous red bill diagnostic. Head dark grey-brown with yellowish collar on back of neck. Body pale green-blue above and brownish-yellow below. **Food:** fish, frogs and small birds. **Voice:** noisy *Kee..kee..kee* repeated many times. **Range:** all India except drier parts of NW. **Habitat:** canals, streams, coastal backwaters in well wooded country.

Stork-Billed Kingfisher

WHITE-THROATED KINGFISHER
(White-Breasted)
Halcyon smyrnensis 28cm. Sexes alike. Chestnut-brown head, neck and under-body below breast; bright turquoise-blue above, often with greenish tinge; black flight-feathers and white wing-patch in flight; white chin, throat and breast distinctive; coral-red beak and legs. Solitary or scattered pairs atop overhead wires, poles, tree-tops; frequently found far from water; drops on to ground to pick prey. **Food:** insects, frogs, lizards, small rodents; only occasionally fish. **Voice:** noisy; loud, crackling laugh, often audible over crowded urban areas; song a longish, quivering whistle, sounding as *kililililili.....* characteristic feature of hot season when bird is breeding; fascinating courtship display. **Range:** all India, south of outer Himalaya. **Habitat:** forest, cultivation, lakes, riversides, coastal mangroves and estuaries.

White-Throated Kingfisher

BLACK-CAPPED KINGFISHER
Halcyon pileata 30cm. Sexes alike. Black cap, white collar and deep blue upperbody render this species unmistakable; white throat, upper breast and dull rufous below; in flight, a conspicuous white wing-patch; deep, daggerlike, coral-red beak. The **Collared** *Todiramphus chloris* (24cm) lacks black cap; white collar bordered by black stripe and greenish-blue upperparts; white underbody, black beak and unmarked wings are further clues. Mostly solitary; a coastal bird, only sometimes wandering inland; has favoured feeding sites; dives for fish but also takes insects from ground. **Food:** fish, crabs, insects, frogs. **Voice:** shrill, fairly loud cackle, quite like the commoner White-Breasted, but unmistakable once heard. **Range:** the coast, from around Bombay south along entire western seaboard and all along the eastern coast, S Sri Lanka. **Habitat:** chiefly coastal areas, mangroves, estuaries; may wander inland, especially along rivers.

Black-Capped Kingfisher

Pied Kingfisher

Blue-Bearded Bee-Eater

Green Bee-Eater

PIED KINGFISHER (Lesser Pied)

Ceryle rudis 30cm. Speckled black-and-white plumage diagnostic; black nuchal crest; double black gorget across breast in malt. The female differs in having a single, broken breast gorget. Solitary, in pairs or in small groups; always around water, either perched on poles, tree-stumps or rocks; hovers when hunting, bill pointed down as wings beat rapidly; dives fast, headlong on sighting fish; batters catch on perch; calls in flight. The **Crested Kingfisher** *C lugubris* of Himalayan streams and rivers can be identified by larger size (41cm), larger crest and white nuchal collar. **Food:** chiefly fish; occasionally tadpoles and water insects. **Voice:** piercing, twittering *chirrruk.. chirruk...* cries in flight, sounding as if the bird is complaining. **Range:** all India, from about 2000m in Himalaya. **Habitat:** streams, rivers, ponds; sometimes coastal areas.

BLUE-BEARDED BEE-EATER

Nyctyornis athertoni 30cm. Sexes alike. Unmarked grass-green above, bluer on forehead; blue along centre of throat to breast appears beardlike, prominent when bird is calling; buffy-yellow below breast, streaked green; tail lacks the long central pins. Pairs or three to four birds; arboreal, rarely descending low; makes short aerial sallies after winged insects; batters prey on perch; usually not an easy bird to observe from close. **Food:** winged insects; observed on *Erythrina* and *Salmalia* flowers. **Voice:** harsh *korrr..korrr* croaking notes, often followed by softer chuckling call. **Range:** outer Himalaya to about 1800m, from Himachal to extreme east; the W Ghats and Nilgiris; forested parts of Madhya Pradesh, E Ghats through Andhra Pradesh, Orissa, Bihar and W Bengal. **Habitat:** forest edges, clearings.

GREEN BEE-EATER

Merops orientalis 21cm including the long central tail-pins. Sexes alike. Bright green plumage; red-brown wash about head; pale blue on chin, throat, bordered below by black gorget; slender, curved black beak; rufous wash on black-tipped flight feathers; elongated central tail-feathers distinctive. Small parties; perches freely on bare branches and overhead telegraph wires; attends also to grazing cattle; launches graceful sorties after winged insects; batters prey against perch before swallowing. **Food:** mostly winged insects; confirmed nuisance to the honey industry. **Voice:** noisy; cheerful trilling notes, chiefly uttered on wing. **Range:** all India, south of about 1800m in outer Himalaya. **Habitat:** open country and cultivation; light forests.

BLUE-TAILED BEE-EATER

Merops philippinus 30cm. Sexes alike. Elongated central tail-feathers. Greenish above, with faint blue wash on wings; bluish rump, tail diagnostic; yellow upper-throat patch with chestnut throat, upper breast; slightly curved black beak, broad black stripe through eyes. The very similar **Blue-Cheeked Bee-Eater** *M persicus* (31cm) has a dull-white and blue-green cheek patch. In good light, the greenish rump and tail help identification. Usually small flocks, frequently in vicinity of water; launches short, elegant flights from wire or tree perch; characteristic flight, a few quick wing-beats and a stately glide. **Food:** winged insects. **Voice:** musical, ringing notes, chiefly uttered in flight. **Range:** exact range of these species not correctly known. **Habitat:** open country, light forests, vicinity of water, cultivation; may occasionally be seen in coastal areas.

Blue-Tailed Bee-Eater

CHESTNUT-HEADED BEE-EATER

Merops leschenaulti 21cm. Sexes alike. Grass-green plumage; chestnut-cinnamon crown, hindneck, upper back; yellow chin, throat; rufous and black gorget. Small gatherings on telegraph wires or bare, upper branches of trees from where the birds launch short aerial sallies; fast, graceful flight; noisy when converging at roosting trees. **Food:** chiefly winged insects, captured in flight. **Voice:** musical twittering notes, mostly uttered on the wing, and sometimes from perch. **Range:** disjunct. Himalayan foothills country, from Dehra Dun to extreme NE; a second population exists in the W Ghats south of Goa; also Sri Lanka. Occasionally may be encountered in the peninsula, especially during the monsoon. **Habitat:** vicinity of water in forested areas.

Chestnut-Beaded Bee-Eater

PIED CUCKOO (Pied Crested)

Clamator jacobinus 33cm. Sexes alike. Black above; noticeable crest; white in wings and white tip to long tail-feathers diagnostic in flight; white underbody. Young birds, seen in autumn, are dull sooty-brown with indistinct crests; white areas dull fulvous. Solidly or in small parties of four to six; arboreal; occasionally descends to ground to feed on insects; arrives just before SW monsoon by end-May, noisy and active, chasing one another; mobbed by crows on arrival. **Food:** insects, including hairy, noxious caterpillars. **Voice:** noisy; loud, metallic *plew...piu...* call-notes; other shrill shrieks. **Range:** chiefly SW monsoon breeding visitor; most of the country south of outer Himalaya. **Habitat:** open forest, cultivation, orchards.

Pied Cuckoo

Common Hawk Cuckoo

Indian Cuckoo

COMMON HAWK CUCKOO
Hierococcyx varius 35cm. Sexes alike. Ashy-grey above; dark bars on rufescent-tipped tail; dull-white below, with pale ashy-rufous on breast; barred below. Young birds broadly streaked dark below; pale rufous barrings on brown upperbody. Solitary, rarely in pairs; strictly arboreal; noisy during May-September; silent after rains. **Food:** chiefly insects; rarely wild fruit and small lizards. **Voice:** famous call-notes; interpreted as *brain-fever...*, uttered untiringly in crescendo: also described as *pipeeha..pipeeha...;* very noisy in overcast weather. **Range:** all India south of Himalayan foothills, uncommon even during rains in arid zones. **Habitat:** forests, open country, near habitation.

INDIAN CUCKOO
Cuculus micropterus 32cm. Slaty-brown above; greyer on head, throat and breast; whitish below, with broadly-spaced black cross-bars; broad subterminal tail-band (characteristic of the non-hawk cuckoos of genus *Cuculus*); the female often has rufous-brown wash on throat and breast; call-notes most important identification clue. Solitary; arboreal, not easy to see; overall appearance very hawk-like, but distinctly weaker-looking flight. The **Eurasian Cuckoo** *C canorus* differs from the Indian Cuckoo by lacking the subterminal black band and has the diagnostic *cuck-koo* call. **Food:** insects, with special fondness for hairy caterpillars. **Voice:** very distinct call; a four-noted mellow whistle, variously interpreted, the best known being *bo.ko.tako* and *crossword..puzzle;* the third note trailing slightly and the fourth a little more; very vocal between April-August coinciding with the breeding of its principal hosts, drongos and orioles; may call for several minutes continuously, often throughout the day if overcast. **Range:** most of India south from Himalaya to about 2500m, excepting the drier and arid parts of NW India; appears to move considerably, especially just before and after the rains. **Habitat:** forest, orchards.

GREY-BELLIED CUCKOO (Indian Plaintive)

Cacomantis passerinus 23cm. Sexes alike. Grey head; grey-brown upperbody; white tail-tip and patch on wing-underside seen in flight; grey throat, upper-breast; paler, almost white below. Female also has hepatic (reddish) phase. Bright chestnut upperbody and throat, with a reddish-brown wash; cross-barred black on back; white below throat, narrowly cross-barred black. Hepatic female very similar to **Banded Bay Cuckoo** *C sonneratii*. Mostly solitary; keeps to foliage but often emerges to launch short sally or to move from one patch to another; active and noisy, chiefly during monsoon. **Food:** insects, specially hairy caterpillars. **Voice:** quite noisy, with good range of calls, a mournful (plaintive) single-noted *piteeer...* call; sometimes a three-noted call, the second note shortest, the third long-drawn; also, a four-noted Indian Cuckoo-like call, but distinctly higher-pitched and shrill; also a longer song of eight or nine notes. **Range:** India, south from Himalaya to about 2500m, excepting arid NW regions; widespread and commoner in forested parts; easily overlooked, thus exact status unclear; moves seasonally. **Habitat:** open forests, orchards and gardens in vicinity of habitation.

Gertrud Denzau

Grey-Bellied Cuckoo

DRONGO CUCKOO

Surniculus lugubris 25cm including tail. Sexes alike. Glossy black plumage; appearance, including forked tail, indistinguishable from Black Drongo; white in under-tail and base of outer tail-feathers diagnostic; very distinctive calls. Young birds dull in colour, speckled white. Solitary; mostly overlooked and mistaken for drongo, but cuckoo-like flight a giveaway; strictly arboreal. **Food:** insects, wild fruit. **Voice:** diagnostic; very noisy during SW monsoon, when it disperses wide; loud, rising five to seven notes, a whistling *pee..pee..pee..pee..pee..*; ends abruptly, only to begin all over again; noisy in overcast weather. **Range:** lower Himalaya but spreads wide during the rains. **Habitat:** open forests; orchards, cultivation with trees.

Tim Loseby

Drongo Cuckoo

ASIAN KOEL

Eudynamys scolopacea 42cm. **Male:** metallic black plumage; greenish beak and crimson eyes. **Female:** dark brown, thickly spotted and barred white; whitish below, dark-spotted on throat, barred below. Solitary or in pairs; arboreal; mostly silent between July and February; fast flight. **Food:** ficus and other fruits; insects, snails, eggs of smaller birds. **Voice:** familiar call of Indian countryside. Very noisy between March and June, coinciding with breeding of crows; loud *kuoo...kuooo..* whistling calls in crescendo by male; *ko.el...* call, the first syllable longish; waterbubbling call of female, and possibly male. **Range:** all India, up to about 1800m in outer Himalaya; uncommon in drier areas. **Habitat:** light forests, orchards, city parks, cultivation and open areas.

Gertrud Denzau

Asian Koel

Sirkeer Malkoha

Greater Coucal

Vernal Hanging Parrot

SIRKEER MALKOHA (Cuckoo)

Phaenicophaeus leschenaultii 45cm including long tail. Sexes alike. Dull olivish-brown plumage; glossy black shaft streaks on breast and head; long, graduated tail, with broad white tips to blackish outer feathers diagnostic in flight; cherry-red beak, with yellow tip. Solitary or in pairs; sometimes four or five birds in the neighbourhood; move mostly on ground, in dense growth; may clamber out on some bush-tops or low trees; flight weak and short. **Food:** insects, fallen fruit, lizards. **Voice:** fairly loud and sharp clicking notes: mostly vocal when breeding, chiefly during the rains; a non-parasitic cuckoo. **Range:** most of India, to about 1800m in the Himalaya; absent in NW India and Kashmir. **Habitat:** open jungle, scrub, ravines, dense growth around habitation.

GREATER COUCAL (Crow-Pheasant)

Centropus sinensis 50cm including tail. Sexes alike. Glossy bluish-black plumage; chestnut wings; blackish, loose-looking, long graduated tail. Female somewhat bigger. Solitary or in pairs; moves amidst dense growth, fanning and flicking tail often; clambers up into trees, but is a poor flier, lazily flying short distances. **Food:** insects, lizards, frogs, eggs and young of other birds, small snakes. **Voice:** loud and resonant *coop.. coop..cooop...* call familiar; occasionally a squeaky call. **Range:** all India, from outer Himalaya to about 2000m. **Habitat:** edge of forest, scrub, cultivation, gardens, derelict patches, vicinity of habitations.

VERNAL HANGING PARROT (Indian Lorikeet)

Loriculus vernalis 15cm. Bright grass-green plumage; short, square tail and bright crimson rump distinctive; small blue throat patch. Female like male, but lacks blue on throat. Solitary or in pairs; occasionally large flocks in flowering and fruiting trees; chiefly arboreal, difficult to locate in canopy; energetic gymnast, moving around branches or hanging upside down to feed; sleeps hanging upside down, like bats; occasionally seen with other birds in mixed parties in canopy. **Food:** nectar, soft fruit-pulp, plant seeds. **Voice:** faint clucking note. **Range:** the Himalaya east of Nepal: peninsula mountains, chiefly the E and W Ghats. Moves a great deal locally. **Habitat:** forest, orchards.

ALEXANDRINE PARAKEET
Psittacula eupatria 52cm including long tail; female smaller. **Male:** rich grass-green plumage; hooked, heavy red beak; deep red shoulder patch; rose-pink collar and black stripe from lower mandible to collar distinctive. **Female:** lacks the collar and black stripe. Yellow under-tail in both sexes. Both small flocks and large gatherings; feeds on fruiting trees in orchards and on standing crop, often causing extensive damage; strong fliers; roosts along with other birds at favoured sites. **Food:** fruits, vegetables, crops, seeds. **Voice:** high-pitched *kreeak...* scream, on wing as well as on perch; popular cage-bird, learning to imitate some notes and human words. **Range:** almost throughout the country, south of Himalayan foothills. **Habitat:** forest, orchards, cultivated areas, towns.

Alexandrine Parakeet

ROSE-RINGED PARAKEET
Psittacula krameri 42cm including long tail. **Male:** grass-green plumage; short, hooked, red beak; rosy-pink and black collar distinctive (obtained only during third year). **Female:** lacks the pink-and-black collar; instead, pale emerald-green around neck. Gregarious; large necks of this species, familiar sight in India; cause extensive damage to standing crops, orchards and garden fruit-trees; also raids grain depots and markets; large roosting colonies, often along with mynas and crows. **Food:** fruit, crops, cereal. **Voice:** shrill *keeak...* screams, somewhat less grating than the larger Alexandrine's. **Range:** all India, south of Himalayan foothills. **Habitat:** light forest, orchards, towns, villages.

Rose-Ringed Parakeet

SLATY-HEADED PARAKEET
Psittacula himalayana 40cm including long tail. Sexes alike, but female lacks red on shoulders. Grass-green plumage; deep slaty-grey head; black chin, narrow neck-ring; blue-green hindneck collar; red shoulder-patch; long, pointed, yellow-tipped tail. The **Grey-Headed Parakeet** *P finschii* of the NE regions is very similar but slightly smaller. Small flocks in forests; arboreal, but often feeds on standing crop; strong flier. **Food:** fruits, acorns, maize; often causes damage. **Voice:** highpitched but pleasant double-noted *tooi..tooi..* call, somewhat interrogative in tone; calls mostly in flight; also a single-noted call. **Range:** Himalaya, to about 2800m; moves considerably, descending very low in winter. **Habitat:** forest, mountainsides, orchards, hillside cultivation.

Slaty-Headed Parakeet

Toby Sinclair

Plum-Headed Parakeet

PLUM-HEADED PARAKEET (Blossom-Headed)

Psittacula cyanocephala 35cm including tail. **Male:** yellowish-green plumage; plum-red head; black and bluish-green collar: maroon-red wing-shoulder patch; white tips to central tail-feathers distinctive. **Female:** dull greyer head; yellow collar; almost non-existent maroon shoulder-patch. Pairs or small parties; arboreal, but descends into cultivation in forest clearings and outskirts; sometimes huge gatherings in cultivation; strong, darting flight over forest. **Food:** fruits, grain, flower nectar and petals. **Voice:** loud, interrogative *tooi....tooi...* notes in fast flight; also other chattering notes. **Range:** all India south of Himalayan foothills. **Habitat:** forest, orchards, cultivation in forest.

Getrud Denzau

Malabar Parakeet

MALABAR PARAKEET (Blue-Winged)

Psittacula columboides 38cm including tail. Pinkish-grey head, back and breast; black chin and neck-ring, along with a blue-green collar; greenish lower-back, rump and upper-wings, middle feathers of long tail; yellow tips to tail-feathers. Blue-green collar absent in female. Pairs or small groups, rarely more than six birds together; a forest bird, chiefly arboreal but sometimes descends to cultivation; strong flight. **Food:** fruits, seeds, standing crop, flower-nectar. **Voice:** loud, high-pitched and somewhat harsh *tchoi....tchwe* call, quite like the commoner Blossom-Headed's but unmistakable once heard. **Range:** restricted to W Ghats from just north of Bombay to extreme south; also some associated hill ranges. **Habitat:** forests, orchards, cultivation, clearings.

INDIAN SWIFTLET (Indian Edible-Nest)

Collocalia unicolor 12cm. Sexes alike. Tiny size. Blackish-brown plumage; slightly-forked tail in flight. The **Himalayan Swiftlet** *C brevirostris* (14cm) is very similar except for the rump which is paler than rest of body. Gregarious and colonial; huge numbers on cliff-sides and caves; swarms leave before dawn in a rush of wings; spends day high over mountains and countryside, hawking insects, often along with other swifts and martins; arrives back to caves and cliff roosts around dusk, when the bats are leaving. **Food:** winged insects. **Voice:** roosting birds keep up incessant, faint chatter. **Range:** W Ghats, south of Ratnagiri; associated hill ranges. **Habitat:** caves, cliffs on rocky, offshore islands.

ASIAN PALM SWIFT

Cypsiurus balasiensis 13cm. Sooty-brown plumage; typical swift wings, long and sickle-like; deeply forked tail diagnostic, specially in flight. Sociable; small parties in open, palm-dotted country; strong in flight, and uttering lively screaming notes on the wing; hawks insects all day, occasionally rising very high; roosts on underside of palmyra frond (leaf). **Food:** winged insects. **Voice:** three note shrill scream, uttered very fast and always on the wing. **Range:** throughout the country, south of Himalayan foothills; also in NE states. **Habitat:** open country, cultivation; this bird's life revolves around the palmyra.

ALPINE SWIFT

Tachymarptis melba 22cm. Sexes alike. Very long, sickle-shaped, pointed wings; dark sooty-brown above; white underbody; broad, brown band across breast diagnostic in flight; dark under tail-coverts. Loose parties dashing erratically at high speed in the skies; extremely strong flier; seen high in skies around dusk, many birds wheeling and tumbling, their shrill screams rending the air; drinks at ponds and puddles by skimming over water surface. **Food:** winged insects; also hawks insects disturbed by forest-fires. **Voice:** shrill *chrrrr....chee..chee...* screams in fast flight; twittering notes at roost sites. **Range:** all India, from about 2500m in Himalaya; uncommon over N Indian plains. **Habitat:** hill-country, cliffsides.

Goren Erkstrom

Alpine Swift

HOUSE SWIFT

Apus affinis 15cm. Sexes alike. Blackish plumage; white rump and throat diagnostic; short square tail and long, sickle-like swift wings. The **Fork-Tailed Swift** *A pacificus* (18cm) has a deeply forked tail. Highly gregarious; on the wing during day, hawking insects, flying over human habitation, cliffs and ruins; strong fliers, exhibiting great mastery and control in fast wheeling flight; frequently utters squealing notes on wing; retires to safety of nest-colonies in overcast weather. **Food:** winged insects. **Voice:** musical squeals on the wing; very vocal at sunset, but also through the day. **Range:** throughout the country from about 2400m in Himalaya. **Habitat:** human habitation, cliffs, ruins.

Otto Pfister

House Swift

Krupakar Senani

Crested Treeswift

Thakur Dalip Singh

Barn Owl

Kamal Sahai

Collared Scops Owl

CRESTED TREESWIFT

Hemiprocne coronata 23cm. **Male:** bluish-grey above, with a faint greenish wash; chestnut sides of face, throat; ashy-grey breast, whiter below. **Female:** like male, but lacks chestnut on head. Backward curving crest and long, deeply-forked tail diagnostic. Pairs or small, scattered parties; fly during day, hawking insects; have favourite foraging areas; flight graceful, not as fast as other swifts, but displaying typical swift mastery; calls from perch and in flight; unlike other swifts, perches on bare, higher branches; drinks in flight from surface of forest pools. **Food:** winged insects. **Voice:** double-noted faint scream; also a parrot-like *kea..kea...* call. **Range:** all India, south of Himalayan foothills; absent in the arid parts of NW India. **Habitat:** open, deciduous forest.

BARN OWL

Tyto alba 35cm. Sexes alike. Dull golden-buff above, finely speckled black and white; white below, often with fine, dark spots; heart-shaped, white facial disc striking. The rather similar **Grass Owl** *T capensis* is dark brown above. Solitary or in pairs; nocturnal, but sometimes hunts during day; normally rests during day, mostly in a tree-cavity, dense creepers or some dark loft; perches upright; flies silently, mostly under 4m from ground; pounces on prey. **Food:** rodents, small birds, bats and large insects. **Voice:** long-drawn, wild shriek; a variety of snoring, hissing notes. **Range:** almost all India, south of Himalayan foothills. **Habitat:** grasslands, cultivation, human habitation, even town-centres.

COLLARED SCOPS OWL

Otus bakkamoena 25cm. Small ear-tufts and upright posture. Sexes alike. Greyish-brown above, profusely marked whitish; buffy nuchal collar diagnostic; buffy-white underbody, streaked and mottled dark. The very similar **Eurasian Scops Owl** *O scops* lacks nuchal collar. Solitary or in pairs; remains motionless during day in thick, leafy branches or at junctions of stems and branches; very difficult to spot; flies around dusk. **Food:** insects, small lizards and rodents; also small birds. **Voice:** a single note *wut...wut....,* rather questioning in tone; calls through the night, often for 20 minutes at stretch, a *wut..* every two to four seconds. **Range:** throughout country from about 2400m in the Himalaya. **Habitat:** forests, cultivation, orchards, trees in vicinity of habitation.

EURASIAN EAGLE OWL (Great Horned Owl)
Bubo bubo 56cm. Sexes alike. Brown plumage, mottled and streaked dark and light; prominent ear-tufts; orange eyes; legs fully-feathered. The **Brown Fish Owl** *B zeylonensis* (56cm) is darker and has white throat patch and naked legs. Solitary or pairs; mostly nocturnal; spends day in leafy branch, rock-ledge or an old well; flies slowly but considerable distances when disturbed; emerges to feed around sunset, advertising its arrival with its characteristic call. **Food:** rodents; also reptiles, frogs and medium-sized birds. **Voice:** deep, booming *bu..boo..* call; snapping calls at nest. **Range:** throughout country, from about 1500m in the Himalaya. **Habitat:** ravines, cliffsides, riversides, scrub and open country.

Eurasian Eagle Owl

DUSKY EAGLE OWL (Dusky Horned Owl)
Bubo coromandus 58cm. Sexes alike. Pale grey-brown plumage, profusely spotted, streaked and marked with white, mostly below; dark shaft-stripes; prominent ear-tufts and dull yellow eyes diagnostic. The Brown Fish Owl is deep rufous-brown, thickly streaked, and has bright yellow eyes and naked legs. Mostly pairs, sometimes three to four scattered; has favoured roost-sites in large, leafy trees; may call and fly during daytime. **Food:** small animals, birds, frogs, insects. **Voice:** deep, hollow, somewhat eerie hoot of five to eight notes fading towards end; interpreted as *wo..wo..wo..wo..o.o.o.* **Range:** most of the country south of outer Himalaya; status in extreme south of country unclear. **Habitat:** groves, light forest, roadside leafy trees, vicinity of habitation.

Dusky Eagle Owl

MOTTLED WOOD OWL
Strix ocellata 48cm. Sexes alike. Tawny-grey above, profusely mottled with black, white and buff; whitish facial disc, with narrow chocolate-black barrings forming concentric circles; white spots on crown, nape; whitish throat; buffy below, barred black. The **Brown Wood Owl** *S leptogrammica* (46cm) has white supercilium. The **Tawny Owl** *S aluco* (45cm) has streaked underparts. Solitary or in pairs; nocturnal, spends day in dense foliage of large trees; leaves roost after sunset. **Food:** rats, mice, squirrels; also pigeons and lizards. **Voice:** loud, hooting note. **Range:** all India, from Himalayan foothills south; absent in arid NW parts and much of NE. **Habitat:** forests, orchards, vicinity of habitation, cultivation.

Mottled Wood Owl

Jungle Owlet

JUNGLE OWLET (Barred)

Glaucidium radiatum 20cm. Lacks ear-tufts. Sexes alike. Darkish brown above, barred rufous and white; flight-feathers barred rufous and black; white moustachial stripe, centre of breast and abdomen; remainder of underbody barred dark rufous-brown and white. The **Asian Barred Owlet** *G cuculoides* (23cm) of the Himalaya is slightly larger and has abdominal streaks. Solitary or in pairs; crepuscular, but sometimes also active and noisy by day; otherwise spends day in leafy branch; flies short distance when disturbed. **Food:** insects, small birds, lizards, rodents. **Voice:** noisy; musical *kuo.kak..kuo..kak...* call-notes, rising in crescendo for few seconds only to end abruptly, other pleasant bubbling notes. **Range:** throughout country, from about 2000m in Himalaya; probably absent in extreme NE states. **Habitat:** forest; partial to teak and bamboo mixed forests.

Spotted Owlet

SPOTTED OWLET

Athene brama 20cm. No ear-tufts. Sexes alike. Greyish-brown plumage, spotted white. Yellowish eyes; broken whitish-buff nuchal collar. Young birds more thickly marked white; darkish streaks below breast, pairs or small parties; roosts during day in leafy branches, tree-cavities or cavity in wall; active in some localities during daytime; disturbed birds fly to neighbouring tree or branch and bob and stare at intruder. **Food:** insects, small rodents, lizards and birds. **Voice:** assortment of scolding and cackling notes, screeches and chuckles. **Range:** throughout country, up to about 1800m in outer Himalaya. **Habitat:** open forests, orchards, cultivation, vicinity of habitation.

Sri Lanka Frogmouth

SRI LANKA FROGMOUTH

Batrachostomus moniliger 24cm. Unusually wide gape and broad, swollen beak diagnostic. **Male:** grey-brown plumage, mottled with brown, buff, black and white. **Female:** overall plumage dull rufous with black-ringed white spots on wing coverts. Little known species; nocturnal and crepuscular; spends day perched motionless like a stump and extremely difficult to spot; on disturbance merely points beak towards sky. Usually noticed when flushed and moves only a few metres. Favours regular perch. **Food:** wide gape indicates that the bird hawks insects; but also reported to catch insects on ground and from branches. **Voice:** chuckling *whuo...* has been described. **Range:** W Ghats south of Coorg and wet zone of Sri Lanka. Rare and unknown. **Habitat:** dense forest.

GREY NIGHTJAR (Indian Jungle)

Caprimulgus indicus 30cm. Plumage in nightjars highly obliterative. Mottled and vermiculated grey-brown, black, buff and white; in some species, white tips to tail in male; calls highly diagnostic. Solitary or several scattered; crepuscular and nocturnal; squats during day, along a branch's length or on rocky ground amidst dry leaves; extremely difficult to spot unless almost stepped upon; flies around dusk, hawking insects in zig-zag flight; settles on cart tracks and roads, where eyes gleam in vehicle headlights. The **Large-Tailed Nightjar** *C macrurus* is slightly larger (33cm) and has more brownish plumage. **Food:** winged insects. **Voice:** somewhat whistling *chuckoo..chuckoo*, up to seven minutes at a stretch, with pauses in between; a quick-repeated, mellow *tuck.tuck.tuck* call, 8 to 50 at a stretch; occasionally a pleasant *uk...kukrooo*, with a slight pause after the shorter first note; vocal between dusk and dawn. Calls help identification. **Range:** all India, up to about 3000m in the Himalaya. **Habitat:** forest clearings, broken scrubby ravines.

Grey Nightjar

SAVANNA NIGHTJAR (Franklin's)

Caprimulgus affinis 25cm. **Male:** grey-brown plumage, mottled dark; a buffy 'V' on back, from shoulders to about centre of back two pairs of outer tail-feathers white with pale-dusky tips; white wing-patches. **Female:** like male, but without white outer tail-feathers, which are barred; conspicuous rufous-buff wing-patches; call most important identification clue. Solitary or several scattered over an open expanse; overall behavior like other nightjars; remains motionless during day on open rocky, grass or scrub-covered ground; sometimes roosts on tree, along length of a branch; flies around dusk, often flying high; drinks often. **Food:** flying insects. **Voice:** calls on wing as well as on perch, a fairly loud, penetrating *sweeesh* or *schweee...*, like whiplash cutting through air; calls every few seconds, often for hours at a stretch; if disturbed during day, may make a harsh, chuckling and faint screeching sound. **Range:** throughout country, south of outer Himalaya to about 2000m; moves considerably locally. **Habitat:** rocky hillsides, scrub and grass country, light forests, dry streams and river-beds, fallow land, cultivation.

Savanna Nightjar

Snow Pigeon

SNOW PIGEON

Columba leuconota 35cm. Sexes alike. Blackish-brown head separated from dull-brown back by whitish collar; extensive white on lower-back and three dark bands in grey wings, both these characteristics seen at rest and in flight; very dark tail has white subterminal band; black beak and red feet. Flocks of variable size gleaning on the ground, frequently around mountain habitations, freshly-sown cultivations and vicinities of melting snow; flight very strong; breeds in large colonies on cliffs and in rock-caves. **Food:** grain, bulbs, seeds. **Range:** the Himalaya, 2800-5000m, may descend to about 1000m in winter. **Habitat:** open meadows, cultivation, mountain habitation, cliff-faces.

Nilgiri Wood Pigeon

NILGIRI WOOD PIGEON

Columba elphinstonii 42cm. Sexes alike. Reddish-brown above; metallic purple-green on upper-back; grey head, underbody; whitish throat; black-and-white chessboard on hindneck diagnostic. Solitary or in small gatherings; arboreal but often descends to forest floor to pick fallen fruit; strong flier, wheeling and turning amidst branches at a fast speed; occasionally along with other frugivorous birds. **Food:** fruits, berries, newer buds. **Voice:** loud *who..* call, like a softer version of *Langur's* call, followed by three to five deep and eerie sounding *who...whu...who....* notes; characteristic call of heavy W Ghats forest. **Range:** W Ghats south from Bombay. **Habitat:** moist evergreen forest; sholas; cardamom plantations.

Oriental Turtle Dove

ORIENTAL TURTLE DOVE (Rufous Turtle)

Streptopelia orientalis 32cm. Sexes alike. Grey-and-black spotted patch on neck sides; rufous-brown back and scapulars, with black markings diagnostic; slaty-grey lower back, rump; whitish border to roundish tail, best seen when tail fanned during landing. Pairs or loose parties, occasionally solitary birds; feeds mostly on ground; rests during hot hours in leafy branches; perches on overhead wires. **Food:** seeds, crops, bamboo seeds. **Voice:** deep and grating *ghur..ghroo..goo....* **Range:** several races, resident and migratory, distributed over much of the Indian region, except the arid NW. **Habitat:** mixed forest, vicinity of cultivation, orchards.

Laughing Dove

LAUGHING DOVE (Little Brown)

Streptopelia senegalensis 26cm. Sexes alike. Pinkish-grey-brown plumage with black-and-white chessboard on sides of foreneck; white tips to outer tail-feathers and broad grey wing-patches best seen in night; small size distinctive. Pairs or small flocks; associates freely with other doves in the huge gatherings at harvest time; feeds mostly on ground, walking about silently. **Food:** grains, grass and weed seeds. **Voice:** somewhat harsh but pleasant *cru.do.do.do.do*. **Range:** almost all India from about 1200m in the outer Himalaya; uncommon in NE states. **Habitat:** open scrub, cultivation, neighbourhood of habitation.

Krupakar Senari

Spotted Dove

SPOTTED DOVE

Streptopelia chinensis 30cm. Sexes alike. Grey and pink-brown above, spotted white; white-spotted black hindneck collar (chessboard) diagnostic dark tail with broad white tips to outer feathers seen in flight; vinous-brown breast, merging into white on belly. Young birds are barred above and lack chessboard. Pairs or small parties on ground; frequently settles on paths and roads, flying further on intrusion; quite tame and confiding in many areas; drinks often; at harvest times, seen along with other doves in immense gatherings. **Food:** grains, seeds. **Voice:** familiar bird-sound of India, a soft, somewhat doleful *crook..cru..croo* or *croo..croo..croo.* **Range:** all India, to about 3500m in the Himalaya. **Habitat:** open forest, scrub, habitation, cultivation.

RED COLLARED DOVE (Red Turtle)

Streptopelia tranquebarica 32cm. Sexes alike. Greyish-brown plumage; lilac wash about head and neck; black half-collar on hind-neck diagnostic; broad whitish tips to brown tail-feathers, seen as a terminal band when fanned during landing; dull lilac breast and ashy-grey underbody. Small parties when not

E. Hanumantha Rao

Red Collared Dove

E. Hanumantha Rao

Eurasian Collared Dove

breeding; often associates with other doves; large gatherings glean in cultivated country; strong flier, chases intruders in territory. **Food:** seeds, grain. **Voice:** characteristic *kukkoo.. kook...*, almost dreamlike in quality; also a strident *koon... koon...* when male displays at onset of breeding. **Range:** most of the country, except extreme NE Himalaya; resident and local migrant; commonest in NW, W and C India. **Habitat:** cultivation, open scrub, dry forest.

 EURASIAN COLLARED DOVE (Indian Ring) *Streptopelia decaocto* 22cm. **Male:** deep ashy-grey head; black hindneck collar; rich wine-red back; slaty grey-brown lower back, rump and upper-tail; whitish tips to all but central tail-feathers. **Female:** much like Ring Dove, but smaller size and more brownish colouration distinctive. Solitary, in pairs or small parties; associates with other doves but is less common; feeds on ground, gleaning on harvested croplands; perches and suns on leafless branches and overhead wires. **Food:** grass and other seeds, cereals. **Voice:** quick-repeated *gru..gurgoo...* call, with more stress on first syllable. **Range:** throughout country, south of the Himalayan foothills. **Habitat:** cultivation, scrub, deciduous country.

Ashok Dilwali

Emerald Dove

Kamal Sahai

Pompadour Green Pigeon

EMERALD DOVE (Green-Winged Pigeon)

Chalcophaps indica 26cm. Sexes alike. Bronze emerald-green upperbody; white forehead, eyebrows; grey crown, neck; white on wing shoulder and across lower-back; whitish rump diagnostic in flight; rich pinkish-brown below; coral red beak and pink-red legs. Solitary or in pairs; moves on forest paths and clearings or darts almost blindly through trees, usually under 5m off ground; difficult to spot on ground. **Food:** seeds, fallen fruit; known to eat termites. **Voice:** deep, plaintive *hoo.oon..hoo.oon.,* many times at a stretch. **Range:** almost throughout country up to about 2000m. **Habitat:** forest, bamboo, clearings; foothills.

POMPADOUR GREEN PIGEON (Grey-Fronted)

Treron pompadora 28cm. **Male:** grey crown, nape; chesnut-maroon back, scapulars; yellow in wings; black wing-shoulder, tail with broad, grey terminal band; bright yellowish-green throat and orangish breast. **Female:** olive-green plumage, without chestnut-maroon on back or orange breast; dull-buff under tail-coverts, streaked greenish. The female **Orange-Breasted Green Pigeon** *T bicincta* has slaty-grey central tail-feathers. Arboreal; small flocks, often with other birds on fruiting trees; occasionally large gatherings; strong flight. **Food:** fruits, berries. **Voice:** rich whistling notes. **Range:** restricted to the forested zones of SW and S India, W Ghats and associated ranges; resident but also shows some local movement. **Habitat:** forest, groves and orchards, edges of forest.

YELLOW-FOOTED GREEN PIGEON (Yellow-Legged Green or Bengal)

Treron phoenicoptera 33cm. Ashy olive-green above; olivish-yellow collar, band in dark slaty tail; lilac-red shoulder patch (mostly absent in female); yellow legs and underbody. Female slightly duller. The nominate (northern) race has grey lower breast and belly. Small necks; mostly arboreal, rarely coming to salt-licks or cropland; remains well hidden in foliage but moves briskly; has favourite feeding trees. **Food:** fruits, berries. **Voice:** rich, mellow whistling notes. **Range:** south roughly of line from S Rajasthan to N Orissa; some difficulty in interpreting the exact range of this and northern races. **Habitat:** forests, orchards, city parks, cultivated village vicinities.

Krupakar Senani

Yellow-Footed Green Pigeon

WEDGE-TAILED GREEN PIGEON

Treron sphenura 35cm. Yellowish-green plumage and wedge-shaped tail. **Male:** rufous-orange on crown; deep maroon on back, scapulars; pale-orangish breast. **Female:** lacks rufous-orange on crown and maroon on upperbody. The **Pin-Tailed Green Pigeon** *T apicauda* is slightly larger (42cm) and has elongated central tail-feathers. Small flocks; mostly arboreal, feeding in foliage of fruiting trees; gymnastically reaching out to fruit; occasionally feeds at salt-licks on ground. **Food:** fruits, berries. **Voice:** rich, mellow whistling notes; also soft *coo...coo...* notes in summer. **Range:** Himalaya, from Kashmir to extreme NE; foothills to about 2800m; moves altitudinally; found south of Brahmaputra river. **Habitat:** mostly broad-leafed hill forests.

Green Imperial Pigeon

Indian Bustard

Lesser Florican

GREEN IMPERIAL PIGEON

Ducula aenea 43cm. Sexes alike. A large forest pigeon. Greyish head, neck and underbody with a distinct pinkish wash; metallic bronze-green upperbody, unbanded tail; chocolate-maroon under-tail; reddish legs. Pairs or small parties on fruiting trees, not infrequently with other species; chiefly arboreal but comes to ground, at salt-licks and water; strong flight; has favourite feeding spots. **Food:** fruit, berries. **Voice:** deep chuckling notes, quite pleasant-sounding and somewhat ventriloquistic. **Range:** forested parts of N India, from Garhwal terai eastwards; forested regions of C and E India, W Ghats south of Bombay; resident in many areas but also moves considerably. **Habitat:** forests.

INDIAN BUSTARD (Great)

Ardeotis nigriceps **Male:** 120cm. Black crown, short crest; sandy-buff upperbody, finely marked black; white below; black band on lower-breast. **Female:** 92cm; smaller size; breast gorget broken and only rarely full. Scattered pairs or small parties; shy, difficult to approach; enters immediate vicinity of *Bishnoi* villages and other rural habitation; fast runner; hides in shade of bushes; flies low over ground. **Food:** grain, seeds, tubers; also insects, rodents, snakes and lizards. **Voice:** loud *whonk...,* often audible for over a mile. **Range:** resident and local migrant; distant areas of Rajasthan, Gujarat, Maharashtra, Karnataka; numbers and erstwhile range much reduced today. **Habitat:** open grassland and scrub; semi-desert.

LESSER FLORICAN (Likh)

Sypheotides indica **Male:** 45cm. Black and white plumage; narrow, upcurving plumes on head striking. **Female:** slightly larger than male; pale sandy-buff, profusely streaked, mottled with dark brown and black; black crown, with pale median stripe. Winter male like female, but more white in wings diagnostic. Solitary or in pairs; in breeding season, several males display over wide, open grasslands; extremely difficult bird to observe, keeps to dense grass growth; tight sitter, runs through cover, but flies far and strongly when flushed; range and numbers much reduced today. **Food:** chiefly insects; also shoots, seeds. **Voice:** rattling call of displaying male, likened to sound made by rubbing tongue on palate; audible for considerable distances; calls during display jump. **Range:** moves considerably; breeds during monsoon in parts of C India; not much data for winter range. **Habitat:** tall grassland, cultivation.

SIBERIAN CRANE

Grus leucogeranus 140cm. Sexes alike. Snow-white plumage striking; naked-red face; black in-flight feathers. Young birds, which also arrive in winter, have buff-brown-cinnamon in plumage; complete head feathered. Pairs or small flocks; the flock size wintering in India (Bharatpur in Rajasthan) has been falling over the years, with barely a dozen birds arriving; spends most of its time in shallow water, feeding with head submerged; the bird is of much concern to conservationists. **Food:** shoots, tubers, aquatic seeds; perhaps also insects. **Voice:** vocal; its loud trumpeting calls may be heard in winter too; musical *koonk...koonk..* in flight. **Range:** winter visitor; rather uncommon, today restricted only to Bharatpur; sporadically recorded in parts of N India, Bihar; southernmost record is around Nagpur. **Habitat:** open marshes, jheels.

Siberian Crane

SARUS CRANE

Grus antigone 165cm. Sexes alike, but female slightly smaller; grey plumage; naked red head, upper neck; young birds are brownish-grey, with rusty brown on head. Pairs, family parties or flocks; also feeds along with other waterbirds; known to pair for life and usually well protected in northern and west-central India, but habitat loss continues to be grave threat; flies under 40ft off ground. **Food:** fish, frogs, crustaceans, insects, grains, tubers. **Voice:** very loud, far-reaching trumpeting, often a duet between a pair; elaborate dancing rituals. **Range:** commoner in N and C India (E Rajasthan, Gujarat, N and C Madhya Pradesh, Gangetic plain). **Habitat:** marshes, jheels, well-watered cultivation, village ponds.

Sarus Crane

DEMOISELLE CRANE

Grus virgo 75cm. Sexes alike. Overall plumage grey; black head and neck; prominent white ear-tufts; long black feathers of lower neck fall over breast; brownish-grey secondaries sickle-shaped and drooping over tail. Young birds have grey head and much shorter drooping secondaries over tail. Huge flocks in winter, often many thousands; feeds early mornings and early evenings in cultivation; rests during hot hours on marsh-edges and sandbanks; flies en-masse when disturbed. **Food:** wheat, paddy, gram; does extensive damage to winter crops. **Voice:** high-pitched, sonorous *krook...krook..* calls. **Range:** winter visitor; commonest in NW India and over E Rajasthan, Gujarat and Madhya Pradesh, though sporadically over much of the country. **Habitat:** winter crop-fields, sandy river-banks, ponds.

Demoiselle Crane

Common Crane

COMMON CRANE

Grus grus 140cm. Sexes alike. Pale slaty-grey plumage; slight red on crown when seen from close range; black face, throat and white stripe on sides of head, neck; black flight-feathers and dark, drooping tail plumes diagnostic. Gregarious in winter; feeds in mornings and evenings in cultivation; rests during day; rather shy and suspicious, ever alert; slow, but strong flight. **Food:** shoots, tubers, grain, insects; also watermelons in some areas. **Voice:** loud, strident trumpeting *krr..oohk..:* calls on ground and from high in skies; also other harsh, screeching notes. **Range:** winter visitor; commonest in NW India, progressively less towards the east, rarely straying south of S Maharashtra and N Andhra Pradesh. **Habitat:** cultivation of wheat, gram, groundnut; also riverbeds.

Black-Necked Crane

BLACK-NECKED CRANE

Grus nigricollis 150cm. Sexes alike. Female slightly smaller. black head, neck; dull-red lores, complete crown; small white patch around eye; greyish plumage; black wing-tips, drooping plumes. Pairs or small necks, up to 70 birds seen together in Bhutan; barely three to five pairs breeding in Indian region (Ladakh); inhabits high-altitude open marshes and lakesides; where much revered by locals; dancing displays commence around March, flies high during afternoons, calling loudly. **Food:** fallen grain, shoots, tubers, insects and possibly molluscs. **Voice:** loud, trumpet-like calls, higher-pitched than Sarus Crane's. **Range:** breeds only in Ladakh within Indian limits; possibly in parts of Arunachal Pradesh. A larger population inhabits the Tibetan plateau; up to a hundred birds winter in parts of C and E Bhutan. **Habitat:** high-altitude marshes, lakesides, open cultivation.

SLATY-LEGGED CRAKE

Rallina eurizonoides 25cm. Sexes alike. Rich, cinnamon chocolate-brown head, neck and breast; white on chin and throat; darkish rufous-brown above; banded black and white below breast; slaty legs. Solitary or in pairs; semi-nocturnal; shy, sneaking into dense cover at the slightest sign of disturbance; flies into tree when suddenly flushed; walks upright, with cocked tail. **Food:** insects, molluscs, seeds, shoots of certain marshland plants. **Voice:** noisy during SW monsoon, when breeding; mix of double-noted and harsh, single-note crying calls; noisier at night. **Range:** throughout the Indian region. **Habitat:** well-watered areas, usually in and around jungles.

WATER RAIL

Rallus aquaticus 28cm. Sexes alike. Brown upperparts streaked with black; dirty-white throat and chin with grey breast and belly barred black and white. Long red bill diagnostic. Young have distinct white barring on wings. Mostly solitary though mate is usually nearby; unobtrusive, secretive and cautious; moves with head held high but vanishes into reeds and low growth on slightest suspicion; legs dangle behind in flight. **Food:** molluscs, insects, shoots of marsh plants. **Voice:** shrill squeal sometimes heard early morning. **Range:** breeds in Kashmir spreading to the Indo-Gangetic plains in winter. *Rallidae* tend to be generally overlooked by bird-watchers but are in fact commoner than they appear. **Habitat:** marshes, reedbeds, paddy cultivation, ponds.

Water Rail

BROWN CRAKE

Amaurornis akool 28cm. Sexes alike, but female slightly smaller. Darkish olive-brown upperbody, wings and tail; white chin and throat fade into ashy-grey underparts; browner on breast, flanks and abdomen. Solitary or pairs; mostly crepuscular, extremely elusive and secretive; feeds in early mornings and late evenings on edges of jheels, flicking the stub tail and generally moving very suspiciously. **Food:** insects, molluscs, seeds of marshland plants. **Voice:** mostly silent, but a plaintive note and a long-drawn, vibrating whistle have been described. **Range:** resident and local migrant; south from Kashmir lowlands down through the peninsula, at least to Mysore and Orissa. **Habitat:** reed-covered marshes, irrigation channels, dense growth on jheels.

Brown Crake

WHITE-BREASTED WATERHEN

Amaurornis phoenicurus 32cm. Sexes alike. White forehead, sides of head; dark slaty-grey above; silky white below; slaty-grey sides of breast, flanks; rufous on vent and under tail-coverts. Solitary or in small parties; often around village ponds and tanks, occasionally derelict patches in towns; jerks stumpy tail as it walks with long strides; climbs trees easily, especially when breeding. **Food:** insects, worms, molluscs, shoots of marsh plants. **Voice:** very noisy when breeding during rains, a series of loud croaks and chuckles, the commonest being a harsh *krr..khkk...*; often calls through the night; silent during dry season. **Range:** south from Himalayan foothills through the country. **Habitat:** reed-covered marshes, ponds and tanks, monsoon cultivation and streams.

White-Breasted Waterhen

Spotted Crake

Purple Swamphen

Common Moorhen

SPOTTED CRAKE
Porzana porzana 22cm. Sexes alike. Olive-brown above, with a rufescent wash, streaked black; grey supercilium, sides of head and neck; whitish chin, throat; greyish breast spotted white; white barring on grey-brown flanks. Solitary or pairs; crepuscular; skulks and very difficult to spot; in some areas, can be approached if one remains very quiet and still; moves amidst reed beds and jheel vegetation; gently and warily sneaks under leaf or dense growth if disturbed. The **Ruddy-breasted Crake** *P fusca* has a chestnut face with upperparts dark olive brown. **Food:** insects, worms, seeds of aquatic plants. **Voice:** unrecorded, said to be silent. **Range:** winter visitor over most of the country, south to about central Karnataka. **Habitat:** reed-covered jheels, vegetation in and around marshes.

PURPLE SWAMPHEN (Purple Moorhen)
Porphyrio porphyrio 4cm. Sexes alike. Purplish-blue plumage; long red legs with oversized toes distinctive; thickish red beak; bald red forehead (casque); white under stumpy tail, seen when tail flicked up; bald red patch on forehead smaller in female. Small parties amidst reeds and other vegetation on marsh and jheels; sometimes large gatherings on vegetation-covered waterbodies; walks on floating growth, swims rarely; rather tame in some areas. **Food:** vegetable matter, seeds, tubers; known to damage paddy crop; insects, molluscs, small frogs also eaten. **Voice:** noisy when breeding, a mix of cackling and hooting notes. **Range:** mostly resident; south, throughout the country, from about 1500m in Kashmir. **Habitat:** vegetation and reed-covered jheels, tanks.

COMMON MOORHEN
Gallinula chloropus 32cm. Sexes alike. Dark grey head, neck; dark brownish-olive above; slaty-grey below, white centre of abdomen; fine white border to edge of wing; bright red frontal shield and base of beak with greenish-yellow tip diagnostic; greenish legs. Usually in small parties; commoner in winter; moves amidst marsh vegetation, jerking tail; good swimmer, jerks head as it swims. **Food:** seeds and tubers of water plants, insects, molluscs, small fish and frogs. **Voice:** occasional loud, harsh *pruck...:* noisy when breeding, uttering loud croaking notes. **Range:** throughout the country, from about 2400m in Himalaya; breeds commonly in Kashmir, but also in parts of the peninsula. **Habitat:** reed covered ponds, tanks, jheels.

COMMON COOT

Fulica atra 42cm. Sexes alike. Slaty-black plumage; stout ivory-white beak and flat forehead-shield distinctive. Almost tailless and duck-like appearance. Gregarious; much more abundant in winter when numbers greatly augmented by winter visitors; huge gatherings on jheels, ponds and placid stretches of rivers; wavelike sound of a huge flock of coots flying or paddling over water, amidst much chuckling sounds; dives underwater; much hunted, especially in winter, when this species serves as staple diet for many locals; patters along water surface, rising with some difficulty. **Food:** seeds, shoots of aquatic plants: paddy, insects, molluscs. **Voice:** loud *kraw*; chuckling sounds. **Range:** all India; resident and winter visitor. **Habitat:** reed-fringed jheels, tanks, slow-moving rivers.

Common Coot

E. Hanumantha Rao

CHESTNUT-BELLIED SANDGROUSE (Indian)

Pterocles exustus 28cm, with tail. **Male:** sandy-buff above, speckled brown and dull yellow, black gorget and choco-black belly. **Female:** buffy above, streaked and barred darker; black-spotted breast: rufous and black-barred belly, flanks. Pointed central tail-feathers and black wing-underside distinctive in flight. Huge gatherings at waterholes in dry season; regularly arrives at water; strictly a ground bird, squatting tight or shuffling slowly; rises en masse. **Food:** seeds of grasses and weeds. **Voice:** deep, clucking *kurt..ro..* call-note; uttered mostly on wing. **Range:** all India except NE and extreme south. **Habitat:** open areas, semi-desert fallow land.

Joanna Van Gruisen

Chestnut-Bellied Sandgrouse

Goren Ekstrom

Black-Bellied Sandgrouse

BLACK-BELLIED SANDGROUSE (Imperial)

Pterocles orientalis 40cm. **Male:** mottled sandy-grey above; rufous-chestnut sides of neck, upper throat; black throat, pectoral gorger, belly and flanks; buff-brown band between gorget and belly. **Female:** mottled pink-fawn plumage; black line below yellow throat: black belly, flanks. Whitish underside of wings distinctive. Gregarious, regularly arrives at water-sites, rises almost straight from ground. **Food:** grass and weed seeds; grain. **Voice:** noisy on arrival on ground; clucking call-notes. **Range:** abundant but erratic winter visitor to NW India; sporadically in Gangetic plain and C India. **Habitat:** semi-desert areas, fallow lands.

Rishad Naoroji

Painted Sandgrouse

PAINTED SANDGROUSE (Close-Barred)

Pterocles indicus 28cm. **Male:** white and black on forehead, crown; chestnut, fawn and black (three-coloured) breast band. **Female:** lacks the head and breast colours of male. Both sexes have a close-barred plumage and lack the pinlike central feathers in tail. Pairs or half a dozen birds together; large flocks around end-monsoon; mostly flies when almost stepped upon; comes regularly to water in small flocks; also runs on ground. **Food:** grass and weed seeds; occasionally termites. **Voice:** chuckling notes in flight and on ground; soft, clucking note when flushed. **Range:** commoner in NW, W and C India, east to Bihar, Orissa; absent in NE and uncommon in Gangetic plain. **Habitat:** scrub-covered hillsides, open, dry forest.

Joanna Van Gruisen

Solitary Snipe

SOLITARY SNIPE

Gallinago solitaria 30cm. Sexes alike. Cryptic coloured marsh-bird with plump body and very long beak. Dense plumage, brown, buff, black and fulvous, with some chestnut markings above. The various species of snipe are not easy to distinguish in field. Flight style and numbers of feathers in tail help identification. This species has 18 feathers, but this character only helpful when bird in hand. The **Wood Snipe** *G nemoricola* of the Himalaya is very similar but somewhat darker and heavier and slower in flight. Usually solitary; secretive and silent; mostly seen only when flushed; short, erratic flight when flushed. **Food:** small snails, worms, aquatic insects. **Voice:** fairly loud *pench..* call in flight. **Range:** a mountain bird; breeds about 2800-4500m in Himalaya, Ladakh and Kashmir to NE India; moves lower in winter, sporadically in parts of eastern plains. **Habitat:** dense growth along marshy mountain streams.

COMMON SNIPE (Fantail)

Gallinago gallinago 28cm. Sexes alike. Cryptic coloured marsh-bird, brownish-buff, heavily streaked and marked buff, rufous and black; dull-white below. Fast, erratic flight; 14 or 16 tail-feathers; whitish wing-lining distinctive, but not easily seen. The **Pintail Snipe** *G stenura* is very similar and usually distinguished only in hand. Usually several in dense marsh-growth; very difficult to see unless flushed; probes with long beak in the ooze, often in shallow water; feeds mostly during mornings and evenings. **Food:** small molluscs, worms, insects. **Voice:** loud *pench* call when flushed. **Range:** breeds in parts of W Himalaya: mostly winter visitor over the subcontinent, commoner in N and C India. **Habitat:** marshlands, paddy cultivation, jheel edges.

Common Snipe

BLACK-TAILED GODWIT

Limosa limosa 40cm. Sexes alike. Female slightly larger. Grey-brown above; whitish below; very long, straight beak; in flight, broad, white wing-bars, white rump and black tail-tip distinctive. In summer dull rufous-red on head, neck and breast with close-barred lower breast, flanks. The **Bar-Tailed Godwit** *L lapponica* has slightly upcurved beak; at night, lack of white wing-bars and barred black-and-white tail help identification. Gregarious, often with other large waders; quite active, probing with long beak; wades in water often, the long legs barely visible; fast and graceful, low flight. **Food:** crustaceans, worms, molluscs, aquatic insects. **Voice:** an occasional, fairly loud *kwika..kwik*. **Range:** winter visitor. The Bar-Tailed is commoner along the western seaboard, between Ratnagiri and Bombay. **Habitat:** marshes, estuaries, creeks.

Greater Spotted Eagle

EURASIAN CURLEW

Numenius arquata 58cm. Sexes alike. A large wader. Sandy-brown upperbody, scalloped fulvous and black; white rump and lower back; whitish below, streaked black; very long, downcurved beak. The very similar **Whimbrel** *N phaeopus* is smaller; has a blackish crown with white stripe through centre and white stripes on sides of head. Mostly solitary; feeds with other large waders; runs on ground, between tidemarks, occasionally venturing in very shallow water; a truly wild and wary bird, not easy to approach close. **Food:** crustaceans, insects, mudskippers. **Voice:** famed scream; a wild, rather musical *cour...lee* or *cooor..lee..* the first note longer. **Range:** winter visitor; sea coast west to east. **Habitat:** rivers, estuaries, creeks, large remote marshes.

Eurasian Curlew

Common Redshank

COMMON REDSHANK
Tringa totanus 28cm. Sexes alike. Grey-brown above; whitish below, faintly marked about breast; white rump, broad band along trailing edge of wings; orange-red legs and base of beak. In summer, browner above, marked black and fulvous, and more heavily streaked below. The **Spotted Redshank** *T erythropus* is very similar but lacks complete white band along trailing edge of wings in flight. Small flocks, often with other waders; makes short dashes, probing and jabbing deep in ooze; may also enter water, with long legs completely submerged; rather alert and suspicious bird. **Food:** aquatic insects, crustaceans, molluscs. **Voice:** quite musical, fairly loud and shrill *tleu.ewh.ewh*, mostly in flight or during take-off; very similar to Greenshank's call, but more shrill and high-pitched. **Range:** breeds in Kashmir, Ladakh above 3000m; winter visitor over the country; fairly common. **Habitat:** marshes, creeks, estuaries.

Common Greenshank

COMMON GREENSHANK *Tringa nebularia* 36cm. Sexes alike. Grey-brown above; long, slightly upcurved, blackish beak; white forehead, underbody; in flight, white lower back, rump and absence of white in wings diagnostic; long, greenish legs. In summer, darker above, with blackish centres to feathers. The **Marsh Sandpiper** *T stagnatilis* is very similar but smaller and has distinctly longer legs; also has distinctive call. Either solitary or small groups of two to six birds, often with Redshanks and other waders; feeds at edge of water but may enter water to belly level. **Food:** crustaceans, molluscs, aquatic insects. **Voice:** wild, ringing *tew.tew.tew..*, much like Redshanks, but less shrill; occasionally single note, heard when disturbed. **Range:** winter visitor, fairly common, most of India. **Habitat:** marshes, estuaries, creeks.

WOOD SANDPIPER
Tringa glareola 20cm. Sexes alike. Grey-brown above, closely spotted white; slender build; white rump, tail; white below; brown on breast, no wing-bar. Summer: dark olive-brown above, spotted white. The **Green Sandpiper** *T ochropus* is stouter, more shy, much darker, glossy brown-olive above; in flight, white rump contrasts strikingly with dark upperbody; blackish

below wings diagnostic. Small to medium-size flocks, often with others; quite active, probing deep into ooze or feeding at edge. **Food:** crustaceans, insects, molluscs. **Voice:** quite noisy; sharp, trilling notes on ground; shrill, somewhat metallic *chiff.chiff.* calls when flushed; sometimes a loud, sharp *thuie..* call. *T ochropus* has distinct, wild ringing calls when flushed. **Range:** winter visitor to most of India. **Habitat:** wet cultivation, marshes, tidal creeks, mudflats.

Wood Sandpiper

COMMON SANDPIPER

Actitis hypoleucos 20m. Sexes alike. Olive-brown above, more ash-brown and streaked-brown on head, neck sides; brown rump white below, lightly streaked-brown on breast; in flight, narrow, white wing-bar and brown rump. In summer is darker above and speckled. One to three birds, either by themselves or scattered amidst mixed wader flocks; quite active, makes short dashes, hobbing, wagging short tail; usually flies low over water, the rapid wing-beats interspersed with short glides ('vibrating flight') helping identification of the species. **Food:** crustaceans, insects, molluscs. **Voice:** Shrill *twee..tse.tse.tse* note, usually when flushed; longish, trilling song. **Range:** breeds in Himalayas, Kashmir to Garhwal to about 3000m plus; winter visitor all over India. **Habitat:** freshwater marshes, lakes, tidal areas, creeks.

Common Sandpiper

GREATER PAINTED-SNIPE

Rostratula benghalensis 25cm. Polyandrous. **Br Female:** metallic olive above, thickly marked buff and black; buff stripe down crown-centre; chestnut throat, breast, sides of neck, white below breast. **Br Male:** duller overall; lacks chestnut. Sexes difficult to distinguish when not in breeding plumage. Crepuscular and nocturnal; solitary or a few scattered birds; feeds in squelchy mud but also moves on drier ground; runs on landing; **Food:** insects, crustaceans, molluscs and vegetable matter. **Voice:** common call a long-drawn, mellow note that can be likened to the noise made by blowing into a bottle-mouth. **Range:** resident, throughout country from about 2000m in the Himalaya. **Habitat:** wet ooze, marshes, such areas where there is a mix of open water, ooze and heavy, low cover.

Greater Painted-Snipe

Joanna Van Gruisen

Pheasant-Tailed Jacana

PHEASANT-TAILED JACANA

Hydrophasianus chirurgus. **Male:** 30cm, with 14cm tail when breeding; breeding plumage choco-brown and white; golden yellow on hindneck. When not breeding is dull-brown and white, also has blackish necklace and lacks long tail; very long toes diagnostic. Solitary or pairs when breeding; small flocks in winter; purely aquatic, moving on vegetation-covered pond surface; unusually long toes enable it to trip on the lightest of floating leaves; quite confiding on village ponds. **Food:** mostly seeds, tubers, roots; also insects, molluscs. **Voice:** loud *mewing* call when breeding, two birds often calling in duet. **Range:** throughout country, from about 1500m. **Habitat:** ponds and jheels covered with floating-vegetation.

Rishad Naoroji

BRONZE-WINGED JACANA

Metopidius indicus 30cm. Sexes alike. Female slightly larger. Glossy black head, neck, breast; glistening bronze-green back, wings; broad white stripe over eyes; chestnut rump, tail; long legs with massive toes distinctive. Immature birds have rufous-brown crown; black terminal band to tail and whitish underbody, tinged rufous-buff around breast. Small gatherings during winter and summer, keeps to leafy, floating growth on jheel beds, village tanks; wary, moves slowly and silently; flies low, with long legs trailing. **Food:** tubers, seeds of aquatic plants; also insects, crustacea, molluscs. **Voice:** loud harsh notes; also a shrill piping call. **Range:** most of India, excepting some NW regions. **Habitat:** vegetation-covered jheels, ponds.

Bronze-Winged Jacana

EURASIAN THICK-KNEE (Stone-Curlew)

Burhinus oedicnemus 40cm. Sexes alike. Sandy-brown plumage, streaked dark; whitish below breast; thickish head, long, bare yellow legs and large eye-goggles diagnostic; white wing-patch in flight. Solitary or in pairs; strictly a ground bird; crepuscular and nocturnal; rather quiet, sitting for long hours in same patch, where seen regularly; colouration and nature makes it difficult to spot; squats tight or runs in short steps when located and disturbed, moving suspiciously. **Food:** small reptiles, insects, slugs: also seeds. **Voice:** a plaintive, curlew-like call at dusk and thereafter; also sharp *pick...pick..* notes. **Range:** drier parts of country, from about 1200m in outer Himalaya. **Habitat:** light, dry forest, scrub, dry riverbanks, ravinous country, orchards and open *babool* clad areas.

Eurasian Thick-Knee

GREAT THICK-KNEE (Great Stone Plover)

Esacus recurvirostris 50cm. Sexes alike. Sandy-grey above; thick-set head and enormous-looking, somewhat upturned, black and yellow beak; large goggle-eyes surrounded by white, two black bands on face; white below, washed grey on neck, breast; white in flight-feathers, visible in night. Solitary or pairs on open barrenland, river banks or rocks in mid-river; mostly crepuscular and partly nocturnal; spends day under strong sun resting, and usually very difficult to spot; extremely wary. **Food:** crabs, molluscs, small insects; also lizards. **Voice:** harsh call-note, somewhat whistle-like; wild, piping calls at night, especially when breeding (February to April, sometimes till mid-May). **Range:** almost all India, south of terai; uncommon in NE regions. **Habitat:** dry, open country; barrenlands, river banks, rocky areas, islands in jheels.

Great Thick-Knee

EURASIAN OYSTERCATCHER

Haematopus ostralegus 42cm. Sexes alike. Pied plumage. Black head, upperparts, breast; white below; long orange beak and pinkish legs distinctive. White on throat in winter. White rump and broad wing-bar conspicuous in flight. Young birds are browner. Commoner on sea coasts, frequently associates with other waders; runs and probes ooze; beak highly specialised for feeding on molluscs. **Food:** molluscs, crabs, worms. **Voice:** piping *kleeeep...* in flight; also a shrill whistle, often double-noted, uttered on ground as well as in flight. **Range:** winter visitor, specially to the coastal regions; more common on western seaboard. **Habitat:** rocky and sandy coastal areas.

Eurasian Oystercatcher

Joanna Van Gruisen

E. Hanumantha Rao

Sharad Gaur

Black-Winged Stilt

BLACK-WINGED STILT

Himantopus himantopus 25cm. **Male:** jet-black mantle, pointed wings (above and below); rest of plumage glossy white. **Female:** dark brown where male is black; black wing underside; black spots on head; duller overall in winter. Very long pink-red legs diagnostic, extend much beyond tail in flight. Gregarious; large numbers, often along with other waders on a wetland; long legs enable it to enter deeper water; clumsy walk; submerges head when feeding; characteristic flight silhouette. **Food:** aquatic insects, molluscs, vegetable matter. **Voice:** shrill notes in flight, very tern-like; noisy when breeding. **Range:** resident and local migrant over most of country, from about 1800m in W Himalaya. **Habitat:** marshes, salt-pans, tidal creeks, village ponds, also riversides.

Pied Avocet

PIED AVOCET

Recurvirostra avosetta 45cm. Sexes alike. Long legged. Black and white plumage, long bluish legs and long, slender upcurved beak diagnostic. (The Black-winged Stilt has reddish legs, long straight beak and glossy back and wings.) In flight, the long legs extend much beyond the tail. Usually gregarious, only sometimes two to three birds scattered over waterbody; frequently enters shallow water; characteristic sideways movement of head when feeding, the head bent low as upcurved beak sweeps along bottom ooze; also swims and 'up-ends', ducklike. **Food:** aquatic insects, minute molluscs, crustaceans. **Voice:** loud, somewhat fluty *klooeet* or *kloeep* call, mostly on wing; also some harsh, screaming notes. **Range:** breeds in Kutch, N Balochistan; winter visitor, sporadically over most parts of India, commoner in NW regions. **Habitat:** freshwater marshes, coastal tidal areas, creeks.

Little Ringed Plover

LITTLE RINGED PLOVER

Charadrius dubius 16cm. Sexes alike. Sandy-brown above; white forehead; black bands on head, breast and white neck-ring diagnostic; white chin, throat; lack of wing-bar in flight and yellow legs and ring around eye additional clues. Small numbers, runs on ground, on ooze and drying jheels, walks with characteristic bobbing gait, picking food from ground; when approached close, flies rapidly, low over ground, zig-zag flight accompanied by a whistling note. **Food:** insects, worms, tiny crabs. **Voice:** a *few...few..* whistle, high-pitched but somewhat plaintive. **Range:** resident and local migrant: throughout country south from Himalayan foothills. **Habitat:** shingle-covered river banks, tidal mudflats, estuaries, lake edges.

YELLOW-WATTLED LAPWING

Vanellus malarbaricus 28cm. Sexes alike. Jet black cap, bordered with white; sandy-brown upperbody; black band in white tail; in night, white bar in black wings; black chin, throat; sandy-brown breast; black band on lower breast; white below; yellow lappets above and in front of eyes and yellow legs diagnostic. Solitary or in pairs, rarely small gatherings; sometimes with the commoner Red-Wattled; as a rule, prefers drier habitat; quiet and unobtrusive; feeds on ground, moving suspiciously. **Food:** mostly insects. **Voice:** short plaintive notes; on the whole a quiet bird; quick-repeated notes when nest site intruded upon. **Range:** from NW India south through country; does not occur in extreme NE. **Habitat:** dry, open country.

Yellow-Watted Lapwing

RIVER LAPWING (Spur-Winged)

Vanellus duvaucelii 30cm. Sexes alike. Black forehead, crown, crest drooping over back; sandy grey-brown above; black and white wings; black chin, throat, with white border; grey-brown breast band; white below with black patch on belly; black spur at bend of wing. Usually pairs in close vicinity; may collect into small parties during winter, sometimes with other waders; makes short dashes or feeds at water's edge; often remains in hunched posture, when not easy to spot; slow flight; reported to swim and dive. **Food:** crustaceans, insects, small hogs. **Voice:** rather like Red-Wattled, only a bit softer and less shrill; also a sharp *deed..did..did..* **Range:** breeds in parts of E and C India, including Orissa, Andhra Pradesh and E Madhya Pradesh; may disperse in winter. **Habitat:** stony river-beds, sandbanks; sometimes collects around jheels in winter.

River Lapwing

RED-WATTLED LAPWING

Vanellus indicus 35cm. Sexes alike. Jet-black head, neck, breast; bronze-brown upperbody; white below, continuing to broad bands up the neck-sides towards eyes; fleshy crimson facial wattles diagnostic. Solitary or pairs when breeding; often large flocks in winter; moves on open ground, feeds during mornings and evenings; vigilant species, its loud cries heralding any new activity in an area; feeds late into evening. **Food:** insects, seeds and tubers. **Voice:** noisy; its loud, piercing *did ye do it..* calls amongst the most familiar bird-calls of India; dive-bombs at intruders when breeding, shrieking wildly. **Range:** throughout India, from about 2000m in W Himalaya. **Habitat:** open country, roadsides, village outskirts, edge of jheels.

Red-Watted Lapwing

Thakur Dalip Singh

White-Tailed Lapwing

WHITE-TAILED LAPWING
Vanellus leucurus 28cm. Sexes alike. Pink-brown above, with grey-white forehead, supercilium; ash-grey chin, throat, turning dark-grey on breast; yellow legs; in night, white rump, tail, black and white in wings diagnostic. The **Sociable Lapwing** *V gregarius* has brown crown, stripe through eyes; in flight, dark subterminal tail-band, large white patch in dark wings. Small to medium-size flocks, often with other waders; makes short runs when feeding; less boisterous and active than the commoner Red-wattled, but overall similarity in habits. **Food:** molluscs, water insects, worms. **Voice:** mostly silent in winter except for an occasional soft, double-noted whistle. **Range:** winter visitor, NW India; smaller numbers east to Uttar Pradesh, parts of Bihar, C India. **Habitat:** open marshy areas, edges of lakes and jheels.

M.K. Kuppuraj

Indian Courser

INDIAN COURSER
Cursorius coromandelicus 26cm. Sexes alike. Bright rufous crown; white and black stripes above and through eyes to nape; sandy-brown above; chestnut throat, breast and black belly; long, whitish legs; in flight, dark underwings. Small parties in open country; strictly a ground-bird, runs in short spurts and feeds on ground, typical plover-style, suddenly dipping body; when disturbed, flies strongly for short distances and lands; can fly very high. **Food:** black beetles, other insects. **Voice:** soft hen-like clucking call in flight, when flushed. **Range:** most of the country south of the Himalaya, but distribution rather patchy; absent in NE. **Habitat:** open scrub, fallow land, dry cultivation.

Mohir Aggarwal

Small Pratincole

SMALL PRATINCOLE
Glareola lactea. Sexes alike. Brown forehead; sandy-grey above; black stripe from eye to beak; white, squarish tail, tipped black; smoky-brown underbody has a rufous wash; whiter on lower breast and abdomen; long, narrow wings and short legs. The **Collared Pratincole** *G pratincola* is larger, with forked tail and black loop on throat. Gregarious; large flocks over an open expanse, close to water; very swallow-like in demeanour; strong and graceful flight over water surface catching insects on wing; fly high in late evening. **Food:** insects, taken on wing. **Voice:** soft, but harsh call-notes in flight. **Range:** resident and local migrant; all India south of outer Himalaya, from about 1800m. **Habitat:** large, quiet riversides, sandbars, marshy expanses, coastal swamps, tidal creeks.

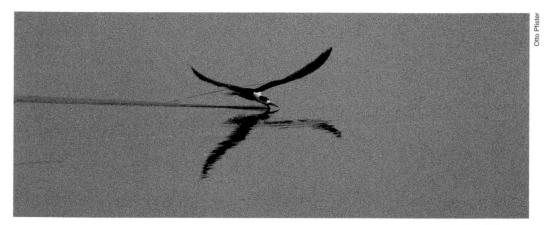

Otto Pfister

Indian Skimmer

INDIAN SKIMMER

Rynchops albicollis 40cm. Slender, pointed-winged and tern-like. Sexes alike, but female slightly smaller. Pied plumage, blackish-brown above, contrasting with white underbody; white forehead, neck-collar, wing-bar; yellowish-orange beak, with much longer lower mandible; red legs. Solitary or loose flocks flying over water; characteristic hunting style is to skim over calm waters, beak wide open, the longer-projecting lower mandible partly submerged at an angle, to snap up fish on striking; many rest together on sandbars. **Food:** chiefly fish. **Voice:** a shrill scream; twittering cries at nest colony. **Range:** commoner in N and C India, east to Assam; less common south of Maharashtra, N Andhra Pradesh. **Habitat:** large rivers, especially fond of placid waters.

BLACK-HEADED GULL

Larus ridibundus 45cm. Sexes alike. **Winter:** when in India, greyish-white plumage; dark ear-patches; white outer flight-feathers, with black tips. **Summer breeding:** coffee-brown head and upper neck, sometimes acquired just before emigration. The **Brown-Headed Gull** *L brunnicephalus* is larger and has white patches (mirrors) on black wing-tips. Highly gregarious; large flocks on sea coast, scavenging in harbour; wheels over busy seaside road or a beach; large numbers rest on rocky ground and sand; follow boats in harbour. **Food:** offal, fish, prawns, insects, earthworms. **Voice:** noisy; querulous *kree..ah* screams. **Range:** winter visitor; commoner on western seaboard; also strays inland, both on passage and for short halts. **Habitat:** sea coast, harbours, sewage outflows, garbage dumps.

B. Dasgupta

Black-Headed Gull

Joanna Van Gruison

Caspian Tern

CASPIAN TERN

Sterna caspia 50cm. Sexes alike. A large tern. Pale-grey above; jet-black cap in summer, streaked white in winter; unmarked white below. Large size, stout, coral-red beak, black legs and feet, and slight tail-fork diagnostic. Young birds are barred brown above. Two to four birds flying over estuaries and creeks or resting on sandbanks at water's edge; rarely gathers into large flocks; when hunting, hovers over water, beak pointing down; on spotting quarry, plunges headlong. **Food:** chiefly fish; also crabs and prawns. **Voice:** loud, raucous *kreahh..krraa..* uttered in fligght. **Range:** winter visitor over most of the Indian coast; breeds in Sri Lanka and W Pakistan. **Habitat:** coastal regions; lagoons, estuaries, backwaters.

I.A. Babu

River Tern

RIVER TERN

Sterna aurantia 42cm, with tail. Sexes alike. Very light grey above; jet-black cap, nape when breeding; white below; narrow, pointed wings, deeply forked tail; bright yellow, pointed beak and red legs diagnostic. In winter, black on crown and nape reduced to flecks. Solitary or small flocks, flying about erratically; keeps to riversides, calm waters, large tanks; scans over water, plunging if possible prey is sighted; rests on riverbanks, often dozens together; noisy and aggressive, especially at nesting colonies (March to mid-June). **Food:** fish, aquatic insects; also crabs, other crustaceans and molluscs. **Voice:** an occasional harsh, screeching note. **Range:** most of India; commoner in N and C India. **Habitat:** inland water bodies, rivers, tanks; almost completely absent on the seacoast.

Joanna Van Gruisen

Whiskered Tern

WHISKERED TERN

Chlidonias hybridus 26cm. Sexes alike. Black markings on crown; silvery-grey-white plumage; long, narrow wings and slightly-forked, almost squarish tail; short red legs and red beak distinctive. Summer: jet-black cap and snow-white cheeks (whiskers); black belly. At rest, close wings extend beyond tail. Large numbers flying about a marsh or tidal creek, leisurely but methodically, beak pointed down; dive from about 5m height but turn when just about to touch the ground, perhaps picking up some insect in the process; also hunt flying insects over standing crops. **Food:** insects, crabs, small fish, tadpoles. **Voice:** sharp, wild notes. **Range:** breeds in Kashmir and Gangetic plain; common in winter over the country. **Habitat:** inland marshes, wet cultivation, coastal areas, tidal creeks.

OSPREY

Pandion haliaetus 55cm. Sexes alike; female larger. Dark brown above; some white on head; white below; brown breast 'necklace', seen at rest and in flight; in overhead flight, white body with breast band, long, narrow black tipped, barred wings with black carpal (wrist) patches. Young birds have upper body marked white. Solitary or in scattered pairs; mostly around water; perches on a stake or tree top; circles over water; hovers characteristically; dives with feet dangling; often splashes into water; carries fish on to perch. **Food:** fish, often heavier than the bird itself. **Voice:** short, nasal scream; calls rarely. **Range:** resident in parts of the Himalaya, between about 2000 and 3500m; winter visitor over India. **Habitat:** lakes, rivers, coastal lagoons.

Osprey

BLACK BAZA (Indian Black-Crested)

Aviceda leuphotes 32cm. Sexes alike. Black upperparts, including long crest, foreneck, upper-breast; broad white breast-band followed by a black and chestnut band below; buff-white lower breast, flanks, barred chestnut; black abdomen; pale underside of tail. Solitary or small flocks in tall forests; more active in cloudy weather and at dusk; makes sorties after winged insects from perch high up in forest tree; occasionally hovers. **Food:** insects, small lizards, frogs, small birds. **Voice:** plaintive squeal, very much like Pariah Kite's. **Range:** uncommon resident; Kerala and some parts in adjoining Karnataka; NE India, east of E Nepal to about 1200m. **Habitat:** evergreen forest, clearings, streams, foothills.

Black Baza

ORIENTAL HONEY-BUZZARD

Pernis ptilorhyncus 67cm. Sexes alike. Slender head and longish neck distinctive; tail rarely fanned. Highly variable phases. Mostly darkish-brown above; crest rarely visible; pale brown underbody, with narrow whitish bars; pale underside of wings barred; broad dark subterminal tailband; two or three more bands on tail; tarsus unfeathered. Solitary or in pairs, perched on forest trees or flying; often enters villages and outskirts of small towns. **Food:** bee larvae, honey, small birds, lizards; occasionally robs poultry. **Voice:** high-pitched, long-drawn *weeeeeu...* may call during the night. **Range:** resident and local migrant; all India to about 2000m in the Himalaya. **Habitat:** forest, open country, cultivation, vicinity of villages.

Oriental Honey-buzzard

Black-Shouldered Kite

Black Kite

BLACK-SHOULDERED KITE (Black-Winged)

Elanus caeruleus 32cm. Sexes alike. Pale grey-white plumage, whiter on head, neck and underbody; short black stripe through eyes; black shoulder patches and wing-tips distinctive at rest and in flight; blood-red eyes. Young; upperbody tinged brown, with pale edges to feathers. Usually solitary or in pairs; resting on exposed perch or flying over open scrub and grass country; mostly hunts on wing, regularly hovering like a Kestrel to scan ground; drops height to check when hovering, with legs held ready. **Food:** insects, lizards, rodents, snakes. **Voice:** high-pitched squeal. **Range:** all India, to about 1500m in outer Himalaya. **Habitat:** open scrub and grass country; light forest.

BLACK KITE (Pariah Kite)

Milvus migrans 60cm. Sexes alike. Dark brown plumage; forked tail, easily seen in flight; underparts faintly streaked. The **Black Kite** *M m lineatus* breeds in Himalaya and winters in N and C India, is slightly larger and has conspicuous white patch on underwing, visible in overhead flight. Common and gregarious; commoner near man, thriving on the refuse generated, often amidst most crowded localities; roosts communally. **Food:** omnivorous; garbage, dead rats, earthworms, insects, nestlings of smaller birds, poultry. **Voice:** loud, musical whistle, often uttered on wing during breeding season. **Range:** resident; all India to about 2200m in Himalaya, co-existing with Black-Eared in some localities. **Habitat:** mostly neighbourhood of humans.

Brahminy Kite

BRAHMINY KITE

Haliastur indus 50cm. Sexes alike. White head, neck, upper back and breast; rest of plumage a rich, rusty-chestnut; brownish abdomen and darker tips to flight feathers visible mostly in flight. **Young:** brown, like Pariah Kite, but with rounded tail. Solitary or small scattered parties; loves water; frequently scavenges around lakes and marshes; also around villages and towns. **Food:** mostly stranded fish; also frogs, insects, lizards, mudskippers, small snakes, rodents. **Voice:** loud scream. **Range:** resident and local migrant; all India, from about 1800m in the Himalaya. **Habitat:** margins of lakes, marshes, rivers, sea coast.

White-Bellied Sea Eagle

WHITE-BELLIED SEA EAGLE

Haliaeetus leucogaster 70cm. Sexes alike; female larger. Ashy-brown above; white head, neck, underparts, tail-end; in overhead flight, wedge-shaped tail, white body, underwing and terminal tail bar contrasting with black flight feathers and tail. Solitary or in pairs; perches on tall tree or poles, overlooking sea or lake; with a great stoop, picks prey from near water surface; indulges in spectacular courtship display; often feeds in nest. **Food:** mostly sea-snakes; fish, including dead ones; also robs poultry. **Voice:** loud metallic screams, mostly when breeding. **Range:** resident; the coast south of Bombay and all along the east coast; flies many miles inland to freshwater lakes, rivers. **Habitat:** sea coast, inland water.

PALLAS'S FISH EAGLE

Haliaeetus leucoryphus 80cm. Sexes alike; female larger. Dark brown plumage; buffy-golden head, neck and breast; darkish tail and contrasting broad, white band confirms identity. Young birds are much darker above, paler below. Solitary or in pairs; perches atop tall trees or poles, mostly near or in the middle of a lake or river; picks fish from surface in its talons; often pirates the catch of other birds; robs nestlings at heronries. **Food:** fish, frogs, turtles, wildfowl, nestlings of herons and other water birds. **Voice:** loud screams; very noisy when breeding. **Range:** resident; local migrant; N India, to about 1800m in Himalaya; along Gangetic plains to E India; Chilka Lake. **Habitat:** jheels, large rivers.

Pallas's Fish Eagle

Gertrud Denzau

Grey-headed Fish Eagle

GREY-HEADED FISH EAGLE (Himalayan)
Ichthyophaga icthyaetus 75cm. Sexes alike. Dark brown plumage; grey head, neck and throat; pale brown crown, nape; pale brown breast; white flanks, abdomen and tail with broad black terminal band distinctive in overhead flight. The **Lesser Fish** *I nana* is smaller and has pure grey head; lacks pure-white in tail when seen from below. Mostly solitary; sits straight on lookout perches, usually on trees over and around forest streams or pools; captures fish off surface; does not plunge. **Food:** predominantly fish; sometimes birds, squirrels. **Voice:** loud, ringing cry; noisy when breeding. **Range:** resident; from Delhi east through Gangetic plains to Assam and further east; south through the peninsula. **Habitat:** lakes, rivers in forested country.

Nitin Rai

Lammergeier or Bearded Vulture

LAMMERGEIER or BEARDED VULTURE
Gypaetus barbatus 125cm. Wingspan of about 2.5m. Sexes alike. Silvery-black above with white shaft stripes; rust-white head, neck, black bristly "beard" under chin; white below with a rusty wash; in overhead flight, long, narrow wings and long, black wedge-shaped tail. Young birds dark brown with blackish head. Usually solitary; soars high over ravines or glides effortlessly over the slopes; may swoop down on hill-station garbage dumps to snatch away some offal; carries bones and drops on rock to break and eat fragments; feeds sometimes with other vultures. **Food:** refuse, bones. **Range:** resident; the Himalaya, west to east, 1000-5000m; soars higher. **Habitat:** high mountain slopes.

Kamal Sahai

Egyptian Vulture

**EGYPTIAN VULTURE
(Small White Scavenger)**
Neophron percnopterus 65cm. Sexes alike. White plumage; blackish in wings; naked yellow head, neck and throat; yellow bill; thick ruff of feathers around neck; wedge-shaped tail and blackish flight feathers distinctive in overhead flight. The nominate race of NW India is slightly larger and has dark horny bill. Several usually together, perched atop ruins, earthen mounds or just walking on ground; glides a lot but rarely soars high; sometimes with other vultures. **Food:** garbage, carrion, insects, stranded turtles, the bird being specially adept at opening live turtles. **Range:** all India; plains to about 2000m in the Himalaya. **Habitat:** open country; vicinity of human habitation.

WHITE-RUMPED VULTURE (Indian White-Backed)

Gyps bengalensis 90cm. Sexes alike. Blackish brown plumage; almost naked head has whitsh-ruff around base; white rump (lower back) distinctive, when perched and often in flight; in overhead flight, white underwing coverts contrast with dark underbody and flight feathers. Young birds are brown and show no white on underwing in flight. Common and gregarious; seen with other vultures and crows at carcass, slaughter houses, garbage dumps. When resting, the head and neck are dug into shoulders; soars high on thermals; several converge onto a carcass; basks in sun; wades and bathes in shallow water. **Food:** mostly scavenges on carcasses. **Voice:** loud screeches when feeding. **Range:** resident; all India, to about 2800m in the Himalaya. **Habitat:** open country.

White-rumped Vulture

LONG-BILLED VULTURE (Indian Long-Billed)

Gyps indicus 90cm. Sexes alike. Pale-brown plumage; hair-like feathers on naked head and neck seen at close range; ruff of white feathers round base of neck, very dull sandy-brown below; in overhead flight, pale underbody and underwing diagnostic. The Himalayan race *Gi tenuirostris* has bald head, neck. Gregarious, frequently seen with other vultures and crows at carcasses and garbage dumps; less common than the White-backed but similar in habits. **Food:** scavenges on carcasses, offal. **Voice:** appears rather silent, even when feeding. **Range:** common in the drier parts of India (Rajasthan, Gujarat, most of C India, south of Gangetic plains); *G i tenuirostris* occurs along foothills, from Kashmir to Assam. **Habitat:** open country habitation, forest; breeds on cliffs.

Long-billed Vulture

HIMALAYAN GRIFFON

Gyps himalayensis 125cm. Sexes alike. Pale sandy-brown above; very pale buff-white below with broad, white shaft streaks; in overhead flight, the massive size, almost whitish underbody and contrasting black flight feathers and tail. Young birds are darker brown above. One to six birds sail motionless over high country; soars to immense heights on thermals; follows cattle graziers in high altitudes; several converging on a carcass; fixed rest-sites on rock faces. **Food:** chiefly scavenges on carcasses. **Voice:** cackling screeches at carcass site. **Range:** resident; Himalaya, between about 600-3000m; forages much higher; recorded over 5000m. **Habitat:** barren, high altitude country; around mountain settlements.

Himalayan Griffon

Red-Headed Vulture

Short-Toed Snake Eagle

Eurasian Marsh Harrier

RED-HEADED VULTURE (King Vulture)

Sarcogyps calvus 85cm. Sexes alike. Black plumage with white on thighs and breast; naked red head, neck and feet; in overhead flight, the white breast, thigh patches and grey-white band along wings distinctive; widely-spread primaries. Young birds are darkish-brown with white abdomen and undertail. Mostly solitary but two to four may be seen at a carcass along with other vultures, usually does not mix with the rest. **Food:** chiefly scavenges on carcasses. **Voice:** reportedly a hoarse croak. **Range:** resident; all India, to about 2800m in the Himalaya; uncommon. **Habitat:** open country, village outskirts.

SHORT-TOED SNAKE EAGLE

Circaetus gallicus 65cm. Sexes alike, but female larger. Brown above; whitish below; pale brown across throat, breast; banded tail; terminal band broad; in overhead flight, the pale silvery-white underwings and darker head and breast distinctive; overall, a thick-set eagle. Usually solitary; surveys low, like harriers; hovers to check for prey, frequently soars high; tremendous dive for prey; perches on tree-tops or poles. **Food:** snakes, lizards, frogs, rodents, large insects. **Voice:** a plaintive, loud scream. **Range:** resident; all India, to about 1200m in outer Himalaya; absent in NE. **Habitat:** open country, cultivation.

CRESTED SERPENT EAGLE

Spilornis cheela 75cm. Sexes alike; female larger. Dark brown plumage; roundish, pied crest, visible when erected; pale brown below, finely spotted white; in overhead flight, the dark body, white bars along the wings and white tail band confirm identity; characteristic call. Solitary or in pairs, flying over forest, often very high, calling frequently; perches in a leafy branch; swoops down on prey, snatching in talons; raises crest when alarmed. **Food:** snakes, lizards, birds, rodents, squirrels. **Voice:** loud whistling scream, *keee..kee..ke..*, the first note long-drawn. **Range:** resident; all India, to about 3000m in the Himalaya; Andamans. **Habitat:** forested country.

EURASIAN MARSH HARRIER

Circus aeruginosus 55cm. **Male:** dark brown plumage; dull rufous head, breast; silvery grey wings, tail; black wing-tips (best seen in flight). **Female (and young):** choco-brown; buff on head and shoulders; like Pariah Kite, but tail rounded (not forked). Solitary or in pairs; sails low over a marsh, grassland or

Crested Serpent Eagle

cultivation; often drops onto ground, frequently vanishing in dense grass and reed growth; perches on mounds or edge of marshes. **Food:** fish, rodents, frogs, small waterbirds, insects. **Range:** winter visitor; common; all India, south of foothills country; commoner in N India. **Habitat:** marshes, jheels, wet cultivation.

PIED HARRIER
Circus melanoleucos 48cm. **Male:** pied black, white and grey. Black head, back, throat, breast; grey tail, wings; black primaries; black band on wings above (across median coverts). **Female:** dark brown above; pale white nape patch, rump; pale buffy-rufous below; marked underside of flight feathers; overall appearance like other female harriers, and species identification not always easy. Solitary or in pairs; methodically surveys open grassy country; flies low, almost floats over; occasionally hovers for a few seconds. **Food:** rodents, lizards, frogs, insects. **Range:** resident in Manas and adjoining areas in Assam; winter visitor over parts of E India and erratically in parts of C and S India. **Habitat:** grassy areas, cultivation, reedy edges of jheels.

Pied Harrier

Manjunath Hegade

Crested Goshawk

CRESTED GOSHAWK

Accipiter trivirgatus 42cm. Sexes alike, female larger. Dark brown above; slaty-grey crown, crest; white below, streaked on breast; barred with rufescent below breast; white throat, under tail-coverts; black mesial stripe. Like Shikra, remains hidden in leafy branch, preferably around a forest clearing; pounces on prey; has favoured hunting grounds; often soars over forest. **Food:** middle-size birds such as pigeons, partridges; also rodents, squirrels. **Range:** resident; two races in India, one found from the Himalaya south to Godavari river, the other resident in the W Ghats south of Goa. **Habitat:** deciduous and semi-evergreen forest.

Rishad Naoroji

Shikra

SHIKRA

Accipiter badius 32cm. Ashy-grey above; whitish below, close-barred with rust-brown; grey throat-stripe; in flight, the multi-handed tail and roundish wings help identification; golden yellow eyes and yellow legs and feet seen at close range. The migrant **Sparrowhawk** *A nisus* is very similar but closer look reveals the longer legs, rufous cheek patch and absence of mesial stripe in *nisus*. Usually solitary; hides in leafy branch; pounces on unsuspecting prey; occasionally chases small birds; soars over forest. **Food:** rodents, small birds, lizards, large insects; also robs poultry. **Voice:** loud, drongo-like *titew..titew.* **Range:** resident; all India, to 1600m in the Himalaya. **Habitat:** light forest, open country, neighbourhood of villages.

Kamal Sahai

White-Eyed Buzzard

WHITE-EYED BUZZARD

Butastur teesa 45cm. Sexes alike. Ashy-brown above; distinct throat, white with two dark cheek stripes and a third stripe from chin; white nape patch, white eyes and orange-yellow cere visible from close quarters; in flight, a pale shoulder patch from above; from below, the pale underside of roundish wings against a darkish body distinctive. Solitary or scattered pairs; seen on exposed perches, trees, poles or telegraph wires; seems to prefer certain sites; soars high and does aerial displays when breeding. **Food:** rodents, lizards, squirrels, small birds, frogs and insects. **Voice:** musical, plaintive *te..twee.* frequently when breeding. **Range:** resident; all India, to about 1200m in Himalaya. **Habitat:** open, dry forest; cultivated country.

GREATER SPOTTED EAGLE

Aquila clanga 65cm. Sexes alike, but female slightly larger. Deep brown above, with purplish wash on back; somewhat paler below; often has whitish rump; soars on straight wings, with drooping tips; immature birds may have white markings above. The **Lesser Spotted Eagle** *A pomarina* is slightly smaller, with narrower wings and is paler above. Mostly solitary; prefers vicinity of water; perches for long spells on bare trees or on ground; sluggish behavior. **Food:** small animals, waterfowl, small birds. **Voice:** loud shrill *kaek...kaek*, often from perch. **Range:** breeds sporadically in parts of N, E and NC India; spreads south in winter. **Habitat:** tree covered areas in the vicinity of water.

Black-Tailed Godwit

TAWNY EAGLE

Aquila rapax 70cm. Sexes alike, female slightly larger. Variable plumage; adults usually dark brown, with faint pale barrings on short rounded tail; holds tail straight and level with body when in flight; lacks dull white rump of most Spotted Eagles. Adult **Steppe Eagle** *A nipalensis* is very similar but may have pale white wing bars and rump. Difficult to distinguish; solitary or several scattered; sits on ground for long periods eating carrion or offal; lazy, low flight. **Food:** carrion, small animals, birds. **Voice:** loud crackling notes; high pitched call. **Range:** sporadically over parts of the country; *nipalensis* is a winter visitor. **Habitat:** open country, vicinities of villages, towns and cultivation.

Tawny Eagle

BONELLI'S EAGLE

Hieraaetus fasciatus 70cm. Sexes alike, but female larger. Uncrested, long-tailed forest eagle. Dark brown above; buffy-white below, heavily streaked with black; broad subterminal tail-band black; several narrower bands; the pale, streaked body, barred flight feathers and broad band on longish tail distinctive in flight. Solitary or in pairs, flying over forests; pairs often hunt in unison; pounces on prey from lofty perches or strikes in aerial pursuit. **Food:** hares, large ground birds, monitor lizards; also smaller forest birds, squirrels. **Voice:** shrill scream of three to six notes. **Range:** resident; all India, sporadically from about 2400m in the Himalaya. **Habitat:** forest.

Bonelli's Eagle

Otto Pfister

Booted Eagle

M.K. Kuppuraj

Changeable Hawk Eagle

Kamal Sahai

Common Kestrel

BOOTED EAGLE (Booted Hawk Eagle)

Hieraaetus pennatus 52m. Sexes alike; female larger. Our smallest eagle. Has two distinct colour phases. **Light phase:** paler head, uppertail and upper wing-coverts; buffy-white wing lining, underbody and tail with blackish flight feathers distinctive, easily identifiable in flight. **Dark phase:** choco-brown below; pale, banded tail, visible in flight. Upperbody as in light phase. Solitary or in pairs hunting in concert; several may roost together at night. **Food:** small birds, rodents, lizards; robs poultry. **Voice:** loud scream of several notes. **Range:** breeds in the Himalaya (1800-3000m). **Habitat:** open forest; scrub.

CHANGEABLE HAWK EAGLE (Crested)

Spizaetus cirrhatus 70cm. Sexes alike, but female larger. Brown above; white underbody longitudinally streaked all over with brown; prominent occipital crest; the streaked whitish body, broad wings and long, rounded tail distinctive in flight. Solitary, occasionally a pair circles high over forests, especially when breeding; surveys for prey from high, leafy branches near forest clearings. **Food:** partridges, other ground-birds, squirrels, hares, lizards. **Voice:** loud, screaming cry, usually long-drawn. **Range:** resident; all India, south of the Himalaya, where another race, (*limnaeetus*, with very small or no crest and paler below with barred abdomen) may be seen up to 2000m. **Habitat:** semi-evergreen and deciduous forest, clearings.

COMMON KESTREL

Falco tinnunculus 35cm. **Male:** black-streaked ash-grey crown, sides of neck, nape; rufous mantle, black-spotted; cheek-stripe; grey tail has white tip and black subterminal band; streaked and spotted buffy underbody. **Female:** pale rufous above; streaked head and narrowly barred back; paler buff below, densely streaked. **Young:** Like female; thickly streaked below. Solitary or in pairs; on exposed perches overlooking open country; circles in air and pounces into grass and scrub; often hovers when hunting. **Food:** insects, lizards, small rodents. **Voice:** an infrequent clicking sound. **Range:** resident; local migrant; several races; breeds in the Himalaya (commoner in the west); also in W Ghats south of Bombay; hill ranges in S India; winter numbers augmented. **Habitat:** open country; cliffsides.

RED-NECKED FALCON (Red-Headed)

Falco chicquera 35cm. Sexes alike; female larger. Blue-grey above; chestnut sides of head, crown, nape, cheek-stripe diagnostic; wings pointed, outer flight feathers blackish, closely barred with white on inner webs; black-barred grey tail with narrow black bars has a broad,

Red-Necked Falcon

black terminal band edged with white; white below; lightly streaked breast, barred below. Pairs, usually hunt in concert; straight and strong flight; also hunts by driving prey out from leafy branches; occasionally soars high; drinks water on ground. **Food:** small birds, rodents, lizards. **Voice:** shrill trilling screams. **Range:** resident; all India south of Himalayan foothills; commoner in Deccan, sometimes breeds in and around habitation. **Habitat:** avoids dense forest, prefers open country, wide cultivated plains with groups of trees.

Oriental Hobby

ORIENTAL HOBBY (Indian)

Falco severus 28cm A small, robust falcon; miniature Shaheen; slaty-grey above; deep, black head, including cheeks; chestnut underparts, paler on throat. The **Eurasian Hobby** *F subbuteo* has rusty-white underparts, thickly streaked. Solitary or several together; feeds mostly around dusk and dawn, in twilight; flies about erratically, circling, dancing, rising and dropping; charges after prey at tremendous speed; eats on wing or on perch. **Food:** large flying insects; small bats, birds and lizards. **Voice:** shrill trill of three to four notes. **Range:** resident; lower Himalaya.

LAGGAR FALCON

Falco jugger 45cm. Sexes alike; female larger. Dark brown above; white on head; narrow moustache; whitish below, streaked thickly on flanks; in flight, pale breast contrasts with darker flanks and thighs. In young birds, underbody below throat dark brown. Usually a pair, scattered or together perches on tree-tops or poles in open country;

Laggar Falcon

Peregrine Falcon

Little Grebe

Darter

often seen in towns and cities; the pair often hunts in concert, chasing prey; spectacular displays at onset of breeding season. **Food:** small to medium-sized birds, rodents, lizards. **Voice:** two or three note scream, mostly when breeding. **Range:** resident; local migrant; all India, to about 1000m in the Himalaya. **Habitat:** open country; scrub.

PEREGRINE FALCON (Shaheen)

Falco peregrinus 42cm. A powerful, broad-shouldered falcon. Sexes alike; female larger. Slaty-grey above, whitish about cheeks; dark moustachial stripe; rusty-white below, finely cross-barred with dark below breast. The migrant **Peregrine Falcon** *F p japonensis* is whitish below, and frequents the vicinity of jheels and marshes. Solitary or in pairs; wheeling and gliding around steep cliffsides; flight very fast and powerful; dives at prey; indulges in spectacular displays. **Food:** birds such as partridges, quails, pigeons, parakeets. **Voice:** fairly loud, ringing scream. **Range:** resident; all India, to about 3000m in the Himalaya; not found in the semi-arid regions. **Habitat:** mostly rugged, mountainous areas; cliffs.

LITTLE GREBE

Tachybaptus ruficollis 22cm. Sexes alike. India's smallest waterbird, squat and tailless. Plumage silky and compact dark brown above; white in flight feathers; white abdomen. **Breeding:** chestnut sides of head, neck and throat, black chin; blackish-brown crown, hindneck. **Winter:** white chin; brown crown, hindneck; rufous neck. Purely aquatic; seen singly or in small, scattered groups, often diving and swimming beneath the surface. **Food:** aquatic insects, frogs, crustacea. **Voice:** shrill trilling notes and an occasional click. **Range:** all India, to 2000m in Kashmir. Resident in most areas. **Habitat:** village tanks, deep jheels, lakes, reservoirs.

DARTER

Anhinga melanogaster 90cm. Sexes alike. Long, snake-like neck, pointed bill and stiff, fan-shaped tail confirm identity. **Adult:** black above, streaked and mottled with silvery-grey on back and wings; choco-brown head, neck; white stripe down sides of upper neck; white chin, upper throat; entirely black below. **Young:** brown with rufous and silvery streaks on mantle. A bird of deep, fresh water; specialised feeder, the entire structure of the bird modified for following and capturing fish underwater, swims low in water, with only head and neck uncovered;

chases prey below water with wings half open, spearing a fish with sudden rapier-like thrusts. made possible by bend in neck at 8th and 9th vertebrae. Tosses fish into air and swallows head-first. Basks on tree stumps and rocks, cormorant style. **Voice:** loud croaks and squeaks. **Range:** all India, south of the Himalayan foothills. **Habitat:** freshwater lakes, jheels.

LITTLE CORMORANT

Phalacrocorax niger 50cm. Sexes alike. Our smallest and commonest cormorant; short, thick neck and head distinctive; lacks gular patch. **Breeding adult:** black plumage has blue-green sheen; silky white feathers on fore crown and sides of head; silvery-grey wash on upper back and wing coverts, speckled with black. **Non-breeding adult:** white chin and upper throat. Gregarious; flocks in large jheels; swims with only head and short neck exposed; dives often, the hunt can become a noisy, jostling scene; frequently perches on poles, trees and rocks, basks with wings spread open. **Food:** mostly fish, also tadpoles, crustaceans. **Range:** all India, south of the Himalaya. **Habitat:** village tanks, jheels, lakes, rivers and coastal areas.

Little Cormorant

INDIAN CORMORANT (Indian Shag)

Phalacrocorax fuscicollis 65cm. Sexes alike. **Breeding adult:** iridescent bronze-black above; glossy black below; white speckles on head and tuft behind eyes. **Non-breeding adult:** no gloss in plumage; white specks on throat; yellowish gular patch. Distinguished from Large Cormorant chiefly by size. Gregarious; frenetic communal hunting appears like stampede; basks with wings and tail open. **Food:** mostly fish. **Range:** resident; local migrant; all India, south of the Himalayan foothills. **Habitat:** rivers, jheels, also tidal creeks.

Indian Cormorant

GREAT CORMORANT (Large)

Phalacrocorax carbo 80cm. Sexes alike. **Breeding adult:** black plumage with metallic blue-green sheen; white facial skin, throat; bright yellow gular pouch and white thigh patches; silky white plumes on head and neck. **Non-breeding adult:** no white thigh patches; gular pouch less bright. **First year young:** dull brown above, white below. Aquatic. Not a gregarious species outside breeding season; usually one or two birds feeding close by, dives underwater in search of fish. **Range:** resident in most areas; all India, to 3000m in the Himalaya (observed in Kashmir, Ladakh, Nepal). **Habitat:** jheels, lakes, mountain torrents.

Great Cormorant

I.A. Babu

Little Egret

LITTLE EGRET

Egretta garzetta 65cm. Sexes alike. A slender, snow-white waterbird. White plumage; black legs, yellow feet and black bill diagnostic. **Breeding:** nuchal crest of two long plumes; feathers on back and breast lengthen into ornamental filamentous feathers. Small flocks feed at edge of water, sometimes wading into the shallower areas; stalks prey like typical heron, waiting patiently at edge of water. **Food:** small fish, frogs, tadpoles, aquatic insects, crustaceans. **Voice:** an occasional croak. **Range:** resident; all India, from 1600m in outer Himalaya. **Habitat:** inland marshes, jheels, riversides, damp irrigated areas; sometimes tidal creeks.

B. Dasgupta

Western Reef Egret

WESTERN REEF EGRET (Indian Reef Heron)

Egretta gularis 65cm. Sexes alike. A slender heron of rocky sea coast. Has two colour phases. **Dark Phase:** slaty-black plumage; white throat, upper foreneck. **Light Phase:** all white plumage, like Little Egret, but habitat and more solitary nature distinctive; bill brown and yellow or bright yellow; plumes in breeding plumage much like Little Egret. Shy and solitary; more active in twilight; sometimes both phases feed side by side; moves cautiously on tidal ooze; jabs at prey; settles hunched-up on a rock. **Food:** small crabs, insects, fish, mudskippers. **Voice:** an occasional croak. **Range:** resident and local migrant; breeds off Gulf of Kutch; commoner on west coast; rare on the eastern seaboard. **Habitat:** rocky and sandy coast; mudflats.

Joanna Van Gruisen

Grey Heron

GREY HERON

Ardea cinerea 100cm. A long-legged, long-necked bird of open marshes. Sexes alike. Ashy-grey above; white crown, neck, underparts; black stripe through eye continues as long, black crest; black dotted band down centre of foreneck; dark blue-black night feathers; golden-yellow iris at close range. Mostly solitary except when breeding; occasionally enters shallow water; usually stands motionless, head pulled in between shoulders, waiting for prey to come close; characteristic flight, head pulled back and long legs trailing. **Voice:** loud *quaak* in flight; also some croaks and squeaks. **Range:** mostly resident; all India; to 4000m in Ladakh; breeds up to 1750m in Kashmir. **Habitat:** marshes, tidal creeks, freshwater bodies.

PURPLE HERON

Ardea purpurea 100cm. Sexes alike. A slender-necked, lanky bird. Slaty-purple above; black crown, long, drooping crest; rufous neck with prominent black stripe along its length; white chin, throat; deep slaty and chestnut below breast; almost black on wings and tail; crest and breast plumes less developed in female. Solitary; crepuscular; extremely shy but master of patience; freezes and hides amidst marsh reeds; when flushed, flies with neck outstretched. **Voice:** a harsh croak. **Range:** mostly resident, though numbers in some areas increase during winter because of migrants; all India south of Himalaya foothills. **Habitat:** open marshes, reed-covered lakes, riversides.

Purple Heron

GREAT EGRET (Large)

Casmerodius albus 90cm. Lanky, snow-white marsh bird; black and yellow **(breeding)** or yellow **(non-breeding)** beak and black legs; when breeding, long, fine plumes on back. The very similar **Intermediate Egret** *Mesophoyx intermedia*, besides being smaller (80cm), develops plumes both on back and breast during the breeding season. Usually solitary; rarely more than three or four birds scattered over a marsh, towering over other egrets; wades in shallow water but mostly waits silently for prey to come close. **Food:** fish, frogs, crustaceans, aquatic insects. **Voice:** an occasional croak. **Range:** resident and local migrant; not common but widespread over the country. **Habitat:** marshes, jheels, rivers, tidal estuaries.

Great Egret

CATTLE EGRET

Bubulcus ibis 50cm. Sexes alike. A snow-white egret seen on and around cattle, garbage heaps, **Breeding:** buffy-orange plumes on head, neck and back. **Non-breeding:** distinguished from Little Egret by yellow beak; from other egrets by size. Widespread; equally abundant around water and away from it; routinely attends to grazing cattle, feeding on insects disturbed by the animals; follows tractors; scavenges at garbage dumps and slaughter houses. **Food:** insects, frogs, lizards, refuse. **Voice:** mostly silent except for some croaking sounds when breeding. **Range:** resident; all India, to 1800m in outer Himalaya. **Habitat:** marshes, lakes, forest clearings.

Cattle Egret

Indian Pond Heron

INDIAN POND HERON

Ardeola grayii 46cm. Sexes alike. A small heron, commonest of family in India, thick-set and earthy-brown in colour, with dull green legs, bill bluish at base, yellowish at centre with black tip, neck and legs shorter than in true egrets. Difficult to sight when settled. **Breeding:** buff-brown head, neck; white chin, upper throat, longish crest; rich maroon back; buff-brown breast. **Non-breeding:** streaked dark brown head, neck; grey-brown back, shoulders; more white in plumage. Found around water; ubiquitous in the plains in hills up to 1200m; remains motionless in mud or up to ankles in water, or slowly stalks prey. Hunts alone, roosts in groups. **Food:** fish, frogs, crustaceans, insects. **Voice:** a harsh croak, usually when flushed, also squeaks and chatters at nesting colony. **Range:** resident; all India. **Habitat:** marshes, jheels, river-sides, roadside ditches, tidal creeks.

LITTLE HERON (Little Green)

Butorides striatus 45cm. Sexes alike. A grey, black and dark metallic green heron. Slaty-grey above, with a glossy green wash; white cheeks; very dark green forehead, crown, longish crest; grey head, neck; glossy green, grey and white in wings; white chin, centre of throat; ashy-grey below. Solitary, shy and sluggish; mostly crepuscular and nocturnal; sits patiently near water. **Food:** frogs, small fish, crabs, insects. **Voice:** redshank-like *tewn..tewn*. **Range:** resident; uncommon; India south of the Himalaya. **Habitat:** secluded pools.

Little Heron

BLACK-CROWNED NIGHT HERON

Nycticorax nycticorax 60cm. Sexes alike. A small but heavy heron. Plumage mostly grey, black and white; black head, back and drooping crest; white forehead, streak over eye, underbody; very long white feathers extend back from crest; greyish sides of neck, wings, rump and tail; blood-red iris visible at close range. Nocturnal; shy and secretive; roosts in trees during day; at dusk the birds leave the colony in small parties to frequent feeding marshes; feeds through the night until early morning. **Food:** frogs, fish, aquatic insects. **Voice:** harsh raucous *kwock*...in flight. **Range:** resident; all India, to about 2200m in W and C Himalaya. **Habitat:** marshes, forest streams, lakes, tidal creeks. Roosts in trees.

Black-Crowned Night Heron

CINNAMON BITTERN (Chestnut)

Ixobrychus cinnamomeus 38cm. **Male:** dark cinnamon-rufous above; chestnut in wings, paler on underside; whitish chin, throat, fading into dull chestnut below. **Female:** more chestnut-brownish above, darker than male; dull rufous below, streaked dark brown; prominent dark streak down centre of foreneck and breast. Young birds have mottled upper body and more heavily streaked below. Usually solitary; mostly seen when flushed from dense reed-growth; overall appearance and behaviour much like familiar Pond Heron; active during the rains. The slightly smaller **Little Bittern** *I minutus* is common in the Kashmir Valley. **Food:** insects, frogs, also fish. **Voice:** courting male calls during the rains, when breeding. **Range:** almost all India south of the Himalayan terai; moves considerably, especially with the onset of the rains. **Habitat:** marshy areas, dense reed growth, wet cultivation.

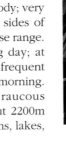

Cinnamon Bittern

GREATER FLAMINGO

Phoenicopterus ruber 140cm. Rose-white plumage; black and scarlet wings; big, downcurved pink beak and legs; characteristic flight, the long legs and neck stretched to full length, with scarlet and black underwing pattern. **Young:** greyish-brown with brown bill. Gregarious; prefers brackish water, lagoons, salt pans; feeds with head immersed; often rests on one leg, neck coiled and head tucked in feathers. **Food:** minute organisms, molluscs, crustaceans, possibly small fish. **Voice:** assortment of cackles when feeding together, otherwise a loud honk. **Range:** resident; local migrant; breeds in Great Rann of Kutch; sporadically seen all over India. **Habitat:** brackish water lagoons, estuaries, freshwater jheels.

Greater Flamingo

Gertrud Denzau

Lesser Flamingo

LESSER FLAMINGO
Phoenicopterus minor 100cm. Smaller size, much deeper rose-pink plumage and dark bill distinguish it from its larger cousin; shorter red legs. **Female:** slightly smaller; no crimson on breast, back. **Young:** grey-brown. Highly social, often seen with Large, prefers heavily saturated brine, lagoons, salt and brackish lakes; peculiar feeding style, the submerged head swinging from side to side as it walks in foot-deep water; bill specially adapted for filter-feeding. **Food:** almost restricted to feeding on algae and diatoms; perhaps also insect larvae. **Range:** first found breeding in Great Rann only in 1974; erratically found in many parts of W and C India. **Habitat:** restricted to high brine concentration, brackish lakes, salt pans, lagoons.

Joanna Van Gruisen

Black-Headed Ibis

BLACK-HEADED IBIS (White)
Threskiornis melanocephalus 75cm. Sexes alike. White plumage; naked black head; long, curved black bill; blood-red patches seen on underwing and flanks in flight. **Breeding:** long plumes over neck; some slaty-grey in wings. **Young:** head and neck feathered; only face and patch around eye naked. Gregarious; feeds with storks, spoonbills, egrets and other ibises; moves actively in water, the long, curved bill held partly open and head partly submerged as the bird probes the nutrient-rich ooze. **Food:** frogs, insects, fish, molluscs, algal matter. **Voice:** loud booming call; nasal grunts reported during breeding season. **Range:** resident; local migrant; all India, from terai south. **Habitat:** marshes; riversides.

Toby Sinclair

Black Ibis

BLACK IBIS
Pseudibis papillosa 70cm. Sexes alike. Glossy black plumage; slender, blackish-green, downcurved beak; red warts on naked black head; white shoulder patch; brick-red legs. The **Glossy Ibis** *Plegadis falcinellus* is deep maroon-brown above, with purple-green gloss from head to lower-back; feathered head and lack of white shoulder-patch distinctive. Small parties, spends more time on the drier edges of marshes and jheels; when feeding in shallow water, often feeds along with other ibises, storks, spoonbills. **Food:** small fish, frogs, earthworms, insects, lizards, crustaceans. **Voice:** two to three note loud nasal screams, uttered in night; also on nest. **Range:** resident; NW India, east through Gangetic plains; south to Karnataka. **Habitat:** cultivated areas; edges of marshes.

EURASIAN SPOONBILL

Platalea leucorodia 65cm. Sexes alike, female slightly smaller. Snow-white plumage; large, flat, spatula-shaped, black bill with yellow tip; longish, black legs; cinnamon-buff patch on lower foreneck; small red-yellow throat patch. **Breeding:** a long, white crest of pointed plumes. Highly gregarious and social; peculiar feeding manner, bird wading quickly, its partly-open half-immersed beak sweeping from side to side; sometimes indulges in frenetic feeding bouts; rests on bare ground during hot hours of day; feeds till past sunset. **Food:** frogs, small fish, crustaceans, vegetable matter. **Voice:** mandible clattering and short grunts when breeding. **Range:** resident; winter visitor in some areas; all India south of terai. **Habitat:** marshes, riversides, jheels, creeks.

Eurasian Spoonbill

Toby Sinclair

GREAT WHITE PELICAN (Rosy)

Pelecanus onocrotalus 75cm. Sexes alike but female slightly smaller. Rose-tinged white plumage; pink feet and yellowish tuft on breast; black primaries and underside of secondaries; forehead feathers continue in pointed wedge above bill. The very similar **Dalmatian Pelican** *Pelecanus crispus* can be distinguished by its dark grey feet and dusky white wing underside. Purely aquatic, huge numbers gathering to feed together; rarely settles on land; strong flier, flocks often flying to great heights. **Food:** almost exclusively fish. **Voice:** grunts and croaks rarely heard. **Range:** resident in Rann of Kutch; winters in parts of N, S and SE India. **Habitat:** large jheels, lakes, coastal lagoons.

Great White Pelican

R.K. Gaur

SPOT-BILLED PELICAN (Grey)

Pelecanus philippensis (roseus) 150cm. Sexes alike. Whitish plumage sullied with grey-brown; pink on lower back, rump and flanks; white-tipped brown crest on back of head; black primaries and dark brown secondaries distinctive in flight; flesh coloured gular pouch has a bluish-purple wash; at close range the blue spots on upper mandible and on gular pouch confirm identity of species. Purely aquatic; seen singly as well as in large gatherings, driving the fish into shallow waters before scooping up the prey in the gular pouches. **Range:** breeds in the well-watered parts of S, SE and E India but population spreads in non-breeding season. **Habitat:** large jheels, lakes.

Spot-Billed Pelican

E. Hanumantha Rao

Painted Stork

PAINTED STORK

Mycteria leucocephala 95cm. Sexes alike. **White plumage:** blackish-green and white wings; blackish-green breast band and black tail; rich rosy-pink wash on greater wing coverts; large, slightly curved bill orangish-yellow. **Young:** pale dirty brown, the neck feathers edged darker; lacks breast band. Common and gregarious; feeds with beak partly submerged, ready to grab prey; when not feeding, settles hunched-up outside water; regularly soars high on thermals. **Food:** fish, frogs, crustaceans. **Voice:** characteristic mandible-clattering of storks; young in nest have grating begging calls. **Range:** resident and local migrant, from terai south through the country's well-watered regions. **Habitat:** inland marshes, jheels, occasionally riversides.

ASIAN OPENBILL (Open-Billed Stork)

Anastomus oscitans 80cm. Sexes alike. India's smallest stork. White plumage, lightly washed with smoky-grey in non-breeding birds; glistening purplish-greenish black on wings and tail; long, thick beak with curved mandibles and a wide gap along the centre. **Young:** dark smoky-brown; darker brown mantle. Widespread over well-watered regions; associates with other storks and herons when feeding; soars along with other birds; exact function of gap in mandibles uncertain. **Food:** mostly molluscs; also frogs and crabs. **Voice:** only mandible-clattering and some moaning sounds at nest. **Range:** resident and local migrant; all India south of terai. **Habitat:** marshes, jheels.

Asian Openbill

WOOLLY-NECKED STORK (White-Necked)

Ciconia episcopus 105cm. Sexes alike. A large black and white stork with red legs. Glossy black crown, back, breast and huge wings, the black parts having a distinct purplish-green sheen; while neck, lower abdomen and undertail coverts; long, stout bill black, occasionally tinged crimson. In young birds, the glossy black is replaced by dark brown. Solitary or in small scattered parties, silently feeding along with other storks, ibises and egrets; stalks on dryland too; settles on trees; soars high on thermals. **Food:** lizards, frogs, crabs, large insects. **Voice:** only clattering of mandibles. **Range:** resident all India, up to about 1400m in the Himalaya. **Habitat:** marshes, cultivation, wet grasslands.

Woolly-Necked Stork

WHITE STORK

Ciconia ciconia 105cm. Sexes alike. All white plumage; black night feathers; red bill and legs confirm identity and help distinguish from the Openbill. Young birds have black parts replaced by brown. Small scattered parties stalk around sedately for food in open marsh or fallow land; usually protected in India due to religious sentiment, yet a shy and wary bird; in winter, enters cultivation; soars high on thermals. **Food:** lizards, frogs, fish, insects including locusts. **Voice:** only clattering of mandibles. **Range:** winter visitor, arriving by mid-September and leaving around end-March; commoner in NW and C India, and in the Indo-Gangetic plains; less common south of the Deccan. **Habitat:** marshes, fallow land, cultivation.

White Stork

BLACK-NECKED STORK

Ephippiorhynchus asiaticus 135cm. Sexes alike. India's largest stork. Unmistakable. Massive black beak; glossy blue-green-black head, neck and tail; rest of body white; in flight, white wings have broad black band along their length; red legs. Solitary or in pairs, feeding in a marsh or perched atop a tree; shy and wary; occasionally a family may be seen feeding close by, parents with young; wades into deeper water than other storks; soars high on thermals. **Food:** fish, frogs, lizards, small turtles, insects. **Voice:** only clattering of mandibles. **Range:** resident; though widespread in the Indian region, this species is becoming uncommon. **Habitat:** marshes, jheels, large rivers.

Black-Necked Stork

GREATER ADJUTANT (Adjutant Stork)

Leptoptilos dubius 140cm. Sexes alike. Plumage whitish-grey and black; naked red **(breeding)** or yellow-brown **(non-breeding)** head, neck; massive beak; long, naked gular pouch. Silvery-grey wing-band and white ruff around base of neck when breeding. The **Lesser Adjutant** *L javanicus* lacks the gular pouch. Usually small parties but many gather at garbage dumps; upright, soldier-like walk; often feeds along with other storks, kites, vultures. **Food:** snakes, lizards, frogs, fish, offal; also crustaceans, small birds. **Voice:** an occasional loud croak; bill-clattering. **Range:** local migrant; breeds over NE areas, Burma; spreads during monsoon over parts of N India, Indo-Gangetic plains. **Habitat:** marshlands, cultivation, mangrove, vicinity of habitation.

Greater Adjutant

Indian Pitta

Asian Fairy Bluebird

Blue-Winged Leafbird

INDIAN PITTA

Pitta brachyura 19cm. Sexes alike. A multi-coloured, stub-tailed, stoutly built bird; bright blue, green, black, white, yellowish-brown and crimson; white chin, throat and patch on wing-tips and crimson vent distinctive. Solitary or pairs; small flocks on migration, before and after monsoons; spends much time on ground, hunting for insects amidst the leaf-litter and low herbage; quietly flies into a tree branch if disturbed; shows fondness for shaded, semi-damp areas. **Food:** chiefly insects. **Voice:** loud, lively whistle, *wheeet..peu;* very vocal when breeding (rains); also a longish single note whistle. **Range:** almost all India, with considerable seasonal movement, particularly before and after the rains; breeds commonly over N and C India, also elsewhere. **Habitat:** forests, orchards; cultivated country.

ASIAN FAIRY BLUEBIRD

Irena puella 28cm. Male: glistening blue above; deep velvet-black sides of face, underbody, wings; blue under tail-coverts. **Female:** verditer blue plumage; dull black lores, flight-feathers. Pairs or small loose bands; spends the day either in leafy, tall branches; descends into undergrowth to feed on berries or hunt insects; utter their two-noted calls while flitting; amongst trees; seen along with other birds. **Food:** fruits, insects, flower-nectar. **Voice:** common call a double-noted *wit..weet..*; also a *whi..chu..*; **Range:** disjunct distribution; one population in W Ghats and associated hills south of Ratnagiri; another in E Himalaya, east of extreme SE Nepal; Kumaon foothills; Andaman & Nicobar Islands. **Habitat:** evergreen forests, sholas.

BLUE-WINGED LEAFBIRD
(Gold-Mantled Chloropsis)

Chloropsis cochinchinensis 18cm. **Male:** green plumage; blue in wings; yellow-green forehead; black from nostrils, base of eyes to lower throat; bright purple-blue moustachial stripes; dull yellow-green band around black throat. **Female:** pale blue-green (not black) mask; greenish-blue moustachial stripe. Solitary or pairs in leafy canopy; often in mixed-hunting parties, a noisy bully on flowering trees. The **Orange-bellied Leafbird** *C hardwickii* is found between 600-2500m along the Himalaya. **Food:** insects, flower-nectar, fruits. **Voice:** noisy; excellent mimic; a mix of its own notes and imitations of other birds' calls, notably of drongos, bulbuls, shikras and cuckoo-shrikes. **Range:** most of India, except arid NW areas of Punjab, Rajasthan, N and W Gujarat. Range of this and *aurifrons* overlaps in the forested areas of W and E Ghats. **Habitat:** light forests, gardens.

GOLDEN-FRONTED LEAFBIRD (Chloropsis)
Chloropsis aurifrons 19cm. Leaf-green plumage, golden-orange forehead; blue shoulder patches, dark blue chin blackish in southern races; cheeks; black lores, ear-coverts, continuing as a loop around blue throat. Pairs in leafy canopy; lively birds, actively hunts in foliage; their wide range of whistling and harsh notes immediately attracting attention; owing to greenish plumage, difficult bird to see in foliage; **Food:** insects, spiders, flower-nectar. **Voice:** noisy; wide assortment of whistling notes, including imitations of several species; commonest call a drongo or shikra-like *che..chwe..* **Range:** from about 1600m in Garhwal Himalaya east; Bihar, Orissa, south along E Ghats and up the W Ghats and adjoining areas. **Habitat:** towns.

Golden-Fronted Leafbird

BAY-BACKED SHRIKE
Lanius vittatus 18cm. Sexes alike. Deep chestnut-maroon back; broad black forehead band, continuing through eyes to ear-coverts; grey crown, neck, separated from black by small white patch; white rump distinctive; black wings with white in outer flight feathers: white underbody, fulvous on breast and flanks. Solitary or in scattered pairs in open terrain; keeps lookout from a perch on some tree-stump, overhead wire or bushtop. **Food:** insects, lizards, small rodents. **Voice:** harsh *churr*; lively warble of breeding male, sometimes imitates other bird calls. **Range:** all India, from about 1800m in the Himalaya; absent in the NE. **Habitat:** open country, light forests and scrub.

Bay-Backed Shrike

LONG-TAILED SHRIKE (Rufous-Backed)
Lanius schach 25cm. Sexes alike. Pale grey from crown to middle of back; bright rufous from then on to the rump; black forehead, band through eye; white 'mirror' in black wings; whitish underbody, ringed pale rufous on lower breast, flanks. Mostly solitary; boldly defends feeding territory; keeps lookout from conspicuous perch; pounces on to ground on sighting prey; said to store surplus in 'larder', impaling prey on thorns; nick-named **Butcher-bird**. **Food:** insects, lizards, small rodents, birds. **Voice:** noisy; harsh mix of scolding notes, shrieks and yelps; excellent mimic; rather musical song of breeding male. **Range:** three races; undergo considerable seasonal movement; all India, from about 2700m in the Himalaya. The *L s tricolor* has a black head and small white patch on wings, breeds in the Himalaya east of Garhwal. **Habitat:** open country cultivation, edges of forest, vicinity of habitation, gardens; prefers neighbourhood of water.

Long-Tailed Shrike

Kamal Sahai

Great Grey Shrike

Otto Pfister

Eurasian Jay

Joanna Van Gruisen

Yellow-Billed Blue Magpie

GREAT GREY SHRIKE

Lanius excubitor 25cm. Sexes alike. Bluish-grey above; broad black stripe from beak through eyes; black wings with white mirrors; black and white tail; unmarked, white underbody. Mostly in pairs in open areas; remains perched upright on bush-tops or overhead wires or flies low, uttering a harsh scream; surveys neighbourhood from perch and pounces on prey; batters and tears prey before swallowing; impaling surplus prey on thorns; a wild and wary bird. **Food:** insects, lizards, small birds, rodents. **Voice:** harsh, grating *khreck..* call; a mix of other harsh notes and chuckles; pleasant, ringing song of breeding male. **Range:** the drier areas of NW, W and C India, across Gangetic plain to W Bengal; south to Tamil Nadu. **Habitat:** open country, semi-desert, scrub, edges of cultivation.

EURASIAN JAY

Garrulus glandarius 33cm. Sexes alike. Pinkish-brown plumage; velvet-black malar stripe; closely black-barred, blue wings; white rump contrasts with jet black tail. The **Black-headed Jay** *G lanceolatus* of the W Himalaya, east to about C Nepal, has black cap, black and white face, and white in wings. Small, noisy bands, often along with other Himalayan birds; common in Himalayan hill-stations; inquisitive and aggressive; mostly keeps to trees, but also descends into bush and onto ground; laboured flight. **Food:** insects, fruits, nuts. **Voice:** noisy; guttural chuckles, screeching notes and whistles; good mimic. **Range:** Himalaya, west to east; 1500-2800m, somewhat higher in the east; may descend low in winter. **Habitat:** mixed temperate forests.

YELLOW-BILLED BLUE MAGPIE

Urocissa flavirostris 66cm including long tail, body size about that of pigeon. Sexes alike. Purple-blue plumage; black head; breast; white nape patch, underbody; very long, white-tipped tail; yellow beak and orange legs. The **Red-billed Blue Magpie** *U erythrorhyncha* (70cm) has more white on nape; red beak, legs; appears to be restricted to the Himalaya between Himachal and E Nepal and some parts of north-east India. Pairs or small bands, flying across clearings, entering hill-station gardens, one bird following another; arboreal, but also hunt low in bushes; even descend to ground, the long tail cocked as the bird hops about. **Food:** insects, fruit, lizards, eggs, small birds. **Voice:** noisy; great mix of metallic screams, loud whistles and raucous notes, often imitating other birds. **Range:** Himalaya, west to east; 1500-3600m; may descend low in winter. **Habitat:** forests, gardens, clearings.

RUFOUS TREEPIE (Indian)

Dendrocitta vagabunda 50cm, including tail. Sexes alike. Rufous above; sooty grey-brown head, neck; black, white and grey on wings, best seen in night; black-tipped, grey tail, long and graduated. Pairs or small parties; often seen in mixed hunting parties, appearing as leader of pack; feeds up in trees, but also descends low into bushes and onto ground to pick termites; bold and noisy, rather tame and confiding in certain areas, such as Ranthambhore, Bharatpur, Sariska; inquisitive, like other crow-family birds. **Food:** insects, lizards, small birds, eggs, fruit, flower-nectar; kitchen scraps in some areas. **Voice:** common call a fluty three-note *goo.ge.lay* or *ko.ki.la*; harsh, guttural notes often uttered. **Range:** almost all India, up to about 1500m in outer Himalaya. **Habitat:** forests, gardens, cultivation, habitation.

Rupin Dang

Rufous Treepie

BLACK-BILLED MAGPIE (Eurasian Common Pied)

Pica pica 52cm, including long tail. Sexes alike. Pied bird. Glossy black head, neck, upper-back, wings; tail glossed bronze-green and purple-blue; white scapulars, lower-back (rump), belly; black under-tail. The Tibetan race *bottanensis* can be identified by its black rump. Usually several in vicinity; moves on ground, perches on fence-posts, trees, house-tops; frequents high-mountain villages; typical crow, bold and aggressive, but also extremely alert; flicks tail often. **Food:** almost omnivorous; refuse, insects, fruit, grain, small animals. **Voice:** loud, grating *chak..chak* calls; also other piping notes. **Range:** high NW Himalaya, Chitral, N Kashmir, Ladakh, Himachal Pradesh; the Tibetan race is found in Bhutan and Arunachal: 1500-4700m. **Habitat:** open valleys, cultivation, habitation.

Sunjoy Monga

Black-Billed Magpie

SPOTTED NUTCRACKER

Nucifraga caryocatactes 32cm. Sexes alike. Choco-brown plumage, thickly speckled with white; dark central tail-feathers, tipped white; white outer tail and under tail-coverts; heavy, pointed beak distinctive. The race *hemispila*, found between Kangra and CE Nepal, has smaller white spots; rump lacks white spots. Small parties in temperate forest; keeps to tree-tops but readily descends onto ground; rather wary; flies short distances across glades; rather noisy, usually attracting attention by its calling. **Food:** seeds of pine, spruce; nuts, acorns; occasionally insects. **Voice:** noisy; guttural *kharr..kharr.* **Range:** Himalaya; 1800-4000m, sometimes descending to about 1200m in winter. **Habitat:** coniferous, oak, rhododendron forest.

Sue Earle

Spotted Nutcracker

Joanna Van Gruisen

Red-Billed Chough

RED-BILLED CHOUGH

Pyrrhocorax pyrrhocorax 45cm. Sexes alike. Glossy black plumage; coral-red curved beak, legs. The **Yellow-billed** or **Alpine Chough** *P graculus* (38cm) has yellow beak and red legs. Highly gregarious; feeds in cultivation; probes ground and dung for insects; does not hesitate to rob corn stored in attics of upland houses; flocks often fly high into the skies, rising on thermals, playing and dancing in air currents in wild splendour; tame and confiding in some areas; cheerful companions to the high-mountain trekker. **Food:** insects, barley grain, wild-berries. **Voice:** melodious, high-pitched *cheeao..cheeau..*; also a loud *kew..kew..*; other squeaky notes. **Range:** high Himalaya; 2200-4000m; may descend to about 1500m in severe winter; the eastern race could be encountered at 6000m in summer. **Habitat:** cliffsides, alpine pastures, cultivation, vicinity of mountain habitation.

Sunjoy Monga

House Crow

HOUSE CROW

Corvus splendens 43cm. Sexes alike. Black plumage; grey collar, upper back and breast; glossy black on forehead, crown and throat. The **Jackdaw** *C monedula* (33cm) is similar to the House Crow, but is smaller, thicker-necked and white-eyed. An integral and conspicuous part of India, street-smart, sharp, swift, sociable, sinister, the crow is almost totally commensal on man; snatches food from table, shops; mobs other birds; performs important scavenging services; occasionally flies very high into skies, either when flying long-distance; communal roost-sites. **Food:** omnivorous, robs young birds from nest; drives other birds from flowering trees. **Voice:** familiar *caw* call; occasionally a pleasant *kurrrrr* note; several other notes. **Range:** all India, reaching about 2500m in the Himalaya. **Habitat:** habitations rural and urban; cultivation, forest edges.

Toby Sinclair

Large-Billed Crow

LARGE-BILLED CROW (Jungle)

Corvus macrorhynchos 48cm. Sexes alike. Glossy black plumage; heavy beak, with noticeable culmen-curve. The **Carrion Crow** *C corone* of NW mountains is confusingly similar. Solitary or in groups of two to six; commoner around villages and only small numbers in urban areas; overall not as 'enterprising' as the familiar House Crow; in forested areas, its behaviour often indicates presence of carnivore-kills. **Food:** omnivorous. **Voice:** harsh *khaa..khaa* calls; several variations on this among the various races of this crow. **Range:** all India, to about 4500m in the Himalaya; absent in extreme W Rajasthan and parts of Punjab. **Habitat:** forests, rural habitations; small numbers in towns and cities.

ASHY WOODSWALLOW (Swallow-Shrike)

Artamus fuscus 19cm. Sexes alike. Slaty-grey plumage, greyer on head; paler on rump, underbody; short square tail, tipped white; white under tail coverts; somewhat heavy-looking bird, rather swallowlike in appearance, but wings much shorter and broader. Small numbers in open country; perches on leafstalks, overhead wires or flies characteristically, a few wingbeats and a glide; hunts flying insects; quiet during hot hours, feeds mostly in mornings and evenings. **Food:** winged insects. **Voice:** harsh *chey...chey...or chaek..chaek..* call, often uttered in flight; short song occasionally when breeding, a mix of harsh and melodious notes. **Range:** India, roughly east and south from WC Gujarat to roughly Shimla; widespread but not continuously distributed; up to about 1800m in outer Himalaya. **Habitat:** open country, edges of forest.

S. Kartikeyan

Ashy Woodswallow

EURASIAN GOLDEN ORIOLE

Oriolus oriolus 25cm. **Male:** bright golden-yellow plumage; black stripe through eye; black wings and centre of tail. **Female:** yellow-green above; brownish-green wings; dirty-white below, streaked brown. Young male much like female. Solitary or in pairs; arboreal, regularly visits fruiting and flowering trees; hunts insects in leafy branches; usually heard, surprisingly not often seen, despite bright colour. **Food:** insects, fruit, nectar. **Voice:** fluty whistle of two or three notes, interpreted *pee.lo.lo,* the middle note lower; harsh note often heard; rich, mellow song when breeding, somewhat mournful; doesn't sing often. **Range:** summer visitor to the Himalayan foothills to about 2600m; spreads in winter to plains; breeds also in many parts of peninsula. **Habitat:** forest, orchards, gardens around habitation.

R.K. Gaur

Eurasian Golden Oriole

BLACK-HOODED ORIOLE (Black-Headed)

Oriolus xanthornus 25cm. Sexes alike. Golden-yellow plumage; black head diagnostic; black and yellow wings, tail; deep pink-red beak seen at close quarters. Pairs or small parties; strictly arboreal, only rarely descending into lower bushes or on ground, active and lively, moves a lot in forest, chases one another, the rich colours striking against green or brown of forest; very vocal; associates with other birds in mixed parties, visits fruiting and flowering trees. **Food:** fruits, flower nectar, insects. **Voice:** assortment of melodious and harsh calls; commonest is a fluty two or three noted *tu.hee* or *tu.yow.yow..* also a single, mellow note. **Range:** all India, from about 1000m in the Himalayan foothills. **Habitat:** forests, orchards, gardens, often amidst habitation.

Krupakar Senani

Black-Hooded Oriole

Otto Pfister

Large Cuckooshrike

LARGE CUCKOOSHRIKE

Coracina macei 28cm. **Male:** grey above; broad, dark stripe through eyes to ear-coverts; black wings, tail: greyish breast, whitish below. **Female:** barred grey-and-white below; paler stripe through eyes. Pairs or small bands of 4-6 birds; characteristic flight over forest, few wing-beats and a glide, often calls in flight; flicks wings on perching; keeps to upper branches, but may descend into bush; very active and noisy when breeding (March-June). **Food:** insects, larvae, flower-nectar, fruits. **Voice:** noisy; a two-noted ringing whistle, *ti..treee...*, the second note long-drawn and higher; somewhat like Blossom-headed Parakeet's call. **Range:** most of India, from about 2200m in the Himalaya; absent in the drier, semi-desert regions of Kutch, C and N Rajasthan, and much of NW India. **Habitat:** forests, gardens, tree-dotted cultivation.

Krupkar Senani

Black-Headed Cuckooshrike

BLACK-HEADED CUCKOOSHRIKE

Coracina melanoptera 20cm. **Male:** grey plumage; black head, wings, tail, the latter white-tipped, except on middle feathers; pale grey below breast, whiter on abdomen, vent. **Female:** brown plumage; whitish-buff below barred dark-brown till abdomen; lacks black head. Solitary or in pairs, only occasionally several together; often part of mixed-hunting bands; keep for most part to leafy, upper branches, probes the foliage for insects; methodically checks foliage before flying off to another grove or forest patch. **Food:** chiefly insects; also berries and flower-nectar. **Voice:** silent for most of year; breeding male has whistling song, up to a dozen notes, frequently uttered. **Range:** all India east and south of line from Mt Abu to W Uttar Pradesh; a Himalayan race is found in parts of Punjab, Himachal and hill regions of Uttar Pradesh, to about 2000m. Undergoes considerable seasonal migration. **Habitat:** forests, gardens, groves.

Krupakar Senani

Small Minivet

SMALL MINIVET

Pericrocotus cinnamomeus 15cm. **Male:** dark-grey head, back, throat; orange-yellow patch on black wings; black tail; flame-orange breast; orange-yellow belly, under tail. **Female:** paler above; orange rump; dusky white throat, breast ringed with yellow; yellowish belly, undertail. Pairs or small flocks; keep to tree-tops, actively moving amidst foliage; flutters and flits about in an untiring hunt for small insects, often in association with other small birds; also hunt flycatcher style. **Food:** chiefly insects; sometimes flower nectar. **Voice:** soft, low *swee..swee..* notes uttered as birds hunt in foliage. **Range:** most of India, from about 900m in outer Himalaya; absent in arid parts of Rajasthan. **Habitat:** forests, groves, gardens, tree-dotted cultivation.

SCARLET MINIVET

Pericrocotus flammeus 20cm. **Male:** glistening black head, upper back; deep scarlet lower back, rump; black and scarlet wings, tail; black throat, scarlet below. **Female:** rich yellow forehead, supercilium; grey-yellow above; yellow and black wings, tail; bright yellow underbody. Pairs or small parties; sometimes several dozen together; keeps to canopy of tall trees; actively flits about to hunt for insects; also launches aerial sallies after winged insects; often seen in mixed-hunting parties of birds; spectacular sight of black, scarlet and yellow as flock flies over forest, especially when seen from above. **Food:** insects, flower-nectar. **Voice:** pleasant, two-note whistle; also a longer, whistling warble. **Range:** disjunct; several isolated races; (1) Himalaya, to about 2500m. (2)W Ghats and adjoining belt. (3) Bengal, S Bihar, W Madhya Pradesh, Orissa, N Andhra. **Habitat:** forests, gardens, groves.

Krupakar Senani

Scarlet Minivet

White-Throated Fantail

Krupakar Senani

WHITE-THROATED FANTAIL (Flycatcher)

Rhipidura albicollis 17cm. Sexes alike. Slaty-brown plumage, including underbody; shorter, white supercilium; white throat; tips to all but central tail-feathers. The **White-spotted Fantail Flycatcher** races *albogularis* and *vernayi* have a white-spotted slaty band across breast; also, whitish-buff belly, less white in tail-tip. Overall behaviour not appreciably different from White-Browed Flycatcher's. **Voice:** shorter and weaker whistling song than White-browed; a harsh *chukrrr...* note. **Range:** outer Himalaya, to about 1800m; NE regions; absent through Indo-Gangetic plain west to NW parts of country; two races from Orissa to Godavari river; most widespread is the White-Spotted race *albogularis*, found all over peninsular India, south of a line from Mt Abu, across the Vindhya and south along the edge of E Ghats. **Habitat:** light forests, groves, gardens amidst habitation, scrub.

White-Browed Fantail

Joanna Van Gruisen

WHITE-BROWED FANTAIL (Flycatcher)

Rhipidura aureola 17cm. Sexes alike, but female slightly duller. Dark brown above; black crown, sides of face; white forehead, broad stripe (brow) to nape; two white-spotted wing-bars, white edges to tail; black centre of throat, sides of breast; white, sides of throat, underbody. Solitary or in pairs; lively bird, flits about tirelessly in low growth and middle levels, fans tail, flicks wings or bursts into a whistling trill; makes short hunting dashes in air; quite tame and confiding. Food: insects. **Voice:** lively whistle of six to eight notes; grating *chuck··chuck..chuckrrr* note, usually when disturbed and agitated. **Range:** most of the country, south of the Himalayan foothills; absent in arid parts of NW India. **Habitat:** forests, orchards, gardens, tree-dotted cultivation.

Black Drongo

Sunjoy Monga

BLACK DRONGO

Dicrurus macrocercus 32cm including tail. Sexes alike. Glossy black plumage; long, deeply forked tail. The **Ashy Drongo** *D leucophaeus* (30cm) is grey-black, and more of a forest-bird, breeding in Himalaya and a winter visitor to the peninsula. Usually solitary, sometimes small parties; keeps lookout from exposed perch; drops on ground to capture prey, launches short aerial sallies, rides atop grazing cattle, follows cattle, tractors, gas-cutters, fires; thus consumes vast numbers of insects; bold and aggressive species. **Food:** chiefly insects; supplements with flower nectar, small lizards. **Voice:** harsh *tiu-tiu* also *cheece cheece*. **Range:** all India, up to about 1800m in outer Himalaya. **Habitat:** open country, orchards, cultivation.

WHITE-BELLIED DRONGO
Dicrurus caerulescens 24cm. Sexes alike, blackish-blue above; longish, forked tail; grey-brown throat, breast; white belly, under tail-coverts. The **Bronzed Drongo** *D aeneus* is of the same size, but is glossy black all over, with a bronze-green and purple sheen. Pairs or small bands of up to four birds, sometimes in association with other birds; arboreal and noisy; makes short flights after winged insects; often hunts till very late in evening. **Food:** insects, flower-nectar. **Voice:** assortment of pleasant, whistling calls and some grating notes. **Range:** most of India south and east of a line from SE Punjab to around Kutch; east to Bengal; occurs to about 1500m in the hills. **Habitat:** forests, groves, vicinity of habitation.

White-Bellied Drongo

SPANGLED DRONGO (Hair-Crested)
Dicrurus hottentottus 30cm including tail. Sexes alike. Glistening blue-black plumage, fine hair-like feathers on forehead; longish, downcurved, pointed beak; diagnostic tail, square-cut and inwardly-bent (curling) towards outer-ends. Solitary or scattered pairs, strictly arboreal forestbird; small numbers may gather on favourite flowering trees like *Erythrina, Salmalia, Bombax*; rather aggressive, often seen in mixed hunting parties of birds. **Food:** chiefly flower-nectar; also insects, more so when there are young in nest. **Voice:** noisy; a mix of whistling, metallic calls and harsh screams. **Range:** lower Himalaya foothills, east of Kumaon; down through NE India, along E Ghats, Orissa, Bastar, through to W Ghats, up north to Bombay, occasionally even further north. **Habitat:** forests.

Spangled Drongo

GREATER RACKET-TAILED DRONGO
Dicrurus paradiseus 60cm, including outer-tail extensions of about 30cm. Actual size, about myna's. Sexes alike. Glossy blue-black plumage; prominent crest of longish feathers, curving backward; elongated, wire-like outer tail-feathers, ending in 'rackets' diagnostic. Solitary or in pairs, sometimes small gatherings; arboreal forest bird, but often descends into low bush; moves a lot in forest; confirmed exhibitionist, both by sight and sound; extremely noisy, often vocal long before sunrise; bold and aggressive, seen mobbing bigger birds 100m over forest. The **Lesser Racket-Tailed Drongo** *D remifer* (38cm) is found in lower Himalaya, east of Garhwal. **Food:** mostly insects; also lizards, flower nectar. **Voice:** noisiest bird of forest; amazing mimic; wide variety of whistles, screams, perfect imitations of over a dozen species. **Range:** forested parts of India, roughly east and south of line from S Gujarat to Kumaon; up to about 1400m. **Habitat:** forests; also forest-edges, orchards.

Greater Racket-Tailed Drongo

Black-Naped Monarch

Asian Paradise-Flycatcher

BLACK-NAPED MONARCH (Flycatcher)

Hypothymis azurea 16cm. **Male:** lilac-blue plumage; black patch on nape, gorget on breast; slight black scaly markings on crown; sooty on wings, tail; white below breast. **Female:** ashy-blue, duller; lacks black on nape and breast. Solitary or pairs in forest, often amidst mixed-hunting parties; extremely active and fidgety, flits and flutters about, often fans tail slightly; calls often as it moves about, the calls often the first indication of its presence. **Food:** insects. **Voice:** common call a sharp, grating, high-pitched *chwich.chweech* or *chwae.chweech* slightly interrogative in tone, the two notes quickly uttered; has short, rambling notes when breeding. **Range:** India south of outer Himalaya, to about 1200m, east of Dehra Dun; absent in arid NW, and N India. **Habitat:** forest, bamboo, gardens.

ASIAN PARADISE-FLYCATCHER

Terpsiphone paradisi **Adult Male**: 50cm including tail-streamers. Glossy blue black head, crest, throat; black in wings; silvery-white body, long tail-streamers. In rufous phase white parts replaced by rufous-chestnut. **Female** and **Young Male:** 20cm. No tail-streamers; shorter crest; rufous above; ashy-grey throat, nuchal collar; whitish below. Solitary or pairs; makes short sallies, flits through trees, the tail streamers floating; strictly arboreal, sometimes descending into taller bushes; cheerful disposition. **Food:** insects, spiders. **Voice:** sharp, grating *chwae* or *chchwae...* call; melodious warbling song and display of breeding male. **Range:** Himalaya, foothills to about 1800m, rarely 2500m; N India, south to Bharatpur absent in a broad belt across Gangetic plain; widespread in peninsular India. **Habitat:** light forests, gardens, open country.

COMMON IORA

Aegithina tiphia 14cm. **Male:** greenish above (rich black above, with yellowish rump, in summer breeding plumage); black wings, tail; two white wing bars; bright yellow underbody. **Female:** yellow-green plumage; white wing-bars; greenish-brown wings. Pairs keep to leafy branches, often with other small birds; moves energetically amidst branches in their hunt for insects, caterpillars; their rich call-notes often a giveaway of their presence in an area. **Food:** insects, spiders; also flower-nectar. **Voice:** renowned vocalist; wide range of rich, whistling notes; single or two-note long-drawn *wheeeeeee* or *wheeeeeee..chu* is a common call; another common call is a three-note whistle. **Range:** all India, from about 1800m in the

Himalaya; absent in arid NW, desert regions of Rajasthan, Kutch. **Habitat:** forest, gardens, orchards, tree-dotted cultivation, habitation.

COMMON WOODSHRIKE

Tephrodornis pondicerianus 16cm. Sexes alike. Greyish-brown plumage; broad whitish supercilium and dark stripe below eye distinctive: white outer tail-feathers seen when bird flies. Dark stripe may be slightly paler in female. The **Large Woodshrike** *T gularis* is larger (23cm) and has white outer tail-feathers. Pairs or small parties, quiet for greater part of year, vocal when breeding (February-May); keeps to middle-levels of trees, hopping about sometimes coming to ground. **Food:** insects; also flower-nectar. **Voice:** whistling *wheet..wheet...* and an interrogative, quick-repeated *whi..whi..whi..whee* thereafter; other trilling, pleasant notes when breeding. **Range:** most of the country, south of Himalayan foothills; commoner in low country. **Habitat:** light forests, edges of forest, cultivation, gardens in and around habitation.

Kurpakar Senani

Common Woodshrike

M.K. Kuppuraj

Common Iora

White-Throated Dipper

WHITE-THROATED DIPPER

Cinclus cinclus 20cm. Sexes alike. Stub-tailed, squat bird. Slaty above; choco-brown head, nape; scaly-brown markings on back, rump; white throat, breast striking; choco-brown belly. The **Brown Dipper** *C pallasii* is entirely choco-brown, with prominent white eye-ring. Solitary or pairs over a stretch of gushing, icy torrent; settles on slippery rocks amidst water; plunges and swims against current; walks on bottom; very restless and energetic, bobs and moves body from side to side; swift, fast flight, low over water; noisy. **Food:** aquatic insects. **Voice:** shrill *dzchit..dzcheet* call, audible over roaring waters; calls mostly in low flight over water; call usually heard long before bird sighted; sharp lively song. **Range:** Himalaya; 2500-4800m; sometimes to 2000m in winter. **Habitat:** rocky, icy torrents, glacial lakes.

Blue-capped Rock Thrush

BLUE-CAPPED ROCK THRUSH (Blue-Headed)

Monticola cinclorhynchus 17cm. **Male:** blue crown, nape; black back, broad stripe through eyes to ear-coverts, blue throat, shoulder patch; white wing-patch and chestnut rump distinctive; chestnut below throat. Back feathers edged fulvous in winter. **Female:** unmarked olive-brown above; buffy white below, thickly speckled with dark-brown. The female Blue Rock Thrush is grey-brown above, has yellow-brown vent and a dull wing-bar. Solitary or in pairs; an elusive forest bird; moves in foliage in mixed parties or rummages on ground, amidst leaf-litter; best seen when it emerges in clearing. The **Rufous-tailed Rock Thrush** *M saxatilis* (19cm) lacks the black eye stripe and has a diagnostic rufous tail. **Food:** insects, flower-nectar, berries. **Voice:** mostly silent in winter, save for an occasional harsh single or double-noted call; rich song of breeding male. **Range:** breeds in the Himalaya, 1000-2500m, sometimes higher; winters in W Ghats, from Narmada river south; sporadic winter records from C Indian forests. **Habitat:** shaded forests, groves.

BLUE ROCK THRUSH

Monticola solitarius 23cm. **Male:** blue plumage; brown wings, tail; pale fulvous and black scales more conspicuous in winter; whiter on belly in winter. **Female:** duller, grey-brown above; dark shaft-streaks; black barrings on rump; dull white below, barred brown. Solitary; has favoured sites, often around habitation; perches on rocks, stumps, roof-tops; has a rather upright posture; flies on to ground to feed, but sometimes launches short aerial sallies. **Food:** insects, berries; rarely flower-nectar. **Voice:** silent in winter; short, whistling song of breeding male. **Range:** breeds in the Himalaya, from extreme west to east Nepal; 1200-3000m, perhaps higher; winters from foothills, NE, south throughout peninsula; uncommon in Gangetic plains. **Habitat:** open rocky country, cliffs, ravines, ruins, habitation.

Blue Rock Thrush

MALABAR WHISTLING THRUSH

Myophonus horsfieldii 25cm. Sexes alike. Deep blue-black plumage, more glistening on wings, tail; bright, cobalt-blue forehead, shoulder-patch. Solitary or in pairs; a lively bird of hilly, forested country; keeps to forest streams. Peculiar stretching of legs and raising of tail; often encountered on roadside culverts, from where it bolts into nullah or valley. **Food:** insects, crustaceans, snails, frogs, berries. **Voice:** renowned vocalist; especially vocal during the rain, a rich, whistling song, very human in quality, nick-named 'whistling schoolboy'; its fluty notes float over the roar of water; also, a harsh, high-pitched *kreeee* call. **Range:** hills of W India, from Mt Abu, south all along W Ghats, to about 2200m; also parts of Satpuras. **Habitat:** forest streams, waterfalls, gardens.

Malabar Whistling Thrush

BLUE WHISTLING THRUSH

Myophonus caeruleus 34cm. Sexes alike. Deep purple-blue plumage, speckled all over with lighter but bright blue; brighter blue forehead, shoulder-patch, edge of wings and tail; whitish-blue spots on tips of median wing-coverts; yellow beak. Solitary or pairs on Himalayan streams and gorges; common all along Himalaya; hops on boulders in the middle of roaring torrent or dashes through forest; also moves on ground, far from water; seen at most hill-stations, often enters houses; remarkable songster. **Food:** aquatic insects, snails, earthworms, crabs. **Voice:** screechy *zseeet... tzee..tzee..* often audible over roar of water; loud, musical song of whistling notes; loud *kreee* call. **Range:** the Himalaya, 1200-3800m, but ascending to about 4400m. **Habitat:** forest streams, gorges, hill-stations.

Blue Whistling Thrush

M.I. Fernandes

Orange-Headed Thrush

Tim Loseby

Plain-Backed Thrush

Otto Pfister

Tickell's Thrush

ORANGE-HEADED THRUSH (Ground Thrush)

Zoothera citrina 21cm. Blue-grey above; orangish-rufous head, nape, underbody; white ear-coverts with two dark-brown vertical stripes; white throat, shoulder-patch. The **Orange-Headed** nominate race has entire head rufous-orange. Usually in pairs; feeds on ground, rummaging in leaf-litter and under thick growth; occasionally associates with laughing-thrushes and babblers; vocal and restless when breeding. **Food:** insects, slugs, small fruit. **Voice:** loud, rich song, often with a mix of other birds' calls thrown in; also a shrill, screechy *kreeee...* call. **Range:** peninsular India south of a line from S Gujarat across to Orissa; the nominate race breeds in the Himalaya, NE; winters in foothills, terai, parts of E India, Gangetic plains and south along E Ghats. **Habitat:** shaded forests, bamboo, groves, gardens.

LONG-TAILED THRUSH (Mountain)

Zoothera dixoni 27cm. Plain olive-brown above; two dull buffy wing-bars and a larger wing-patch seen best in flight; buffy throat, breast, flanks, the rest white, boldly spotted dark brown. The confusingly similar **Plain-Backed Thrush** *Z mollissima* has very indistinct wing-bars; it has a shorter tail but this character not very useful in field. The **Scaly Thrush** *Z dauma* (26cm) has a distinctly spotted back. Pairs or several together in winter; feeds on ground, usually difficult to spot till it takes off from somewhere close-by; flies up into branches if disturbed. **Food:** insects, snails. **Voice:** mostly silent; *mollissima* has a loud, rattling alarm-note. **Range:** the Himalaya, east of C Himachal; breeds about 2000-4000m; descends to about 1000m in winter. **Habitat:** timber-line forest, scrub in summer; heavy forests in winter.

TICKELL'S THRUSH

Turdus unicolor 22cm. **Male:** light ashy-grey plumage; duller breast and whiter on belly; rufous under-wing coverts in flight. **Female:** olive-brown above; white throat, streaked on sides; tawny flanks and white belly. Small flocks on the ground, sometimes along with other thrushes; hops fast on ground, stops abruptly, as if to check some underground activity; digs worms from under soil; flies into trees when approached too close. **Food:** insects, worms, small fruit. **Voice:** rich song; double-noted alarm call; also some chattering calls. **Range:** breeds in the Himalaya, 1500-2500m, east to C Nepal, and perhaps Sikkim; winters along foothills east of Kangra, NE, and parts of C and E peninsular India. **Habitat:** open forests, groves.

GREY-WINGED BLACKBIRD
Turdus boulboul 28cm. **Male:** black plumage; large, grey wing-patch diagnostic; yellow eye-ring and orangish beak. **Female:** olive-brown plumage; wing-patch pale brown. The female Blackbird is darker in plumage. Solitary or small parties, sometimes with other thrushes in winter; a shy bird, taking to trees on slight suspicion; feeds on ground, picks insects or digs worms. **Food:** insects, worms, small fruit. **Voice:** distinct chuckling notes; rich, loud and fluty song; guttural *churrr...* note. **Range:** the Himalaya, breeds 1800-2700m; descends to about 1200m in winter, sometimes into foothills and adjoining plains. **Habitat:** broadleafed heavy forests; in winter, also scrub, secondary growth.

Grey-Winged Blackbird

EURASIAN BLACKBIRD
Turdus merula 25cm. **Male:** lead-grey above, more ashy-brown below; blackish cap distinctive; darker wings, tail; reddish-orange beak and yellow eye-rims distinctive. **Female:** dark ashy-brown above; browner below, with a grey wash; streaked dark-brown on chin, throat. The Black-capped race *T m nigropileus* of the W Ghats, Abu and parts of Vindhyas, has a more distinct black cap; in the Himalayan race *T m maximus* (27cm), the male is entirely black with yellow beak; female is dark brown. Solitary or pairs, sometimes with other birds; Rummages on forest floor but also moves up in leafy branches; rather confiding. **Food:** insects, small fruit, earthworms. **Voice:** loud, melodious song of breeding male: sings from high tree-perch; very vocal in evening; great mimic; screechy *kreeee* during winter; also a harsh *charr* note. **Range:** various races make this a widespread species in the Indian region. **Habitat:** forests, ravines, gardens.

Eurasian Blackbird

DARK-THROATED THRUSH
Turdus ruficollis 25cm. **Male:** grey-brown above; black lores, malar area, sides of neck, throat, breast; white below; white streaks in winter. **Female:** browner above; dull ashy-brown breast, flanks, streaked brown; rest of underbody white, streaked blackish on sides of throat, upper-breast. The male **Red-Trruficollis** has rufous-chestnut throat, breast and much of tail. Gregarious; often along with other thrushes; hops on ground, flies into branches only when disturbed. **Food:** insects, earthworms, small fruit. **Voice:** harsh but thin *schwee* call-note; chuckling *wheech..which....* **Range:** common winter visitor to Himalaya. **Habitat:** forest-edges, cultivation, scrub, fallow-land.

Dark-Throated Thrush

Gould's Shortwing

GOULD'S SHORTWING

Brachypteryx stellata 13cm. Sexes alike. Chestnut above blackish lores; finely barred, grey and black below, with diagnostic triangular spots on lower breast, belly; rufous wash on flanks, vent; short tail characteristic. Mostly solitary; keeps generally to ground, amidst dense undergrowth in evergreen hill forest, but occasionally ascends bush-tops and low branches; may be approached close in some localities, but on the whole a shy and silent bird. **Food:** insects, grubs; possibly also grit. **Voice:** usually silent, save an occasional, sharp *tik..tik* call. **Range:** Himalaya east of Kumaon; breeds above 3000m, to about 4200m; descends in winter to 1500m; recorded at 500m in Sikkim. **Habitat:** dense growth in forest; also boulders in alpine country.

White-Bellied Shortwing

WHITE-BELLIED SHORTWING (Rufous-Bellied)

Brachypteryx major 15cm. Sexes alike. Deep slaty-blue; above; black lores; cobalt-blue over eye (forehead); slaty-blue throat, breast; white belly-centre; rest of underbody, rusty-rufous, more olive-brown on sides. Solitary or in pairs; an unobtrusive, elusive bird of shaded areas, where it is difficult to spot; moves in dense undergrowth, hopping about; emerges late in evening on jungle paths and clearings; may ascend to low branches, especially when disturbed, but returns soon to ground. **Food:** insects. **Voice:** loud call-notes and rich whistling song-notes, uttered round the year, though more frequently when breeding (April-June). **Range:** restricted to southern W Ghats, Palnis, Ashambu Hills. **Habitat:** sholas; evergreen forests.

Brown-Breasted Flycatcher

RUSTY-TAILED FLYCATCHER (Rufous-Tailed)

Muscicapa ruficauda 14cm. Sexes alike. Dull-brown plumage; pale eye-ring and rufous tail diagnostic; ashy throat, breast; whitish belly. The **Brown-breasted Flycatcher** *M muttui* (13cm) which winters in SW India, has white throat and lacks rufous tail. Mostly solitary, rarely pairs together; hunts in leafy canopy, snapping insects as it flits about; on perch often flicks wings and jerks body; sometimes seen with other small birds, but even then maintains a distance and is rather subdued. **Food:** insects. **Voice:** soft somewhat mournful note occasionally uttered; sings when breeding in the Himalaya. **Range:** breeds in W Himalaya, east to C Nepal; 2100-3600m; winters in SW India, south of Kanara; erratically in hilly-forests of C India. **Habitat:** forest edges.

RED-THROATED FLYCATCHER
(Red-Breasted)

Ficedula parva 13cm. **Male:** dull-brown above; white in tail conspicuous in night or when tail is flicked; rufous-orange chin, throat; whitish below. **Female:** white throat; pale-buff breast. The adult male **Kashmir Flycatcher** *F subrubra* has black border to red throat, breast. Solitary or in scattered pairs in shaded areas; may descend to ground, but prefers low and middle branches; flicks wings and lifts tail; launches short aerial sallies; hunts till late in evening; calls often. **Food:** tiny flying insects. **Voice:** sharp clicking sound; also a double *tick..tick* call; pleasant song when breeding (extralimital). **Range:** winter visitor, arriving by early September; all India south of the Himalayan foothills. **Habitat:** forests; gardens.

Otto Pfister

Red-Throated Flycatcher

LITTLE PIED FLYCATCHER

Ficedula westermanni 10cm. **Male:** black above; long, white supercilium and white in wings and tail; white below. **Female:** olive-brown above, with dull wing-bar; bright rufous-brown uppertail; whitish throat, duller grey-white below. The female **Rusty-tailed Flycatcher** *M ruficauda* (14cm) is quite similar, but larger. The female Slaty-blue Flycatcher lacks wing-bar, the female White-browed Blue Flycather is greyer above and lacks wing-bar. Solitary or pairs, often along with other small birds; keeps to middle and upper levels of trees; active, moves from tree to tree; makes short sallies but also hunts on bark crevices. **Food:** insects. **Voice:** rather silent in winter, except for occasional utterance of longish song. **Range:** breeds in the Himalaya 1200-2500m; from around WC Nepal eastwards and in NE; winters in foothills, N India, straying to C and E India. **Habitat:** breeds in Himalayan forests; winters in forested areas, orchards, tree-dotted cultivation.

Gertrud Denzau

Little Pied Flycatcher

Ultramarine Flycatcher

ULTRAMARINE FLYCATCHER
(White-Browed Blue)

Ficedula superciliaris 10cm. **Male:** deep blue above and sides of head, neck, breast, forming a broken breast-band; long, white eyebrow; white in tail; white below. **Female:** dull-slaty above; grey-white below. The eastern race *aestigma* lacks white over eye and in tail. The **Slaty-blue Flycatcher** *F tricolor* male has black on sides of head and lacks white stripe over eye. Solitary or in pairs; seen in mixed parties during winter, active, hunts in characteristic flycatcher-style; rarely ventures in open. **Food:** insects. **Voice:** faint *tick..tick.* in winter; a *chrrr* alarm note; three-syllabled song in the Himalaya. **Range:** breeds in Himalaya, 1800-3200m; winters in N and C India, south to Karnataka and N Andhra Pradesh. **Habitat:** forests, groves, gardens.

Black-and-Orange Flycatcher

BLACK-AND-ORANGE FLYCATCHER

Ficedula nigrorufa 13cm. **Male:** rich orangish-rufous plumage; blackish crown, nape, sides of face, wings. **Female:** like male, but deep olive-brown head; pale eye-ring. Usually solitary, but pairs often close by; not often seen in mixed-hunting parties; keeps to dense, shaded undergrowth, either hopping low or making short flycatcher-sallies from low perch; in its restricted range, quite tame and confiding once spotted. **Food:** insects. **Voice:** soft, gloomy *pee..* call note; a sharp *zit..zit* alarm call; high-pitched, metallic song when breeding. **Range:** very local; restricted to Nilgiris and associated hills in southern W Ghats, commonest above 1500m. **Habitat:** dense, evergreen forest undergrowth, bamboo.

Verditer Flycatcher

VERDITER FLYCATCHER

Eumyias thalassina 15cm. **Male:** verditer-blue plumage, darker in wings, tail; black lores. **Female:** duller, more grey overall. The **Nilgiri Flycatcher** *E albicaudata* of W Ghats is darker-blue with white in tail; the **Pale Blue Flycatcher** *Cyornis unicolor* (16cm) male is uniform blue, with white on belly; female is olive-brown. Solitary or in pairs in winter, sometimes with other birds; restless, flicking tail, swooping about, ever on the move, occasionally descending low; rather more noticeable because of its continuous movement and habit of perching in open exposed positions, like a bare twig on a tree top. **Food:** insects. **Voice:** silent in winter, save for a rare, faint *chwe..* call; rich, trilling notes and song during Himalayan summer. **Range:** breeds in the Himalaya; 1200-3200m; winters in Indian plains, hill-forests of C, E and S India. **Habitat:** open forests, orchards.

RUFOUS-BELLIED NILTAVA

Niltava sundara 15cm. Blue patch on sides of neck. **Male:** deep purple-blue back, throat; dark-blue mask; black forehead; brilliant blue crown, shoulders, rump; chestnut-rufous underbody. **Female:** olivish-brown overall; rufescent tail; white on lower throat diagnostic. The **Vivid Niltava** *N vivida* (18cm) male lacks the blue neck-patch, is slightly larger, and is found only sporadically in the NE. The **Blue-Throated Flycatcher** *Cyornis rubeculoides* (14cm) male has dark blue throat and white belly; it is duller, uniform blue above. Mostly solitary; keeps to undergrowth; highly unobtrusive, seldom seen; often nicks wings like redstart, and bobs body. **Food:** insects. **Voice:** squeaky churring note; occasionally a sharp *psi..psi*; also some harsh notes and squeaks. **Range:** the Himalaya, NE; 1500-3200m; winters in foothills, adjoining plains. **Habitat:** dense forest undergrowth, bushes.

Rufous-Bellied Niltava

WHITE-BELLIED BLUE FLYCATCHER

Cyornis pallipes 15cm. **Male:** indigo-blue above; black lores; bright-blue forehead, supercilium; indigo-blue throat, breast; white below breast. **Female:** deep olive-brown above; chestnut tail; rufous-orange till breast, whiter below. The female Blue-throated Flycatcher has dull-rufescent (not chestnut) tail. Solitary, rarely in pairs; sometimes in mixed parties; mostly silent, unobtrusive, hence overlooked; hunts in low growth, often flicking tail. **Food:** insects. **Voice:** soft true-noted call; longish, squeaky song when breeding; rather silent for most part of year. **Range:** W Ghats, south of Bhimashankar around the latitude of Pune. **Habitat:** dense forest undergrowth.

TICKELL'S BLUE FLYCATCHER

Cyornis tickelliae 14cm. **Male:** dark indigo-blue above; bright blue on forehead, supercilium; darker, almost appearing black on sides of face; rufous-orange throat, breast; whitish below. **Female:** duller overall. The male Blue-throated Flycatcher has dark blue throat. Usually in pairs in shaded areas, often in mixed-hunting parties; vicinity of wooded streams are favoured haunts; flits about intermittently or launches short sorties; has favourite perches; often breaks into fluty song. **Food:** insects. **Voice:** clear, metallic song of six notes, sometimes extending to nine or ten; often uttered in winter too. **Range:** all India, south roughly of a line from Kutch to Dehra Dun east along terai; absent in extreme N, NW India. **Habitat:** shaded forests, bamboo, gardens.

Tickell's Blue Flycatcher

Grey-Headed Canary Flycatcher

GREY-HEADED CANARY FLYCATCHER
Culicicapa ceylonensis 9cm. Sexes alike. Ashy-grey head, throat, breast; darker crown; yellow-green back and yellow rump; yellow in browner wings, tail; yellow below breast. Some Flycatcher Warblers (*Seicercus* spp) are superficially similar to the Grey-headed Flycatcher, but lack grey on throat and breast. Solitary or in pairs, occasionally several in vicinity, especially in mixed parties; a forest-bird, typical flycatcher, excitedly flirting about, launching aerial sallies and generally on the move; wherever this bird is, its cheerful unmistakable calls heard. **Food:** insects. **Voice:** vocal; high-pitched two or three-syllabled calls, *whi..chichee..whi..chiehee;* longer, trilling song; also chattering notes. **Range:** commonly breeds in the Himalaya, 1500-3000m; common in winter over much of the subcontinent. **Habitat:** forests, gardens, orchards.

White-Tailed Rubythroat

WHITE-TAILED RUBYTHROAT (Himalayan)
Luscinia pectoralis 15cm. **Male:** slaty above; white supercilium; white in tail; scarlet chin, throat; jet black sides of throat, continuing into broad breast-band; white below, greyer on sides. **Female:** grey-brown above; white chin, throat; greyish breast. The **Siberian Rubythroat** *L calliope* male lacks black on breast; has white malar stripe; female has brown breast; winters in NE and E India. Solitary; wary, difficult to observe; cocks tail; hops on ground, or makes short dashes; ascends small bush-tops. **Food:** insects, molluscs. **Voice:** short metallic call-note; short, harsh alarm-note; rich, shrill song, occasionally in winter also. **Range:** breeds in the Himalaya, 2700-4600m, winters in N, NE India. **Habitat:** dwarf vegetation, rocky hills, cultivation, damp ground with grass and bush.

Bluethroat

BLUETHROAT
Luscinia svecica 15cm. **Male:** pale brown above; whitish eyebrow; rufous in tail; bright blue chin, throat, with chestnut, occasionally white spot in centre; black and rufous bands below blue; whitish-buff below. **Female:** lacks blue; blackish malar stripe continues into broken gorget of brown spots across breast. Mostly solitary; great skulker, preferring damp areas with good grass and bush growth; cocks tail, straightens up a bit to look around; extremely wary; emerges in open but quickly vanishes into growth; difficult to observe. **Food:** insects. **Voice:** harsh *tack* and a *churr* in winter; rich song in summer, rarely before emigration, by mid-April. **Range:** breeds only in Ladakh, N Kashmir and Spiti; winter visitor over most of country. **Habitat:** damp ground, cultivation, vicinity of canals, jheels.

INDIAN BLUE ROBIN (Blue Chat)

Luscinia brunnea 15cm. **Male:** deep slaty-blue above; white supercilium; blackish lores, cheeks; rich-chestnut throat, breast, flanks; white belly-centre, under-tail. **Female:** brown above; white throat, belly; buffy-rufous breast, flanks. The **White-Browed Bush Robin** *Tarsiger indicus* male has very long, conspicuous supercilium, and completely rufous-orange underbody; it is resident in the Himalaya. Solitary, rarely in pairs; great skulker, very difficult to observe; moves amidst dense growth and hops on ground; jerks and flicks tail and wings often. **Food:** insects. **Voice:** high-pitched *churr* and harsh *tack..* in winter; trilling song of breeding male, sometimes singing from exposed perch. **Range:** breeds in the Himalaya, 1500-3300m. Winters in southern W Ghats, Ashambu Hills and Sri Lanka. **Habitat:** dense rhododendron, ringal bamboo undergrowth in summer. Evergreen forest undergrowth, coffee estates in winter.

Indian Blue Robin

ORIENTAL MAGPIE ROBIN

Copsychus saularis 20cm. **Male:** glossy blue-black and white; white wing-patch and white in outer-tail distinctive; glossy blue-black throat, breast; white below. **Female:** rich slaty grey, where male is black. A familiar bird of India. Solitary or in pairs, sometimes with other birds in mixed parties; hops on ground, preferring shaded areas; common about habitation; when perched, often cocks tail; flicks tail often, especially when making short sallies; active at dusk; remarkable songster, very rich voice. **Food:** insects, berries, flower-nectar. **Voice:** one of India's finest songsters; rich, clear song of varying notes and tones; male sings from exposed perches, most frequently between March and June, intermittently round the year; also has harsh *churr* and *chhekh* notes; a plaintive *sweee...* is a common call. **Range:** all India, up to about 1500m in outer Himalaya; absent in extreme W Rajasthan. **Habitat:** forests, parks, towns.

Oriental Magpie Robin

WHITE-RUMPED SHAMA

Copsychus malabaricus 25cm including tail. **Male:** glossy-black head, back; white rump and sides of graduated tail distinctive; black throat, breast; orange-rufous below. **Female:** grey where male is black; slightly shorter tail and duller rufous below breast. Usually pairs; overall behaviour like Magpie-Robin's; arboreal bird of forest, hill-station gardens; keeps to shaded areas, foliage, only occasionally emerging in open; launches short sallies and hunts till late in evening. **Food:**

White-Rumped Shama

Trevor Price

Krupakar Senani

Krupakar Senani

insects; rarely flower-nectar. **Voice:** rich songster; melodious, three or four whistling notes very characteristic; variety of call notes, including a mix of some harsh notes. **Range:** Himalayan foothills, terai, east of Kumaon; NE India; hill-forests of Bihar, Orissa. SE Madhya Pradesh, E Maharashtra, south along E Ghats to about Cauvery river; entire W Ghats, from Kerala north to S Gujarat. **Habitat:** forests, bamboo, hill-station gardens.

Toby Sinclair

Indian Robin

INDIAN ROBIN

Saxicoloides fulicata 16cm. Several races in India. Males differ in having dark-brown, blackish-brown or glossy blue-back upperbody. This description concerns the race *cambaiensis* of N, NW and C India. **Male:** dark-brown above; white wing-patch glossy blue-black below; chestnut vent, undertail. **Female:** lacks white in wings; duller grey-brown below. Solitary or in pairs in open country, and often in and around habitation; rather suspicious and maintains safe distance between man and itself; hunts on ground, hopping or running in short spurts; when on ground, holds head high and often cocks tail, right up to back, flashing the chestnut vent and undertail. **Food:** insects. **Voice:** long-drawn *sweeeech* or *weeeech* call; a warbling song when breeding; also a guttural *charrr..* note. **Range:** all India, south of the Himalayan foothills; absent in extreme NE. **Habitat:** open country, edges of forest, vicinity of habitations, scrub.

R.K. Gaur

Black Redstart

BLACK REDSTART

Phoenicurus ochruros 15cm. **Male:** black above (marked with grey in winter); grey crown, lower back; rufous rump, sides of tail; black throat, breast rufous below. **Female:** dull-brown above; tail as in male; dull tawny-brown below. The eastern race *rufiventris* has black crown, and is the common wintering bird of India. Mostly solitary in winter, when common all over India; easy bird to observe, in winter and in its open high-altitude summer country; perches on overhead wires, poles, rocks, stumps; characteristic shivering of tail and jerky body movements; makes short dashes to ground, soon returning to perch with catch; rather confiding in summer, breeding in houses, under roofs and in wall crevices. **Food:** insects, mostly taken on ground. **Voice:** squeaking *tictititic..* call, often beginning with faint *tsip..*note; trilling song of breeding male. **Range:** breeds in the Himalaya, 2400-5200m; winters over much of subcontinent. **Habitat:** open country, cultivation.

WHITE-CAPPED WATER REDSTART

Chaimarrornis leucocephalus 19cm. Sexes alike. Black back, sides of head, wings, breast; white crown diagnostic; chestnut rump, tail; black terminal tail-band; chestnut below breast. The male **White-Winged Redstart** *Phoenicurus erythrogaster* (16cm) has completely chestnut tail (no black tip) and prominent white wing-patch. Solitary or pairs on Himalayan torrents; rests on rocks amidst gushing waters, flying very low over the waters to catch insects; jerks and wags tail and dips body; restless bird; interesting display of courting male. **Food:** insects. **Voice:** loud, plaintive *tseeee* call; also a *psit..psit..* call; whistling song of breeding male. **Range:** Himalaya: 2000-5000m; descends into foothills in winter. **Habitat:** rocky streams.

White-Capped Water Redstart

PLUMBEOUS WATER REDSTART

Rhyacornis fuliginosus 12cm. **Male:** slaty-blue plumage; chestnut tail diagnostic; rufous on lower belly. **Female:** darkish blue-grey-brown above; two spotted wing-bars; white in tail; whitish below, profusely mottled slaty. Young birds are brown, also with white in tail. Pairs on mountain rivers; active birds, making short dashes from boulders; move from boulder to boulder, flying low over roaring waters; tail frequently fanned open and wagged; hunts late in evening; maintains feeding territories in winter too. **Food:** insects, worms. **Voice:** sharp *kreee...* call; also a snapping *tzit..tzit*; rich, jingling song of breeding male, infrequently uttered in winter. **Range:** the Himalaya, 800-4000m, but mostly 1000-2800m; also breeds south of Brahmaputra river; in winter may descend into the foothills, terai. **Habitat:** mountain streams, rivers.

Plumbeous Water Redstart

GRANDALA

Grandala coelicolor 22cm. **Male:** glossy purplish-blue plumage; jet black lores, wings and tail. **Female:** brown above, streaked dull-white on head, neck; white in wings; blue wash on rump, upper tail-coverts; brown below, streaked as on head and neck. Gregarious, except when breeding; sometimes all male or female flocks; bird of high mountain country; strong, graceful fliers, circling and floating high in the skies, often many hundreds together; suddenly the birds rain down on to ground; hops on ground, on rocks and meadows. **Food:** insects, fruits, berries. **Voice:** *jeeu..jeeu..* call-note; more quickly and commonly uttered when breeding. **Range:** high Himalaya, from Kashmir to Arunachal; breeds 3900-5400m; descends in winter to about 2800m, rarely lower. **Habitat:** cliffs, high-altitude meadows.

Grandala

Tom Loseby

Little Forktail

Otto Pfister

Spotted Forktail

Common Stonechat

LITTLE FORKTAIL

Enicurus scouleri 12cm. Sexes alike. Black and white plumage. Black above, with white forehead; white band in wings extends across lower back; small, black rump patch; slightly forked, short tail with white in outer feathers; black throat, white below. Solitary or in pairs; a bird of mountain streams, waterfalls and small shaded forest puddles; energetically moves on moss-covered and wet slippery rocks; constantly wags and flicks tail; occasionally launches short sallies, but also plunges underwater, dipper-style. **Food:** aquatic insects. **Voice:** rather silent save for a rarely uttered sharp *tzittzit* call. **Range:** the Himalaya, west to east, breeding between 1200-3700m; descends to about 300m in winter. **Habitat:** rocky mountain streams, waterfalls.

SPOTTED FORKTAIL

Enicurus maculatus 25cm with long tail. Sexes alike. White forehead, forecrown; black crown, nape; black back spotted white; broad, white wing-bar, rump; deeply forked, graduated black and white tail; black till breast, white below. The white-spotted back easily identifies this species from other similar sized forktails in the Himalaya. Solitary or in scattered pairs; active bird, moving on messy boulders at water's edge or in mid-stream; long, forked tail gracefully swayed, almost always kept horizontal; flies low over streams, calling; sometimes rests in shade of forest; commonly seen bird of the Himalaya. **Food:** aquatic insects, molluscs. **Voice:** shrill, screechy *kree* call, mostly in flight; also some shrill, squeaky notes on perch. **Range:** the Himalaya; breeds mostly 1200-3600m; descends to about 600m in winter. **Habitat:** boulder-strewn torrents, forest streams, roadside canals.

COMMON STONECHAT (Collared Bushchat)

Saxicola torquata 13cm. **Br Male:** black above; white rump, wing-patch, sides of neck/breast (collar); black throat; orange-rufous breast. In winter, black feathers broadly edged buff-rufous-brown. **Female:** rufous-brown above, streaked darker; unmarked yellowish-brown below; white wing-patch and rufous rump. Solitary or in pairs in open country; perches on small bush-tops, fence-posts, boulders; restless, makes short trips to ground to capture insects. **Food:** insects. **Voice:** double-noted *wheel..chat* call; soft, billing song of breeding male in Himalaya. **Range:** breeds in Himalaya, 1500-3000m; winters all India except Kerala and much of Tamil Nadu. **Habitat:** dry, open areas, cultivation, tidal creeks.

PIED BUSHCHAT

Saxicola caprata 13cm. **Male:** black plumage; white in wing, rump, belly. **Female:** brown above, paler on lores; darker tail; dull yellow-brown below, with a rusty wash on breast and belly. Solitary or in pairs; perches on a bush, overhead wire, pole or some earth mound; makes short sallies on to ground, either devouring prey on ground or carrying to perch; active, sometimes guards feeding territories in winter; flicks and spreads wings; fascinating display-flight of courting male (April-May). **Food:** insects. **Voice:** harsh, double-noted call serve as contact and alarm call; short, trilling song of breeding male. **Range:** all India, from outer Himalaya to about 1500m. **Habitat:** open country. scrub, cultivation, ravines.

Pied Bushchat

GREY BUSHCHAT (Dark-Grey)

Saxicola ferrea 15cm. **Male:** dark grey above, streaked black; black mask; white supercilium, wing-patch and outer-tail; white throat, belly; dull grey breast. **Female:** rufous-brown, streaked; rusty rump, outer-tail, white throat; yellow-brown below. Solitary or pairs; like other chats, keeps to open country and edge of forest; perches on bush-tops, poles, flirts tail often; regularly seen in an area; flies to ground on spotting insect. **Food:** insects. **Voice:** double-noted call; also a grating *praee..* call; trilling song of male. **Range:** Himalaya, 1400-3500m; descends into foothills and adjoining plains, including Gangetic plains, in winter. **Habitat:** open scrub forest-edges, cultivation.

Grey Bushchat

VARIABLE WHEATEAR (Pied Chat)

Oenanthe picata 17cm. A polymorphic species (occurring in various colour phases). **Male:** pied plumage; occurs in three phases, black-bellied, white-bellied and white-crowned; jet black plumage in all phases, except variation in colours of belly, crown and rump. **Female:** sooty-black, greyish-brown or earthy-brown; belly usually buff-coloured. Mostly solitary, a bird of dry, barren country; frequently bobs body on perch; flies to ground to pick insect; an aggressive bird, chasing others away from favoured feeding grounds. **Food:** insects. **Voice:** pleasant billing notes in winter; good mimic, song of breeding male often an assortment of imitations. **Range:** mostly winter visitor to NW India, west of a line from around Delhi, through Madhya Pradesh to N Maharashtra. **Habitat:** open country, fallow lands, vicinity of villages.

Variable Wheater

Desert Wheatear

DESERT WHEATEAR

Oenanthe deserti 15cm. **Br Male:** sandy above, with whitish rump and black tail; black wings; white in coverts; black throat, head-sides; creamy-white below. **Female:** brown wings, tail, lacks black throat. **Winter Male:** throat feathers fringed white. The **Isabelline Wheatear** *O isabellina* (16cm) is larger, sandy-grey, without black throat. The male **Wheatear** *O oenanthe* is grey above, with white rump, tail-sides and black tail-centre and tip like inverted 'T'; black ear-coverts and wings. Keeps to ground or perches on low bush or small rock; has favoured haunts; colouration makes it difficult to spot. **Food:** insects. **Voice:** in winter an occasional *ch..chett* alarm note; reportedly utters its short, plaintive song in winter also. **Range:** winter visitor over N, C and W India, almost absent south of S Maharastra and Andhra Pradesh; the Tibetan race *oreophila* breeds in Kashmir, Ladakh, Lahaul and Spiti, about 3000-5000m. **Habitat:** open rocky, barren country; sandy areas; fallow lands.

Brown Rock-Chat

BROWN ROCK-CHAT

Cercomela fusca 17cm. Brown above, more rufous below; dark-brown wings, almost blackish tail. Overall appearance like female Indian Robin. Usually pairs, around ruins, dusty villages, rocky hill-sides; often approaches close; tame and confiding; captures insects on ground; rather aggressive when breeding. **Food:** insects; occasionally kitchen-refuse. **Voice:** harsh *chaeck..* note; also a whistling *chee* call; melodious song of breeding male; a good mimic. **Range:** confined to parts of N and C India, from Punjab and Dehra Dun, south to about Narmada river; east to Bihar-Bengal. **Habitat:** dry, open country, rocky hills, ravines, ruins, habitation.

Chestnut-Tailed Starling

CHESTNUT-TAILED STARLING
(Grey-Headed Myna)

Sturnus malabaricus 21cm. Sexes alike. Silvery-grey above, with faint brownish wash; dull rufous till breast, brighter below; black and grey in wings. Sociable; noisy parties in upper branches of trees, frequently along with other birds; incessantly squabbles and moves about. **Food:** flower nectar, fruits, insects. **Voice:** noisy; metallic, whistling call; warbling song when breeding. **Range:** India, roughly east and south from Mt Abu to around Dehra Dun; up to about 1800m in Himalayan foothills. The **White-Headed** race *S erythropygius* breeds SW India, in Karnataka and Kerala, spreading north to Bombay in winter. **Habitat:** light forest, open country, gardens.

BRAHMINY STARLING (Black-Headed Myna)

Sturnus pagodarum 20cm. Sexes alike. A grey, black and rufous myna; black crown, head, crest; grey back; rich-buff sides of head, neck and underbody; black wings and brown tail with white sides and tip distinctive in flight. Female has a slightly smaller crest, otherwise like male. Small parties, occasionally collecting into flocks of 20 birds; associates with other birds on flowering trees or on openlands; walks typical myna-style, head held straight up, confident in looks; communal roosting-sites, with other birds. **Food:** fruits, flower nectar, insects. **Voice:** quite noisy; pleasant mix of chirping notes and whistles, sounding as conversational chatter; good mimic; pleasant warbling song of breeding males. **Range:** all India, to about 2000m in W and C Himalaya. **Habitat:** light forests, gardens, cultivation, vicinity of habitation.

Brahminy Starling

ROSY STARLING (Pastor)

Sturnus roseus 24cm. Sexes alike. Rose-pink and black plumage; glossy black head, crest, neck, throat, upper-breast, wings and tail; rest of plumage rose-pink, brighter with the approach of spring emigration. Gregarious; flocks often contain young birds, crestless, dull brown and sooty; seen also around grazing cattle and damp openlands; overall an aggressive and extremely noisy bird; huge roosting colonies, resulting in deafening clamour before settling. **Food:** grain, insects, flower-nectar. **Voice:** very noisy; mix of guttural screams, chattering sounds and melodious whistles. **Range:** winter visitor to India, particularly common in north, west and central India; arrives as early as end-July; most birds depart around mid-April to early May; absent or uncommon east of Bihar. **Habitat:** open areas, cultivation, orchards, flowering trees amidst habitation.

Rosy Starling

COMMON STARLING

Sturnus vulgaris 20cm. Glossy black plumage, with iridescent purple and green; plumage spotted with buff and white; hackled feathers on head, neck and breast; yellowish beak and red-brown legs. Summer (breeding) plumage, mostly blackish. Several races winter in N India, with head purple or bronze-green, but field-identification of races not very easy in winter. Gregarious, restless birds; feeds on ground, moves hurriedly, digging with beak in soil; entire flock may often take-off from ground, flies around erratically or circles, but soon settles on trees or returns to ground. **Food:** insects, berries, grain, earthworms, small lizards. **Voice:** mix of squeaking, clicking

Common Starling

notes; other chuckling calls. **Range:** the race *indicus* breeds in Kashmir to about 2000m; this and three other races winter over NW and N India, occasionally straying south to Gujarat; quite common in parts of N India in winter. **Habitat:** meadows, orchards, vicinity of habitation, open, fallow land.

Asian Pied Starling

ASIAN PIED STARLING (Myna)

Sturnus contra 23cm. Sexes alike. Black and white (pied) plumage distinctive; orangish-red beak and orbital skin in front of eyes confirm identity. Sociable; small parties either move on their own or associate with other birds, notably other mynas and drongos; rather common and familiar over its range but keeps a distance from man; may make its ungainly nest in garden trees, but never inside houses, nor does it enter houses; more a bird of open, cultivated areas, preferably where there is water; attends to grazing cattle; occasionally raids standing crops. **Food:** insects, flower-nectar, grain. **Voice:** noisy; a mix of pleasant whistling and screaming notes. **Range:** bird of NC, C and E India, south and east of a line roughly from E Punjab, through E Rajasthan, W Madhya Pradesh to the Krishna delta; escaped cage birds have established themselves in several areas out of original range as in and around Bombay. **Habitat:** open cultivation, orchards, vicinity of habitation.

COMMON MYNA

Acridotheres tristis 23cm. Sexes alike. Rich vinous-brown plumage; black head, neck, upper-breast; yellow beak, legs and naked wattle around eyes distinctive; large white spot in dark-brown flight feathers, best seen in flight: blackish tail, with broad, white tips to all but central feathers; whitish abdomen. Solitary, or in scattered pairs or small, loose bands; amongst our commonest, most familiar birds; hardly ever strays far from man and habitation; rather haughty and confident in looks; aggressive, curious and noisy; struts about on ground, picks out worms; attends to grazing cattle, refuse dumps; enters verandahs, kitchens, sometimes even helps itself on dining table. The slightly smaller **Bank Myna** *A ginginianus* (21cm) is pale bluish-grey and brick red naked skin behind and below eye. **Food:** omnivorous; fruits, nectar, insects, kitchen scraps, refuse. **Voice:** noisy; a great mix of chattering notes, one of India's most familiar bird sounds. **Range:** all India, up to about 3500m in the Himalaya. **Habitat:** human habitation, cultivation, light forests.

Common Myna

R.K. Gaur

Toby Sinclair

HILL MYNA (Grackle)

Gracula religiosa 28cm. Sexes alike. Black plumage, with a purple-green gloss; white in flight feathers; orange-red beak; orange-yellow legs, facial skin and fleshy wattles on nape and sides of face. In the southern race *indica*, nape-wattles extend up along sides of crown, the eye and nape wattles distinctly separated. Small flocks in forest; extremely noisy; mostly arboreal, only occasionally descends into bush or onto ground; hops amongst branches, and on ground; large numbers gather on fruiting trees, along with barbets, hornbills, green pigeons. Such sights one of the bird-watching spectacles of the Himalayan foothills. **Food:** fruits, insects, flower-nectar, lizards. **Voice:** amazing vocalist; great assortment of whistling, warbling, shrieking notes; excellent mimic; much sought after cage-bird. **Range:** the northern race is found along lower Himalaya; *indica* is a bird of the W Ghats and Sri Lanka: the race *peninsularis* is restricted to eastern ghats. **Habitat:** forests, clearings.

Hill Myna

CHESTNUT-BELLIED NUTHATCH

Sitta castanea 12cm. **Male:** blue-grey above; black stripe from lores to nape; whitish cheeks, upper throat; all but central tail-feathers black, with white markings; chestnut below. **Female:** duller chestnut below. The male **White-Tailed Nuthatch** *S himalayensis* has much paler underbody and clear white patch at base of tail. Pairs or several, often with other small birds; restless climber, clings to bark and usually works up the tree-stem, hammering with beak; also moves upside-down and sideways; may visit the ground. **Food:** insects, grubs, seeds. **Voice:** loud *tzsib..* call; faint twitter; loud whistle during breeding season. **Range:** lower Himalaya east of Kumaon; to about 1800m; peninsula east of a line from C Punjab to Nasik; also the E Ghats; large gaps in distribution. **Habitat:** open forests, groves, roadside trees, habitation.

Chestnut-Bellied Nuthatch

VELVET-FRONTED NUTHATCH

Sitta frontalis 10cm. **Male:** violet-blue above; jet-black forehead, stripe through eyes; white chin, throat, merging into vinous-grey below; coral-red beak. **Female:** lacks black stripe through eyes. Pairs or several in mixed-hunting parties; creeps about on stems and branches; fond of moss-covered trees; also clings upside-down; active and agile, quickly moves from tree to tree; calls often, till long after sunset; also checks fallen logs and felled branches. **Food:** insects. **Voice:** fairly loud, rapidly-repeated, sharp, trilling *chweet..chwit..chwit* whistles. **Range:** lower Himalaya; widespread over the hilly, forested areas of C, S and E India: absent in the flat and arid regions. **Habitat:** forests; also tea and coffee plantations.

Velvet-Fronted Nuthatch

Wallcreeper

WALLCREEPER

Tichodroma muraria 17cm. Sexes alike. Ashy-grey plumage; brown top of head; whitish chin, throat; large, crimson wing-patch and white spots on flight-feathers diagnostic; black tail, tipped paler, with some white in outer feathers. In summer (breeding) plumage, black chin and throat. Usually solitary, sometimes pairs; jerkily moves up on vertical cliff faces, mudbanks, boulders, flicking wings; suddenly erupts from vertical climb, either to grab some winged insect or move to another face; crimson on wings very prominent in butterfly-like flight. **Food:** insects, spiders. **Voice:** mostly silent, except for an occasional faint cheeping note; short (four-noted) breeding song. **Range:** high Himalaya; breed above 2800m, winters much lower, often in foothills and adjacent plains. **Habitat:** cliffs, mud-walls.

Eurasian Treecreeper

EURASIAN TREECREEPER

Certhia familiaris 12cm. Sexes alike. Fulvous-brown above, spotted white on crown and back; white supercilium; long, pointed unbarred tail distinctive; completely white below, grey-brown on flanks. The other tree-creepers with unbarred tail are the **Brown-throated Treecreeper** *C discolor* and **Rusty-flanked Treecreeper** *C nipalensis* both are much darker above; *discolor* has dark throat; *nipalensis* has a buff breast and tawny flanks. Seen amidst other small birds; creeps up along tree-stems; probes crevices; overall very active. **Food:** insects, spiders. **Voice:** faint *tzi...* or *tsee...* note. **Range:** the Himalaya; 1500m to timber-line. **Habitat:** pine, deodar, fir forests.

BAR-TAILED TREECREEPER (Himalayan)

Certhia himalayana 12cm. Sexes alike. Streaked blackish-brown, fulvous and grey above; pale supercilium; broad fulvous wing-band; white chin, throat; dull ash-brown below; best recognised by dark-brown barring on pointed tail. Solitary or several in mixed parties of small birds; spends almost entire life on tree-trunks; starts from near base; intermittently checks crevices and under moss, picks out insects with curved beak; usually climbs to mid-height, then moves on to another tree; sometimes creeps on moss-clothed rocks and walls. **Food:** insects, spiders. **Voice:** long-drawn squeak, somewhat ventriloquial; loud but short, monotonous song; one of the earliest bird songs, heard much before other birds have begun to sing. **Range:** the Himalaya; east to W Nepal; from about 1600m to timber-line; descends in winter. **Habitat:** Himalayan temperate forests.

Bar-Tailed Treecreeper

SPOTTED CREEPER (Grey)

Salpornis spilonotus 13cm. Sexes alike. Dark brown above, spotted white; whitish supercilium; barred tail; white throat; yellowish-brown below, mottled with dark brown. Mostly solitary, though another bird is usually in vicinity; active, climbing up tree-stems and branches, especially trees that have deep-fissured bark like *khair, babool;* works from near ground level to uppermost branches, probing crevices. **Food:** insects, spiders. **Voice:** whistling song, described as being of volume and timbre of sunbird's. **Range:** large part of central India, from E, SE Rajasthan, much of Gangetic plain, south to C Maharashtra. **Habitat:** open forests, groves.

Spotted Creeper

WINTER WREN

Troglodytes troglodytes 9cm. Sexes alike. A tiny, skulking Himalayan bird. Short, erect, cocked tail distinctive; brown above, closely-barred; paler below, whiter on belly, also barred closely. Usually solitary; very active, but also extremely secretive; jerkily hops on boulders or moves mouselike amidst dense bush, holding tail cocked; takes to dense cover if approached close. **Food:** small insects. **Voice:** quite noisy; fairly loud *zirrr.. tzt..tzzt..* alarm-notes; shrill, rambling song, sometimes uttered in winter too, even in snow. **Range:** the Himalaya; breeds about 2700m, descends to about 1200m in winter, especially in W Himalaya. **Habitat:** thickets, dense cover, messy growth, rocky ground, vicinity of mountain habitation.

Winter Wren

FIRE-CAPPED TIT

Cephalopyrus flammiceps 9cm. **Male:** olive-yellow above; scarlet-orange cap, chin, throat; two yellow wing-bars; yellow throat, breast; whiter-buff below. In winter, no scarlet on crown; duller yellow underbody. **Female:** yellowish rump, wing-bars, edges of outer tail-feathers. Small parties, either on their own or in mixed-hunting parties; extremely active, flits about in canopy foliage, clings sideways and upside-down; overall behaviour very leaf-warbler like. **Food:** small insects, buds. **Voice:** faint, twittering song. **Range:** breeds in W Himalaya, Kashmir to Garhwal; 1800-3700m; winters in C India, mostly Madhya Pradesh and parts of NE Maharashtra, SE Uttar Pradesh. **Habitat:** forested hillsides, orchards.

Fire-Capped Tit

Otto Pfister

Spot-Winged Tit

Kamal Sahai

Great Tit

Krupakar Senani

Black-Lored Tit

SPOT-WINGED TIT (Crested Black)

Parus melanolophus 11cm. Sexes alike. Dark-grey back; black crest, sides of neck; white cheeks, nape-patch; rusty-white double, spotted wing-bars; black throat, upper-breast; slaty belly and rufous flanks, undertail. The **Coal Tit** *P ater* (10cm) also with double spotted wing-bars is yellow-brown below breast; it is found only east of C Nepal. The **Rufous-naped Tit** *P rufonuchalis* (13cm) lacks wing-bars and has more extensive black below. Part of mixed-hunting bands of small birds, restless, forever on the move; hunts high in canopy foliage. **Food:** insects, berries. **Voice:** a double-noted *te..tui* call; faint *tzee..tzee*; also a whistling song. **Range:** W Himalaya, east to W Nepal; 2000-3600m; descends into foothills in winter. **Habitat:** coniferous forest; mixed forest in winter.

GREAT TIT (Grey Tit)

Parus major 13cm. Sexes alike. Grey back; black crown continued along sides of neck to broad black band from chin along centre of underbody; white cheeks, nape-patch, wing-bar and outer feathers of black tail; ashy-white sides. The **White-naped Tit** *P nuchalis* of W India lacks black on neck-sides; has extensive white in wings and sides of body. The **Green-backed Tit** *P monticolus* of the Himalaya has an olive back, white sides of underbody and two wing-bars. Pairs or small bands, often with other small birds; restless, clings upside down, and indulges in all sorts of acrobatic displays as it hunts amongst leaves and branches; holds food fast between feet and pecks at it noisily; tame and confiding. **Food:** insects, small fruit. **Voice:** loud, clear whistling *whee..chi.chee..;* other whistling and harsh notes. **Range:** widespread from Himalaya, foothills to about 3500m; peninsular India from Gujarat, C Rajasthan and Orissa south; absent in broad belt from NW India across Gangetic plains. **Habitat:** open forests, gardens, habitation.

BLACK-LORED TIT (Yellow-Cheeked)

Parus xanthogenys 14cm. Sexes alike. Olive-green back; black crest (faintly tipped with yellow), stripe behind eye, broad central band from chin to vent; bright yellow nape-patch, supercilium, sides of underbody. The **Yellow-cheeked Tit** *P spilonotus* has black streaks on back, yellow lores and forehead. Pairs or small flocks, often with other small birds; arboreal, active; feeds in foliage; sometimes enters gardens. **Food:** insects, berries. **Voice:** cheerful, musical notes; loud tailor-bird like *towit..towit* calls near nest; other two- to four-noted whistling calls; whistling song; also harsh, *charr* and some chattering notes. **Range:** the Himalaya to E Nepal; 1200-2500m, widespread in parts of C, E and W India. **Habitat:** forests, gardens.

SULTAN TIT

Melanochlora sultanea 20cm. **Male:** black above; yellow crown, crest; black throat, upper-breast; yellow below. **Female:** deep olivish wash to black upperbody, throat; crest as in male; some yellow also on throat. Small bands, often along with other birds in mixed hunting flocks; active and inquisitive, clings sideways and upside-down, checks foliage and bark-crevices; feeds in canopy but also descends to tall bush. **Food:** insects, small fruit, seeds. **Voice:** noisy; loud, whistling *cheerie..cheerie*; other shrill whistling notes, often mixed with a harsh *churr* or *chrrchuk*; varied chattering notes. **Range:** the Himalayan foothills, from C Nepal east; NE; foothills to about 1200m sometimes ascending to 2000m. **Habitat:** mixed forests, edges of forest.

Sultan Tit

BLACK-THROATED TIT (Red-Headed)

Aegithalos concinnus 10cm. Sexes alike. Grey back; chestnut-red crown; nape; black and white sides of face, throat; brown wings, tail, the latter with white tip and outer feathers; buffy-yellowish-red below throat. Highly sociable; fidgety, over-active bird, ever-curious, checking out leaves, branches, crevices; several birds together, almost always a part of mixed-hunting bands, though sometimes keep to themselves; rather tame and confiding in many areas. **Food:** insects, small fruits. **Voice:** incessant faint *trr..trrv* and *check..check..* call-notes. **Range:** Himalaya, 500-3500m, occasionally to 4000m; optimum breeding zone about 1300-2600m. **Habitat:** open forests, gardens, secondary growth.

Black-Throated Tit

PLAIN MARTIN (Plain Sand)

Riparia paludicola 12cm. Sexes alike. Long wings and slight tail-fork. Grey-brown above, slightly darker on crown; dark-brown wings, tail; dull-grey below, whiter towards abdomen. The **Sand Martin** *R riparia* (13cm) is white below, with a broad, grey-brown band across breast. A gregarious species, always in flocks, flying around sand-banks along water courses; individual birds occasionally stray far and high; hawks small insects in flight; flocks perch on telegraph wires. **Food:** insects captured in night. **Voice:** a *brret...* call, rather harsh in tone, usually on the wing around nest-colony; twittering song. **Range:** NW and N India, from outer Himalaya, south at least to line from vicinity of Bombay-Nasik to C Orissa; moves considerably locally. **Habitat:** vicinity of water, sand-bank, sandy cliffsides.

Plain Martin

Otto Pfister

Dusky Crag Martin

R.K. Gaur

Wire-Tailed Swallow

Gertrud Denzau

Red-Rumped Swallow

DUSKY CRAG MARTIN

Hirundo concolor 13cm. Sexes alike. Dark sooty-brown above; square-cut, short tail, with white spot on all but outermost and central tail-feathers; paler underbody; faintly rufous chin, throat, with indistinct black streaking. The **Eurasian Crag Martin** *H rupestris* is slightly larger and a paler sandy-brown, much paler below. Breeds in the NW and W Himalaya and winters in N and C India. Small parties; flies around ruins, crags, old buildings, hawking insects in flight; acrobatic, swallow-like flight and appearance; rests during hot hours on rocky ledges or some corner. **Food:** insects, captured on wing. **Voice:** faint chip…, uncommonly uttered. **Range:** nearly through the country, south of Himalayan foothills, to about 1500m. **Habitat:** vicinity of old forts, ruins, old stony buildings in towns.

WIRE-TAILED SWALLOW

Hirundo smithii 14cm; tail-wires nearly 15cm long, shorter in female. Sexes alike. Glistening steel-blue above; chestnut cap; unmarked, pure white underbody distinctive; two long wire-like projections (tail-wires) from outer tail-feathers diagnostic. Solitary or small parties, almost always seen around water, either perched on overhead wires or hawking insects in graceful, acrobatic flight, swooping and banking; often flies very low, drinking from the surface; roosts in reed-beds and other vegetation, often with warblers and wagtails. **Food:** insects captured on wing. **Voice:** soft twittering note; pleasant song of breeding male. **Range:** common breeding (summer) visitor to N India, to about 1800m in the Himalaya; breeds in other parts of country too; widespread over the country, excepting arid zones. **Habitat:** open areas, cultivation, habitation, canals, lakes, rivers.

RED-RUMPED SWALLOW

Hirundo daurica 19cm including tail. Sexes alike. Glossy steel-blue above; chestnut supercilium, sides of head, neck-collar and rump; dull rufous-white below, streaked brown; deeply forked-tail diagnostic. Small parties spend much of the day on the wing; the migrant, winter-visiting race *nipalensis*, is highly gregarious; hawk insects along with other birds; freely perches on overhead wires, thin branches of bushes and trees; hunt insects amongst the most crowded areas of towns, flying with amazing agility, wheeling and banking and stooping with remarkable mastery. **Food:** insects caught on the wing. **Voice:** mournful chirping note; pleasant twittering song of breeding male. **Range:** six races over the subcontinent, including Sri Lanka; resident and migratory. **Habitat:** cultivation, vicinity of human habitations, town centres, rocky hilly areas.

GOLDCREST

Regulus regulus 8cm. **Male:** greyish-olive above; prominent golden-yellow median stripe on crown, bordered by black; two pale yellow-white wingbars; white ring around eyes; yellow in wings, tail; whitish below. **Female:** like male, but yellow stripe on crown. Pairs or small flocks, often along with other small birds in conifer canopy; also hunts in low branches and tall growth; restless bird, moving energetically, occasionally hovers when searching insects. **Food:** insects. **Voice:** highpitched, squeaking *tsi..tsi..* call diagnostic. **Range:** the Himalaya, breeds between 2400-4000m, considerable altitudinal movement, descending to 1500m in winter, sometimes to about 1200m. **Habitat:** coniferous forests; orchards in winter.

Goldcrest

BLACK-CRESTED BULBUL
(Black-Headed Yellow)

Pycnonotus melanicterus 18cm. Sexes alike. Glossy black head, crest and throat; olive-yellow nape, back, becoming brown on tail, yellow below throat. The ssp *gularis* has a ruby-red throat. The **Black-Headed Bulbul** *P atriceps* of NE India and Andamans lacks crest, and has black and yellow bands in tail. Pairs or small bands, sometimes with other birds; arboreal. **Food:** insects, fruit. **Voice:** cheerful whistles; also a harsh *churrr* call four to eight-note song. **Range:** disjunct: (1) Himalaya, from Himachal eastwards; NE; foothills to about 2000m. (2) W Ghats and associated hills south of Goa (**Ruby-Throated** ssp *gularis*); (3) Sri Lanka. **Habitat:** forests, bamboo, clearings, orchards.

Black-Crested Bulbul

RED-WHISKERED BULBUL

Pycnonotus jocosus 20cm. Sexes alike. Brown above, slightly darker on wings, tail; black perky crest distinctive; crimson 'whiskers' behind eyes; white underbody with broken breast-collar; crimson-scarlet vent. Sociable; pairs or small flocks, occasionally gatherings of up to 100 birds; lively and energetic; feeds in canopy, low bush and on ground; enlivens their surroundings with cheerful whistling notes; tame and confiding in some areas; popular cage-bird. **Food:** insects, fruits, flower-nectar. **Voice:** cheerful whistling notes; also harsh, grating alarm notes. **Range:** from Garhwal east along Himalayan foothills to about 1500m commoner south of Satpura mountains in peninsular India; disjunct population in hilly areas of S, SE Rajasthan and N Gujarat. **Habitat:** forests, clearings, gardens and human habitation.

Red-Whiskered Bulbul

Rupin Dang

Himalayan Bulbul

HIMALAYAN BULBUL (White-Eared)

Pycnonotus leucogenys 20cm. Light-brown above; black head, throat; white cheeks: dark-brown tail, tipped-white; yellow vent. The **White-eared Bulbul** *P leucotis* of the Himalaya and foothills has browner head, a front-pointed crest and a short, white superciliary stripe. Pairs or small parties; active birds on the move, attracting attention by their pleasant calls; the Himalayan bird is common in Kashmir, where quite confiding. **Food:** insects, fruits, flower-nectar. **Voice:** pleasant whistling notes. **Range:** NW and N India, south to about Bombay; the nominate race is found in the Himalaya, from the foothills to about 3400m. **Habitat:** open scrub, vicinity of habitation, edges of forest, coastal mangroves.

I.A. Babu

Red-Vented Bulbul

RED-VENTED BULBUL

Pycnonotus cafer 20cm. Sexes alike. Dark sooty-brown plumage; pale edges of feathers on back and breast give scaly appearance; darker head, with slight crest; almost black on throat; white rump and red vent distinctive; dark tail tipped-white. Pairs or small flocks, but large numbers gather to feed; arboreal, keeps to middle levels of trees and bushes; a well-known Indian bird, rather attached to man's neighbourhood; pleasantly noisy and cheerful, lively and quarrelsome, often kept as a pet; indulges in dust-bathing; also hunts flycatcher-style. **Food:** insects, fruits, flower-nectar, kitchen-scraps. **Voice:** cheerful whistling calls; alarm calls on sighting snake, owl or some other intrusion, serving to alert other birds. **Range:** all India, to about 1800m in Himalaya. **Habitat:** light forests, gardens, haunts of man.

M.K. Kuppuraj

White-Browed Bulbul

WHITE-BROWED BULBUL

Pycnonotus luteolus 20cm. Sexes alike. Olive plumage, brighter above; whitish forehead, supercilium, and explosive calls confirm identity· Pairs or small parties; not an easy bird to see; skulks in dense, low growth, from where its chattering calls suddenly explode, seen only momentarily when it emerges on bush tops, or flies low from one bush-patch to another; usually does not associate with other birds. **Food:** insects, fruits, nectar. **Voice:** loud, explosive chatter, an assortment of bubbling, whistling notes and chuckles. **Range:** peninsular India, south of a line from C Gujarat to southern W Bengal, avoids the heavy rainfall hill-zones of W Ghats. **Habitat:** dry scrub, village habitation, light forests and clearings.

YELLOW-BROWED BULBUL

Iole indica 20cm. Sexes alike. Bright yellowish-olive above; bright yellow forehead, sides of face, eyebrow; dark brown wings; olive-yellow tail; bright yellow underbody, olivish wash on flanks. Small parties in forest, often along with other small birds in mixed parties; a bird of the undergrowth, even entering hill-station gardens; moves energetically in the bush, works its way along the stem and leaves, sometimes ascends into the canopy of forest trees; rather vocal and active member of mixed parties. **Food:** fruits, forest berries; also insects, more so when nesting. **Voice:** pleasant, mellow whistling notes; also a harsh alarm note. **Range:** W Ghats south of Pune; Sri Lanka. **Habitat:** dense forests and edges.

Yellow-Browed Bulbul

BLACK BULBUL

Hypsipetes leucocephalus 23cm. Sexes alike. Ashy-grey plumage; black, loose-looking crest; coral-red beak and legs diagnostic; whitish below the abdomen. Flocks in forest, often dozens together; strictly arboreal, keeps to topmost branches of tall forest-trees, rarely comes down into undergrowth; noisy and restless, hardly staying on a tree for a few minutes; feeds on berries, fruits, but also hunts insects flycatcher manner. **Food:** forest berries, fruit, insects, flower-nectar. **Voice:** very noisy; an assortment of whistles and screeches. **Range:** several races; disjunct range; Himalaya, between 800–3200m; parts of NE states; W Ghats, south from Bombay; also Shevaroy Hills in Tamil Nadu; Sri Lanka. **Habitat:** tall forests; hill-station gardens.

Black Bulbul

ZITTING CISTICOLA
(Streaked Fantail Warbler)

Cisticola juncidis 10cm. Sexes alike. Rufous-brown above, prominently streaked darker; rufous-buff, unstreaked rump; white tips to fan-shaped tail diagnostic; buffy-white underbody, more rufous on flanks. Diagnostic calls. Pairs or several birds over open expanse; great skulker, lurking in low growth; usually seen during short, jerky flights, low over ground; soon dives into cover; most active when breeding, during rains; striking display of male, soaring erratically, falling and rising, incessantly uttering sharp, creaking note; adults arrive on nest in similar fashion. **Food:** insects, spiders, possibly some seeds. **Voice:** sharp, clicking *zit..zit* calls; continuously during display in air. **Range:** all India, south of the Himalayan foothills; absent in extreme NW Rajasthan. **Habitat:** open country, grass, cultivation, reed beds; also coastal lagoons.

Zitting Cisticola

Krupakar Senani

Grey-Breasted Prinia

GREY-BREASTED PRINIA
(Franklin's Wren Warbler)

Prinia hodgsonii 11cm. Sexes alike. More grey-brown, less rufous above; long, grey tail, tipped black and white; white underbody; when breeding, soft grey breast-band diagnostic. The **Rufous-Fronted Prinia** *P buchanani* (12cm) can be identified by the rufous head and dark brown tail, tipped black and white. Small bands ever on the move; keep to low growth but often clambers into middle levels; singing males may climb to top of trees; few nearly always present in mixed-hunting parties of small birds; nest like tailor-bird's. **Food:** insects, flower-nectar. **Voice:** noisy when breeding; longish, squeaky song; contact calls, almost continuous squeaking. **Range:** all India south of Himalayan foothills up to about 1800m; absent in arid W Rajasthan. **Habitat:** edge of forests, cultivation, gardens, scrub, often in and around habitation.

Goren Ekstrom

Graceful Prinia

GRACEFUL PRINIA (Streaked Wren Warbler)

Prinia gracilis 13cm. Sexes alike. Dull grey-brown above, streaked darker; very pale around eyes; long, graduated tail, faintly cross-barred, tipped white; whitish underbody, buffy on belly. Plumage more rufous in winter. The **Striated Prinia** *P criniger* (16cm) is larger, dark brown, streaked. **Rufous-Vented Prinia** *P burnesii* (17cm) is rufous-brown above, streaked; whitish below. Small parties moving in low growth; usually does not associate with other birds; restless, flicks wings and tail often; occasionally hunts like flycatcher. **Food:** insects. **Voice:** longish warble when breeding; wing-snapping and jumping display of male; *szeep...szip..* call-note. **Range:** NW Himalayan foothills, terai, south to Gujarat, across Gangetic plain. **Habitat:** scrub, grass, canal-banks, semi-desert.

A.K. Raju

Ashy Prinia

ASHY PRINIA (Wren Warbler)

Prinia socialis 13cm. Sexes alike. Rich, ashy-grey above, with rufous wings and long white-tipped tail; whitish lores; dull buffy-rufous below. In winter, less ashy, more rufous-brown; longer tail; whitish chin, throat. Mostly in pairs; actively moves in undergrowth; often flicks and erects tail; typical jerky flight when flying to another bush; noisy and excited when breeding. **Food:** insects, flower-nectar. **Voice:** nasal *pee..pee..pee..*; song, a loud and lively *jivee..jivee..jivee* or *jimmy..jimmy..,* rather like tailor-bird's in quality, but easily identifiable once heard. **Range:** all India south of Himalayan foothills, from about 1400m; absent in W Rajasthan. **Habitat:** cultivation, edges of forest, scrub, parks, vicinity of habitation.

PLAIN PRINIA (Wren Warbler)

Prinia inornata 13cm. Sexes alike. Pale brown above; whitish supercilium, lores; dark wings, tail; long, graduated tail, with buff tips and white outer feathers; buff-white underbody, tawny flanks, belly. In winter, more rufous above. The **Yellow-Bellied Prinia** *P flaviventris* (13cm) is olivish-green above, with a slaty-grey head; yellow belly and whitish throat distinctive. Pairs or several moving about in low growth: skulker, difficult to see; jerky, low flight, soon vanishing into bush; tail often nicked. **Food:** insects, flower-nectar. **Voice:** plaintive *tee..tee;* also a *krrik..krrik* sound; wheezy song, very insect-like in quality. **Range:** all India, from terai and Gangetic plain southwards; absent in W Rajasthan. **Habitat:** tall cultivation, grass, scrub; prefers damp areas.

Plain Prinia

ORIENTAL WHITE-EYE

Zosterops palpebrosus 10cm. Sexes alike. Olive-yellow above; short blackish stripe through eyes; white eye-ring distinctive; bright yellow throat, undertail; whitish breast, belly. Small parties, occasionally up to 40 birds, either by themselves or in association with other small birds; keeps to foliage and bushes; actively moves amongst leafy branches, clinging sideways and upside-down; checks through leaves and sprigs for insects and also spends considerable time at flowers; calls often, both when in branches and when flying in small bands from tree to tree. **Food:** insects, flower-nectar, berries. **Voice:** soft plaintive *tsee..* and *tseer..* notes; short jingling song. **Range:** all India, from Himalayan foothills till about 2000m; absent in arid parts of W Rajasthan. **Habitat:** forests, gardens, groves, secondary growth.

Oriental White-Eye

BROWNISH-FLANKED BUSH WARBLER (Strong-Footed)

Cettia fortipes montana 11cm. Sexes alike. Rufescent olive-brown above; buffy eyebrow; dark through eyes; dull-whitish below, tinged ashy-brown on throat and buff-brown flanks, under tail. Diagnostic call. The slightly smaller **Pale-Footed Bush Warbler** *C pallidipes* (10cm) has yellowish or flesh-coloured legs (*fortipes* has brownish legs). Solitary, occasionally two birds close by; a loner; shy and secretive, sneaking in undergrowth; rarely seen; usually, call-notes confirm presence. **Food:** insects. **Voice:** loud three-note call; *chak...* or *suck..* note; song of breeding male loud, usually high-pitched, long-drawn whistle, beginning with an Iora-like *whreeeeee*, and

Brownish-Flanked Bush Warbler

Sue Eule

Paddyfield Warbler

Goren Ekstrom

Clamorous Reed Warbler

Tim Loseby

Booted Warbler

ending in an explosive, musical phrase. **Range:** the Himalaya, also NE; breeds above 2000m till about 3300m; Moves down in winter, into foothills, and possibly parts of adjacent plains. **Habitat:** undergrowth on hill-sides, edges of forest, open forest, bamboo; also tea-estates and grasslands.

PADDYFIELD WARBLER

Acrocephalus agricola 13cm. Sexes alike. Rufescent-brown above; brighter on rump; whitish throat, rich buffy below. The **Blyth's Reed Warbler** *A dumetorum* (14cm), is a very common winter visitor, also has whitish throat and buffy underbody, but olive-brown upperbody is distinctive. Solitary, hopping amidst low growth; rarely seen along with other birds; damp areas, especially reed-growth and cultivation are favourite haunts; flies low, but soon vanishes into growth. **Food:** insects. **Voice:** a *chrr..chuck* or a single *chack* note, rather harsh in tone. The Blyth's Reed has a somewhat louder, quicker *tchik..* or *tchi..tchi.* call, and rarely, a warbling song before emigration, around early April. **Range:** winter visitor; common over most of India, south of and including the terai. **Habitat:** damp areas, reed-growth, tall cultivation.

CLAMOROUS REED WARBLER (Indian Great)

Acrocephalus stentoreus 19cm. Sexes alike. Brown above; distinct pale supercilium; whitish throat, dull buffy-white below; at close range, or in hand, salmon-coloured inside of mouth; calls diagnostic. Solitary or in pairs; difficult to see but easily heard; elusive bird, keeps to dense low reeds, mangrove and low growth, always in and around water; never associates with other species; flies low, immediately vanishes into, the vegetation; occasionally emerges on reed or bush tops, warbling with throat puffed out. **Food:** insects. **Voice:** highly vocal; loud *chack, chakrrr* and *khe* notes; distinctive, loud warbling; loud, lively song. **Range:** from Kashmir valley, south through the country; sporadically breeds in many areas, migrant in others. **Habitat:** reed beds, mangrove.

BOOTED WARBLER

Hippolais caligata 12cm. Sexes alike. Dull olive-brown above; short, pale white supercilium; pale buffy-white below. The Blyth's Reed Warbler is brighter olive-brown and mostly frequents bushes. Solitary or two to four birds, sometimes in mixed bands of small birds; very active and agile, hunting amongst leaves and upper branches; overall behaviour very Leaf-warbler like, but calls diagnostic. **Food:** insects. **Voice:** harsh, but low *chak..chak.. churrr* calls almost throughout day; soft, jingling song, sometimes heard before departure in winter grounds. **Range:** winters over peninsula south from Punjab to Bengal; breeds in NW regions, parts of W Punjab. **Habitat:** open country with Acacias and scrub; occasionally light forests.

Common Tailorbird

COMMON TAILORBIRD

Orthotomus sutorius 13cm. Sexes alike. Olive-green above; rust-red forecrown; buffy-white underbody; dark spot on throat-sides, best seen in calling male; long, pointed tail, often held erect; central tail-feathers about 5cm longer and pointed in breeding male, in pairs; rather common amidst habitation, but keeps to bushes, gardens; remains unseen even when at arm's length, but very vocal; tail often cocked, carried almost to the back; clambers up into trees more than other related warblers. **Food:** insects, flower-nectar. **Voice:** very vocal; loud familiar *towit..towit*; song is a rapid version of call, with slight change, loud *chuvee..chuvee..chuvee*, male sings on exposed perch. **Range:** all India, to about 2000m in outer Himalaya. **Habitation:** forest, cultivation, habitation.

LARGE-BILLED LEAF WARBLER

Phylloscopus magnirostris 12cm. Sexes alike. Brown-olive above; yellowish supercilium, dark eye-stripe distinctive; one or two faint wing-bars, not always easily seen; dull-yellow below. The very similar **Greenish Warbler** *P trochiloides* (10cm) is best identifiable in field by call (squeaky, fairly loud *dhciewee* or a *cheee.ee*). Usually solitary, sometimes in mixed parties of small birds; quite active, spends most time in leafy upper branches of medium-sized trees; not easy to sight, but characteristic call-notes help in confirming its presence. **Food:** small insects. **Voice:** distinctive *dir..tee...* call, the first note slightly lower; loud, ringing, five-noted song. **Range:** breeds in the Himalaya, 1800-3600m; winters over most of the peninsula. **Habitat:** forests, groves.

Large-Billed Leaf Warbler

GOLDEN-SPECTACLED WARBLER
(Black-Browed Flycatcher Warbler)

Seicercus burkii 10cm. Sexes alike. Olive-green above; greenish or grey-green eyebrow bordered above with prominent black coronal bands; greenish sides of face, yellow eye-ring; completely yellow below. The **White-Spectacled Warbler** *S affinis* has grey on crown and whitish eye-ring. Small restless flocks, often in

Golden-Spectacled Warbler

Toby Sinclair

Grey-Hooded Warbler

R.K. Gaur

White-Throated Laughingthrush

R.K. Gaur

White-Crested Laughingthrush

association with other small birds; keeps to the low bush and lower branches of trees. **Food:** insects. **Voice:** fairly noisy; sharp *chip..chip..* or *cheup..cheup..* notes. **Range:** breeds in the Himalaya, 2000-3500m; winters in foothills, parts of C and E peninsula, N Maharashtra, S Madhya Pradesh, NE Andhra Pradesh. **Habitat:** forest undergrowth.

GREY-HOODED WARBLER
(Grey-Headed Flycatcher Warbler)

Seicercus xanthoschistos 10cm. Sexes alike. Grey above; prominent, long, white eyebrow; yellowish rump, wings; white in outer-tail seen in flight; completely yellow below. The **Grey-Cheeked Warbler** *S poliogenys* has dark slaty head, white eye-ring and grey chin and cheeks; it is found in Himalaya, east of Nepal. Pairs or small bands, often along with mixed-hunting parties; actively hunts and flits in canopy foliage and tall bushes; highly energetic. **Food:** insects; rarely small berries. **Voice:** quite vocal, loud, high-pitched double-note call; pleasant, trilling song. **Range:** the Himalaya; 900-3000m; altitudinal movement in winter. **Habitat:** Himalayan forests, gardens.

WHITE-THROATED LAUGHINGTHRUSH

Garrulax albogularis 28cm. Sexes alike. Greyish olive-brown above, fulvous forehead, black mark in front of eye, full rounded tail with 4 outer pairs of feathers broadly tipped with white. Below rufous but with conspicuous pure white throat sharply demarcated by a line of olive brown. The white gorget stands out in the gloom of forest floor. **Food:** insects, also berries. **Voice:** continual chattering, warning *twit-tzee* alarm. **Range:** throughout Himalaya, with distinct western race, up to 3000m in summer. **Habitat:** dense forest, scrub, wooded ravines.

WHITE-CRESTED LAUGHINGTHRUSH

Garrulax leucolophus 28cm. Sexes alike. Olive-brown above; pure white head, crest, throat, breast, sides of head; broad, black band through eyes to ear-coverts; rich rufous nuchal collar, continuing around breast; olive-brown below breast. Small parties in forest; moves in undergrowth but readily ascends into upper leafy branches; makes short flights between trees; very noisy; hops on ground, rummaging in leaf-litter. **Food:** insects, berries. **Voice:** very noisy; sudden explosive chatter or 'laughter'; also pleasant two or three-note whistling calls. **Range:** the Himalaya. **Habitat:** dense forest undergrowth, bamboo, wooded nullahs.

STRIATED LAUGHINGTHRUSH

Garrulax striatus 28cm. Sexes alike. Rich-brown plumage, heavily white-streaked, except on wings and rich rufous-brown tail; darkish, loose crest, streaked white towards front; heavy streaking on throat, sides of head, becoming less from breast downwards. Pairs or small parties; often along with other birds in mixed, noisy parties; feeds both in upper branches and in low bush; shows marked preference for certain sites in forest. **Food:** insects, fruits; seen eating leaves. **Voice:** very vocal; clear whistling call of 6 to 8 notes; loud, cackling chatter. **Range:** the Himalaya east of Kulu, 800-2700m parts of NE states. **Habitat:** dense forests, scrub, wooded ravines.

Striated Laughingthrush

NILGIRI LAUGHINGTHRUSH

Garrulax cachinnans 20cm. Sexes alike. Olive-brown above; deep slaty-brown crown; long, white stripe over eye and much shorter streak below; black lores, stripe through and behind eye, chin and throat; rich rufous below throat. Small parties, up to a dozen birds; mostly feeds in undergrowth; also hops about actively in upper branches; often seen in mixed hunting-parties; extremely noisy, both on ground and in trees. **Food:** insects, berries and other fruit. **Voice:** extremely noisy; its chattering 'laughter' calls amongst the most familiar bird-calls of the Nilgiris; many birds call in chorus. **Range:** restricted to the Nilgiris in SW India; above 1000m. **Habitat:** dense, evergreen forests; hill-station gardens.

Nilgiri Laughingthrush

GREY-BREASTED LAUGHINGTHRUSH
(White-Breasted)

Garrulax jerdoni 20cm. Sexes alike. Olive-brown above; black eye-stripe; differs from *cachinnans* chiefly in having cheeks, chin, throat and breast deep grey, slightly streaked on sides; paler rufous below breast. The nominate race, restricted to a small area in Coorg has black chin, cheeks. Small flocks, a dozen or so, often with other birds; feeds in low bushes and on ground, hopping in characteristic laughingthrush manner; extremely noisy, wary and difficult to see, as it rarely emerges in open. **Food:** insects, berries and other fruit. **Voice:** extremely noisy; whistling, chattering 'laughter'; also squeaking alarm notes. **Range:** hilly-forested parts of Kerala, W Tamil Nadu, and SW Karnataka, generally above 1000m. **Habitat:** evergreen forests; sholas; undergrowth.

Grey-Breasted Laughingthrush

Streaked Laughingthrush

Variegated Laughingthrush

Black-Faced Laughingthrush

STREAKED LAUGHINGTHRUSH

Garulax lineatus 20cm. Sexes alike. pale grey plumage, streaked dark-brown on upper back, white on lower back; rufous ear-coverts, wings; rufous-edges and grey-white tips to roundish tail; rufous streaking and white shafts on underbody. Pairs or small bands; prefers low bush and grassy areas, only rarely going into upper branches; hops, dips and bows about; flicks wings and jerks tail often; weak, short flight. **Food:** insects, berries; refuse around hillside habitation. **Voice:** fairly noisy; a near-constant chatter of a mix of whistling and squeaky notes; common call a whistle of two or three notes, *pitt..wee.er.* **Range:** the Himalaya, west to east; 1400-3800m; considerable altitudinal movement. **Habitat:** bushy hill-slopes, cultivation, edges of forest.

VARIEGATED LAUGHINGTHRUSH

Garulax variegatus 25cm. Sexes alike. Olive-brown above; grey, black and white head, face; grey, black, white and rufous in wings, tail; black chin, throat, bordered with buffy-white; narrow white tip to tail, with grey subterminal band. Small flocks, up to a dozen and more on steep, bushy hillsides; keep to undergrowth for most part, but occasionally clambers into leafy branches; wary and secretive, not easily seen; weak flight, as in most laughingthrushes. **Food:** insects, fruits; rarely flower-nectar. **Voice:** noisy; clear, musical whistling notes, three to four syllables; also harsh, squeaking notes. **Range:** the Himalaya, east to C Nepal; 1200-3500m; breeds between 2000-3200m. **Habitat:** forests undergrowth, bamboo; seen in hill-station gardens in winter.

BLACK-FACED LAUGHINGTHRUSH

Garulax affinis 25cm. Sexes alike. Diagnostic-blackish face, throat, part of head and contrast-ing white malar patches, neck-sides and part of eye-ring; rufous-brown above, finely scalloped on back; olivish-golden flight-feathers tipped grey; rufous-brown below throat, marked grey. Pairs or small bands, sometimes with other babblers; moves on ground and low growth, also ascends into middle levels of trees; noisy when disturbed or when snakes or other creatures arouses its curiosity. **Food:** insects, berries, seeds. **Voice:** various high-pitched notes, chuckles; a rolling *whirrr* alarm-call; a four noted, somewhat plaintive song. **Range:** the Himalaya, from W Nepal eastwards; descends to 1500m in winter. **Habitat:** undergrowth in forest; dwarf vegetation in higher regions.

PUFF-THROATED BABBLER (Spotted)

Pellorneum ruficeps 15cm. Sexes alike. Olivish-brown above; dark-rufous cap; whitish-buff stripe over eye; white throat; dull fulvous-white underbody, boldly streaked blackish-brown on breast and sides. Solitary or in pairs; shy, secretive bird of undergrowth; mostly heard, extremely difficult to see; rummages on ground, amidst leaf-litter; hops about, rarely ascends into upper branches. **Food:** insects. **Voice:** noisy when breeding; mellow whistle, two, three or four-noted; best-known call is a four-note whistle, interpreted *he will.beat.you.* **Range:** hilly-forest areas; Himalaya, to about 1500m, east of SE Himachal; NE states; S Bihar, Orissa, Satpura range across C India, E and W Ghats. **Habitat:** forest undergrowth, bamboo, overgrown ravines, nullahs.

Krupakar Senani

Puff-Throated Babbler

RUSTY-CHEEKED SCIMITAR BABBLER

Pomatorhinus erythrogenys 25cm. Sexes alike. Olive-brown above; orangish-rufous (rusty) sides of face, head, thighs, flanks; remainder of underbody mostly pure white; long, curved 'scimitar' beak. Small bands in forest; a bird of undergrowth, hopping on jungle floor, turns over leaves or digs with beak; sometimes hops into leafy branches, but more at ease on ground. **Food:** insects, grubs, seeds. **Voice:** noisy; mellow, fluty whistle, two-noted *cue.pe...cue.pe*, followed by single (sometimes double) note reply by mate; guttural alarm call and a liquid contact note. **Range:** the Himalaya foothills to at least 2200m and possibly to 2600m. **Habitat:** forest undergrowth, ravines, bamboo.

Goren Ekstrom

Rusty-Cheeked Scimitar Babbler

WHITE-BROWED SCIMITAR BABBLER (Slaty-Headed)

Pomatorhinus schisticeps 22cm. Sexes alike. Deep olive-brown above; long, white super-cilium; white throat, breast and belly-centre; long curved, yellow 'scimitar beak. Pairs or small, loose bands in forest; keep to undergrowth, where the bubbling, fluty calls are heard more often than the birds are seen; hops on jungle floor, vigorously rummaging amidst leaf-litter digs with long beak; hop their way into leafy branches, but not for long; scattered birds keep in touch through calls. **Food:** insects, spiders, flower-nectar. **Voice:** fluty, musical whistle, often followed by a bubbling note; often calls in duet. **Range:** hilly forest regions of the country, Himalaya to about 1500m. **Habitat:** mixed forest, scrub, bamboo.

Tawny-Bellied Babbler

TAWNY-BELLIED BABBLER (Rufous-Bellied)

Dumetia hyperythra 13cm. Sexes alike. Olivish-brown above; reddish-brown front part of crown; white throat in western and southern races; nominate race has underbody entirely fulvous. Small, noisy parties in undergrowth; rummages on floor, hopping about, always wary; hardly associates with other birds; great skulkers, difficult to see; any sign of danger and the flock disperses amidst a chorus of alarm notes; soon hop and reunite. **Food:** chiefly insects, occasionally seen on flowering silk-cotton trees; also other flower-nectar. **Voice:** faint *cheep..cheep* contact notes; also a mix of other whistling and chattering notes. **Range:** from SE Himachal east along foothills to peninsular India; absent in arid NW, Punjab plains, NE states. **Habitat:** scrub and bamboo in and around forests.

Striped Tit Babbler

STRIPED TIT BABBLER (Yellow-Breasted)

Macronous gularis 11cm. Sexes alike. Dull olive-brown or olive-grey above; pale rufous cap; light-yellow supercilium; pale yellow below, with fine black streaks, the streaks diminishing towards belly. Usually in small flocks, frequently in mixed-bird parties; very noisy and unusually active for a babbler, moves considerably; sometimes hunts on ground but spends most time in upper branches and tall bush. **Food:** insects. **Voice:** very noisy; variety of loud notes, a mix of harsh chuckles and whistles; a harsh *whaech..whaech*. **Range:** disjunct: (1)E Himalaya, NE: (2)E Ghats, parts of eastern peninsula — Orissa, SE Bihar and Madhya Pradesh, NE Andhra, south to Godavari river; (3) Small zone in S Karnataka. **Habitat:** forests, bamboo, dense grass and bushes.

Yellow-Eyed Babbler

YELLOW-EYED BABBLER

Chrysomma sinense 18cm. Sexes alike. Rufous-brown above; whitish lores, short supercilium; yellow eye (iris) and orange-yellow eye-rim distinctive at close range; cinnamon wings; long, graduated tail; white below, ringed pale fulvous on flanks and abdomen. Pairs or small bands in tall grass and undergrowth; noisy but skulking, suddenly clambers into view for a few seconds, before vanishing once again; works its way along stems and leaves, hunting insects; short, jerky flight. **Food:** insects, larvae; also flower-nectar. **Voice:** noisy when breeding (mostly rains); melodious, whistling notes; also a mournful *cheep..cheep* call. **Range:** all India, from the Himalayan foothills south; absent in arid parts of Rajasthan. **Habitat:** scrub, tall grass, cultivation, edges of forest.

COMMON BABBLER

Turdoides caudatus 23cm. Sexes alike. Dull brown above, profusely streaked; brown wings; olivish-brown tail long and graduated, cross-rayed darker; dull-white throat; pale fulvous underbody, streaked on breast sides. Pairs or small bands in open scrub; skulker, works its way low in bush or on ground; moves with peculiar bouncing hop on the ground, long, loose-looking tail cocked-up; extremely wary, vanishes into scrub at slightest alarm; weak flight, evident when flock moves from one scrub-patch to another. **Food:** insects, flower-nectar, berries. **Voice:** noisy; pleasant, warbling whistles, several birds often in chorus; squeaky alarm-notes; calls on ground and in low flight. **Range:** most of N, NW, W and peninsular India, south of outer Himalaya to about 2000m; east to Bengal. **Habitat:** thorn scrub, open cultivation.

Common Babbler

STRIATED BABBLER

Turdoides earlei 21cm. Sexes alike. Dull brownish above, streaked darker; long, cross-barred tail; buffy-brown below, with fine dark streaks on throat, breast (the Common Babbler has white throat and lacks breast-streaks). The **Striated Grass Bird** *Megalurus palustris* (25cm), with greatly overlapping range, has bolder streaking above, prominent whitish supercilium, and almost white below, streaked below breast. Sociable; parties of up to ten birds keep to tall grass and reed-beds; flies low, rarely drops down to the ground. **Food:** insects, snails. **Voice:** loud, three-noted whistle; also a quick-repeated single whistling-note. **Range:** floodplains of N and NE river systems, especially the larger rivers (Indus, Ganges, Brahmaputra). **Habitat:** tall grass, reed beds, scrub.

Striated Babbler

LARGE GREY BABBLER

Turdoides malcolmi 28cm. Sexes alike. Grey-brown above; dark centres to feathers on back gives streaked look; greyer forehead; long, graduated tail cross-rayed, with white outer feathers, conspicuous in flight; fulvous-grey below. Gregarious; flocks in open country, sometimes dozens together; extremely noisy; moves on ground and in medium-sized trees; hops about; weak flight; at any sign of danger, flock comes together. **Food:** insects, seeds, berries; rarely flower-nectar. **Voice:** very noisy; chorus of squeaking chatter; short alarm-note. **Range:** from E Uttar Pradesh, Delhi environs, south through most of peninsula; east to Bihar; abundant in Deccan. **Habitat:** scrub, open country, gardens, vicinity of habitation.

Large Grey Babbler

Toby Sinclair

Jungle Babbler

Krupakar Senani

Yellow-Billed Babbler

Rupin Dang

Silver-Eared Mesia

JUNGLE BABBLER

Turdoides striatus 25cm. Sexes alike. Dull earth-brown above, lightly streaked on back; dark, rufous-brown tail, loose and longish, faintly cross-rayed; ashy-fulvous below, with pale markings on breast; the race *somervillei* of W coast has reddish-rufous rump, tail-coverts. Gregarious; small parties, 6 to 15 birds; also referred to as 'Satbhai' (Seven brothers); 'Seven sisters' in English, as usually there are five to seven birds in a flock; spends much time on ground, rummaging; sometimes flies into branches above, especially when alarmed, appears ruffled and agitated and breaks into a squeaking chorus; social birds, all come together if one member is in some problem. **Food:** insects, flower-nectar, figs. **Voice:** noisy; chattering chorus. **Range:** all India south of Himalayan foothills. **Habitat:** light forests, scrub, gardens, cultivation, vicinity of habitation.

YELLOW-BILLED BABBLER (White-Headed)

Turdoides affinis 24cm. Sexes alike. Creamy-white crown; dull-brown above, appearing scaly on centre of back; darker wings and cross-barring along tail-centre; dark brown throat, breast, the pale-grey edges to feathers giving scaled appearance; yellowish-buff below breast. Small noisy parties, feeds on ground, turning leaves; if disturbed moves about in a series of short, hopping flights; hops amongst tree branches towards the top, from where a short flight takes the birds to an adjoining tree. **Food:** insects, nectar, figs. **Voice:** noisy; definitely more musical chatter than the commoner Jungle Babbler. **Range:** southern peninsular India — Karnataka, Andhra, Tamil Nadu, Kerala; also Sri Lanka. **Habitat:** forests, dense growth, neighbourhood of cultivation and habitation, orchards.

SILVER-EARED MESIA

Leiothrix argentauris 15cm. Sexes alike. Brightly coloured; black crown; silver ear coverts yellow forehead, orangish throat and breast, crimson upper and under tail-coverts, crimson patch on wing. Female has yellowish tail-coverts. Flocks of up to 20 birds flit from tree to tree; actively searches for insects and berries; tit-like acrobatic behaviour; also flycatcher like sallies. **Food:** seeds, berries and insects. **Voice:** incessant *chirrup* while feeding, also long-drawn *see..see...we..* **Range:** C Himalaya to Arunachal Pradesh. **Habitat:** scrub jungle, open clearances in evergreen forests.

RED-BILLED LEIOTHRIX

Leiothrix lutea 13cm. **Male:** olive-grey above; dull buffy-yellow lores, eye-ring; yellow, orange, crimson and black in wings; forked tail, with black tip and edges; yellow throat, orange-yellow breast diagnostic; scarlet beak. The red on wing is considerably reduced or absent in the western race *kumaiensis.* **Female:** like male, but yellow instead of crimson in wings. Small parties, often part of mixed hunting-parties of small birds in forest; rummages in undergrowth but frequently moves up into branches; lively, noisy bird. **Food:** insects, berries. **Voice:** quite vocal; often utters a wistful, piping *tee.tee.tee;* mix of sudden explosive notes; a musical warble. **Range:** the Himalaya, from Kashmir to extreme NE; 600-2700m. **Habitat:** undergrowth, bushy hillsides, plantations.

Red-Billed Leiothrix

CHESTNUT-TAILED MINLA
(Bar-Throated Siva)

Minla strigula 14cm. Sexes alike. Grey-olive back; slightly tufted yellow-olive cap; whitish ear-coverts, black malar stripe; orange-yellow and black in wings; black tail has chestnut and yellow; dull yellow throat, with thin, black scales. Small flocks, frequently in mixed hunting-parties that characterise the Himalaya; arboreal and active; hunts in canopy or in middle levels: when finished with a tree, flock moves on to another. **Food:** insects, berries, other fruits, nectar. **Voice:** mix of whistling squeaks; loud, four-syllabled song with accent on second syllable. **Range:** Himalaya, east of Kangra (Himachal); 800-3700m; breeding mostly above 1800m. **Habitat:** forests of oak, fir, rhododendron; also bamboo.

Chestnut-Tailed Minla

WHITE-BROWED FULVETTA (Tit Babbler)

Alcippe vinipectus 11cm. Sexes alike. Brown crown, nape; prominent white eyebrow; with black or dark-brown line above; blackish sides of face and white eye-ring; olive-brown above, washed rufous on wings, rump and tail; some grey in wings; whitish throat breast, olive-brown below. The eastern races *chumbiensis* and *austeni* have streaked throat; 6 to 20 birds in low growth or lower branches; energetic, acrobatic birds, often seen in mixed-hunting parties. **Food:** insects, caterpillars, berries. **Voice:** fairly sharp *tsuip...* or *tship..* call; also some harsh churring notes, when agitated. **Range:** the Himalaya from W Himachal; E Himalaya; NE regions; 1500-3500m, over 4000m in some parts; descends to 1200m in severe winter. **Habitat:** scrub in forest, ringal bamboo.

White-Browed Fulvetta

Brown-Cheeked Fulvetta

Rufous Sibia

Whiskered Yuhina

BROWN-CHEEKED FULVETTA (Quaker Babbler)

Alcippe poioicephala 15cm. Sexes alike. Olive-brown above; grey crown, nape distinctive; thin, black stripe through eyes; rufescent-brown wings, tail; dull fulvous underbody. Pairs or small parties, often along with other birds; moves actively in undergrowth and leafy branches, clinging sideways or springing from perch; rather shy in most areas, but occasionally emerges in open. **Food:** insects, spiders, flower-nectar, berries. **Voice:** best known call is the 4 to 8 syllabled song, interpreted as daddy *give-me-chocolate*; harsh *churr..* notes serve as contact calls. **Range:** peninsular India, south from Mt Abu across Pachmarhi (Satpuras) to S Bihar and Orissa. **Habitat:** forests, undergrowth, bamboo; also hill-station gardens in W Ghats.

RUFOUS SIBIA (Black-Capped)

Heterophasia capistrata 20cm. Sexes alike. Rich-rufous plumage; grey-brown centre of back (between wings); black crown, slight, bushy crest, sides of head; bluish-grey wings and black shoulder patch; grey-tipped long tail; black sub-terminal tail-band. Small flocks, sometimes with other birds; active gymnasts, ever on the move; have cheerful calls; hunts in canopy and middle levels, moves amidst moss-covered branches; springs into air after winged insects; sometimes hunts like tree-creepers on stems, probing bark crevices. **Food:** insects, flower-nectar, berries. **Voice:** wide range of whistling and sharp notes; rich song of 6 to 8 syllables during Himalayan summer. **Range:** Himalaya; 1500-3000m sometimes up to about 3500m (Bhutan); descends to 600m in winters. **Habitat:** forest both temperate and broad-leafed.

WHISKERED YUHINA (Yellow-Naped)

Yuhina flavicollis 13cm. Sexes alike. Olive-brown above; choco-brown crown, crest; white eye-ring and black moustache seen from close; rufous-yellow nuchal collar (less distinct in western race); white underbody, streaked rufous-olive on sides of breast, flanks. Flocks, almost always with other small birds; active and restless, flitting about or hunting flycatcher style; moves between undergrowth and middle-levels, sometimes ascending into canopy; keeps up a constant twitter. **Food:** insects, berries, flower-nectar. **Voice:** quite vocal; a mix of soft twittering notes and fairly loud two or three note call, *chee.chi..chew.* **Range:** the Himalaya. **Habitat:** forests.

Lesser Whitethroat

LESSER WHITETHROAT

Sylvia curruca 12cm. Sexes alike. Deep-grey above, washed brownish on back and wings; dark, almost blackish, ear-coverts give masked appearance; glistening white throat; white below, buff-wash on breast, belly. The **Greater Whitethroat** *S communis* (14cm) has rusty wings and lacks the dark ear-coverts; it winters over NW India, south at least to W Gujarat. Mostly solitary; secretive, skulking; moves or creeps in dense bush-growth, including *Acacia* and *Prosopis*; jabs with beak at out of reach insect. **Food:** small insects, caterpillars, nectar of *Acacia, Prosopis* and similar flowers. **Voice:** check note, often uttered as it moves in bush; a mix of soft warbling and rapid rattling outburst. **Range:** winter visitor almost all over India; the race *althaea* breeds in W Himalaya, 1500-3700m **Habitat:** open bush country, *Acacia* and *Prosopis* growth, groves, gardens.

INDIAN BUSHLARK (Red-Winged)

Mirafra erythroptera 14cm. Sexes alike. Yellowish-brown above, streaked black; rich chestnut-rufous on wings, easily seen when bird in flight: pale white chin, throat, dull yellowish-brown below; blackish, triangular spots on breast. Pairs or small flocks; moves quietly on ground, running about or

Indian Bushlark

perching on small stones or bush-tops; squats tight when approached but takes to wing when intruder very close; spectacular display-flight, accompanied by singing, when breeding; indulges in display flights during the night too. **Food:** seeds, tiny insects. **Voice:** faint *cheep..chrep...* call-note; song a faint but lively twittering. **Range:** almost all of N, NW and peninsular India; absent in Kerala, NE. **Habitat:** open cultivation, grass and scrub; fallow lands.

ASHY-CROWNED SPARROW LARK (Finch Lark)

Eremopterix grisea 13cm. Thickish beak. **Male:** sandy-brown above; white cheeks and sides of breast dark chocolate-brown sides of face, most of underbody; dark brown tail with whitish outer feathers. **Female:** sandy-brown overall; dull rufous sides of face and underbody. Mostly loose necks, scattered over an area; pairs or small parties when breeding; feed on ground; fond of dusty areas, where large numbers may squat about; sandy colouration makes it impossible to spot the birds, but when disturbed, large numbers suddenly take wing; superb display flight of male. **Food:** grass seeds, tiny insects. **Voice:** pleasant, monotonous trilling song by male; sings on wing and on ground. **Range:** almost all India, south of Himalayan foothills; moves during the rains; uncommon in heavy rainfall areas. **Habitat:** open scrub, semi-cultivation, fallow river basins, tidal mudflats.

Asby-Crowned Sparrow Lark

RUFOUS-TAILED LARK (Finch Lark)

Ammomanes phoenicurus 16cm. Sexes alike. Dark brown above; rufous-brown below, with brown streaks on throat, breast; rich rufous tail with black band across tip diagnostic. Pairs when breeding; small flocks during winter, occasionally with other larks; difficult to locate because of dull coloration; mostly keeps to ground, running about erratically; flies short distance if disturbed; as with several other larks, there is sudden appearance and disappearance of this species in many localities; display flight of male when breeding (March-May). **Food:** seeds of grass, paddy; small insects, especially during rains and when breeding. **Voice:** song a mix of rich whistling notes and chirps; sings on wing and from perch on earth mounds, stones or low bush. **Range:** commoner east from Kutch to around Delhi; east to Bengal and south to N Andhra. **Habitat:** cultivation, fallow ground, open riversides.

Rufous-Tailed Lark

CRESTED LARK

Galerida cristata 18cm. Sexes alike. Sandy brown above, streaked blackish; pointed, upstanding crest distinctive; brown tail has dull rufous outer feathers; whitish and dull yellowish-brown below, the breast streaked dark brown. The **Malabar** and **Syke's Larks** *G malabarica* (15cm) and *G deva* (13cm) are similar, but overall plumage is darker, more rufous-brown; both are birds of Peninsular and S India. Small flocks, breaking into pairs when breeding; runs briskly on ground, pointed crest carried upstanding; settles on bush-tops, stumps, fences, overhead wires. **Food:** seeds, grain, insects. **Voice:** ordinary call-note a pleasant *tee..ur..;* short song of male during soaring, display flight. **Range:** N, NW India, Gangetic plain; south to Rajasthan, Saurashtra, N Madhya Pradesh. **Habitat:** semi-desert, cultivation, dry grassy areas.

Crested Lark

ORIENTAL SKYLARK (Eastern)

Alauda gulgula 16cm. Sexes alike. Brownish above, the feathers edged yellow-brown with black centres; short, indistinct crest, not often visible; dark brown tail with pale-buff outer feathers; dull-buff below; more yellowish-brown on breast, faintly streaked and spotted darker. Pairs or small parties on ground, running in short spurts; squats when approached and flies low at the last moment, with a chirping note; beautiful aerial song-flight of male when breeding. **Food:** seeds, insects. **Voice:** longish, pleasant warble of male, often imitations of other bird calls thrown in; sings usually when soaring high, and on fluttering descent; also has chirping notes. **Range:** all India, up to about 4000m in Himalaya; half a dozen races over the subcontinent. **Habitat:** grasslands, cultivation, mudflats, fallow lands.

Oriental Skylark

HORNED LARK

Eremophila alpestris 20cm. Large lark of high-mountain country. **Male:** pink brown above, white below; black crown-band with conspicuous black 'hems' on either side; dull yellow-white face, throat; black cheeks and breast-band (gorget) separated by narrow white band distinctive; the western race *albigula* of Gilgit and Chitral has black cheeks continuous with black gorget. **Female:** crown streaked black; overall less black, duller-black cheeks, gorget; tiny 'horns'. Young birds are duller and have spotted plumage. In pairs or small parties; quiet, tame and confiding; makes short runs on ground. **Food:** seeds, grain, small insects. **Voice:** somewhat plaintive,

Horned Lark

soft *tsee..ri..* call; a highpitched, squeaky song of breeding male (May-August). **Range:** high mountain bird. From Chitral, Gilgit east through Ladakh, Lahaul, Spiti to Bhutan and east; breeds at about 3500-5000m (up to snowline); descends in winter. **Habitat:** open barren areas, scrub, meadows.

THICK-BILLED FLOWERPECKER
Dicaeum agile 9cm. Sexes alike. Olive-grey above, greener on rump; white-tipped tail; dull whitish-grey below, streaked brown, more on breast; orange-red eyes and thick, blue-grey beak seen at close range. Solitary or in pairs in canopy foliage; arboreal, restless; flicks tail as it hunts under leaves or along branches; frequents parasitic clumps of *Loranthus* and *Viscum*. **Food:** figs, berries of *Ficus, Lantana, Loranthus* and *Viscum*; also insects, spiders and nectar. **Voice:** loud, sharp *chik..chik.* **Range:** India; south of and including the Himalayan foothills; absent over arid parts of NW India and large tracts of Tamil Nadu. **Habitat:** forests, orchards, gardens.

PALE-BILLED FLOWERPECKER (Tickell's)
Dicaeum erythrorynchos 8cm. Sexes alike. Olive brown above; unmarked grey-white below; pinkish-flesh or yellow-brown beak seen only at close range or in good light. The **Plain Flowerpecker** *D concolor* has a dark beak and a pale super-cilium. Solitary or 2-3 birds in canopy; frequents parasitic *Loranthus* and *Viscum*; flits from clump to clump; strictly arboreal, restless; territorial even when feeding. **Food:** causes much damage to orchards; chiefly berries, spiders and small insects. **Voice:** sharp, loud *chik..chik.* **Range:** from Kangra east along foothills to NE India; peninsular India south of a line from Baroda to S Bihar. **Habitat:** light forests, groves.

FIRE-BREASTED FLOWERPECKER
Dicaeum ignipectus 7cm. **Male:** metallic blue-green-black above; buffy below, with scarlet breast-patch and black stripe down centre of lower breast and belly. **Female:** olive-green above, yellowish on rump; bright buff below; flanks and sides tinged olive. Mostly solitary; arboreal and active; flits about in foliage canopy; attending to *Loranthus* clumps; encounter-ed in restless mixed hunting-bands of small birds in Himala-yan forests. **Food:** berries, nectar, spiders, insects. **Voice:** sharp, metallic *chip..chip* note; high-pitched, clicking song. **Range:** the Himalaya, Kashmir to extreme east; breeds 1400-3000m; winters as low as 300m. **Habitat:** forests, orchards.

Pale-Billed Flowerpecker

Fire-Breasted Flowerpecker

E. Hanumantha Rao

N.J. Redmam

RUBY-CHEEKED SUNBIRD

Anthreptes singalensis 10cm. **Male:** metallic green above; deep coppery-red ear-coverts; rufous-buff throat, breast; pale yellow below. **Female:** olive-green above not metallic, paler underbody; usually some yellow on wings. Young birds similar to female, but very pale rufous (sometimes absent) on throat. Pairs or small loose bands; sometimes associates with other birds; restless; hunts amongst leaves and branches or attends to flowers; calls often in short jumping flight. **Food:** insects, flower-nectar. **Voice:** fairly loud chirping note. **Range:** foothills to about 700-900m, occasionally ascending to over 1000m; E Himalaya (Nepal eastwards) and NE regions. **Habitat:** evergreen forests, bushes.

Ruby-Cheeked Sunbird

PURPLE-RUMPED SUNBIRD

Nectarinia zeylonica 10cm. **Male:** deep chestnut-crimson back; metallic green crown, shoulder-patch; metallic-purple rump, throat; maroon collar below throat; yellow below. **Female:** ashy-brown above, with rufous in wings; whitish throat; yellow below. Usually pairs; very active, flits from flower to flower; occasionally descends into flowering garden bushes. **Food:** flower-nectar, spiders, small insects. **Voice:** *tsiswee...tsiswee..* calls; sharp, twittering song of breeding male, much lower in tone and volume than that of Purple Sunbird. **Range:** peninsular India south of a line from around Bombay, C Madhya Pradesh. S Bihar and Bengal. **Habitat:** open forests, gardens, orchards; also common in towns.

Purple-Rumped Sunbird

CRIMSON-BACKED SUNBIRD (Small)

Nectarinia minima 8cm. **Male:** overall appearance like Purple-rumped; deep maroon back; no metallic-green shoulder patch; metallic purple throat with very broad crimson-maroon collar across lower throat and breast diagnostic; yellow belly. **Female:** olivish above; crimson on rump; pale yellow below. Solitary or pairs; typical sunbird, very active acrobat; flits and hovers in front of flowers; also seen around *Loranthus* clumps. **Food:** flower-nectar, insects, spiders. **Voice:** ordinary call-note rather similar to that of Purple-rumped; short, squeaky song of breeding male. **Range:** restricted to W Ghats from S Gujarat to Kerala; also the Nilgiris, Palnis and associated hill ranges; 300-2000m. **Habitat:** evergreen forests, tea and coffee plantations, hill-station gardens.

Crimson-Backed Sunbird

Krupakar Senani

Purple Sunbird

PURPLE SUNBIRD

Nectarinia asiatica 10cm. **Br Male:** metallic purple-blue above, and on throat, breast; dark purplish-black belly; narrow chestnut-maroon band between breast and belly; yellow and scarlet pectoral tufts, normally hidden under wings. **Female:** olive-brown above; pale yellow below (*zeylonica* female has whitish throat). **Non-br Male:** like female but with broad purple-black stripe down centre of throat to belly. Solitary or in pairs; important pollinating agent. **Food:** nectar, small insects, spiders. **Voice:** more noisy than other sunbirds; loud *chweet..* notes. **Range:** all India, south from Himalayan foothills to about l500m. **Habitat:** open forests, gardens, groves.

Krupakar Senani

Loten's Sunbird

LOTEN'S SUNBIRD

Nectarinia lotenia 13cm. **Male:** metallic purplish-black above; dull-black wings, tail; iridescent green and purple throat and purple breast; crimson-maroon breast band and yellow feather-tufts on breast-sides (armpits) diagnostic. **Female:** olive above; white tips to dark tail; pale yellow below; long, curved beak distinctive. Solitary or in pairs; *Loranthus* flowers are a favourite; this and other sunbirds are important pollinating agents of many flowering trees. **Food:** nectar, small-insects, spiders. **Voice:** fairly loud and sharp *tchit..tchit..* call; quickish song of *chewit.. chewit* notes. **Range:** from Bombay south to W Ghats to about 1400m; east coast and E Ghats; S Karnataka, N Tamil Nadu. **Habitat:** forests, gardens.

CRIMSON SUNBIRD (Yellow-Backed)

Aethopyga siparaja 15cm. **Male:** has longer tail; metallic green crown, tail; deep crimson back, neck-sides; yellow rump not commonly seen; bright scarlet chin to breast striking; olive-yellow belly. **Female:** olive plumage, yellower below. In the W Ghats race *vigorsii*, the male's breast is streaked yellow. Solitary or in pairs; active gymnast; also hovers; moves a lot in forest, between tall bushes and canopy. **Food:** nectar, small insects, spiders. **Voice:** sharp, clicking call-notes; pleasant chirping song of breeding male (June-August). **Range:** disjunct: Himalayan foothills from Kangra east; also parts of S Bihar, NE Madhya Pradesh, Bengal and Orissa; W Ghats between Narmada river and N Kanara, and possibly further south; also NE states and Nicobar Islands. **Habitat:** forests.

Crimson Sunbird

LITTLE SPIDERHUNTER

Arachnothera longirostra 14cm. Sexes alike. Olive-green above; dark tail, tipped white; grey-white throat, merging into yellow-white below; orangish pectoral tufts. Very long, curved beak diagnostic. The much larger **Streaked Spiderhunter** *A magna* (17cm) is olive-yellow, profusely streaked. Usually solitary; sometimes two or three birds in vicinity; active, moving considerably between bush and canopy; wild banana blossoms are a favourite; long, curved beak specially adapted to nectar-diet. **Food:** nectar; also insects and spiders. **Voice:** high-pitched *chee..chee* call; loud *which..which...* **Range:** disjunct: (1) W Ghats south of N Kanara; (2) Small zone in E Ghats (Vishakapatanam); (3) Foothills from SE Nepal eastwards, E Himalaya, much of NE states. **Habitat:** forests, secondary growth, nullahs, sholas.

Little Spiderhunter

HOUSE SPARROW

Passer domesticus 15crn. **Male:** grey crown, rump; chestnut sides of neck, nape; black streaks on chestnut-rufous back, black chin, centre of throat, breast; white ear-coverts. The **Spanish Sparrow** *P hispaniolensis* male has chestnut crown and black streaks on flanks. **Female:** dull grey-brown above, streaked darker; dull whitish-brown below. Small parties to large gatherings: mostly commensal on man, feeding and nesting in and around habitation; feeds in cultivation; hundreds roost together. **Food:** seeds, insects. **Voice:** noisy, a medley of chirping notes; richer notes of breeding male; double and triple brooded. **Range:** all India to about 4000m in the Himalaya. **Habitat:** habitation, cultivation.

House Sparrow

Russet Sparrow

RUSSET SPARROW (Cinnamon Tree)
Passer rutilans 1.5cm. **Male:** rufous-chestnut above, streaked black on back; whitish wing-bars; black chin, centre of throat, bordered with dull yellow. **Female:** brown above, streaked darker; pale supercilium, wings-bars, dull ashy-yellow below. The **Eurasian Tree Sparrow** *P montanus* male has black patch on white ear-coverts and lacks yellow on throat sides. Gregarious mountain bird; mostly feeds on ground, picking seeds; may associate with other finches; often perches on dry branches, overhead wires. **Food:** seeds, insects. **Voice:** chirping notes; *swee..* Indian Robin-like call. **Range:** the Himalaya; NE; breeds at 1200-2600m, to about 4000m in NE; descends in winter. **Habitat:** cultivation, edges of forests, mountain habitations.

Chestnut-Shouldered Petronia

CHESTNUT-SHOULDERED PETRONIA (Yellow-Throated Sparrow)
Petronia xanthocollis 14cm. **Male:** dull brown-ish-grey above; chestnut shoulder-patch and white wing-bars diagnostic; lemon-yellow throat patch seen in good light. **Female:** rufous shoulder-patch and paler, often smaller, yellow throat-patch. Gregarious during monsoon and winter; moves considerably in some areas; keeps to tall, leafy trees in forest; may escape notice if not for its characteristic, frequent chirping; feeds on ground and also on flowering trees. **Food:** seeds, nectar, insects. **Voice:** pleasant chirping notes, a good aid in spotting and identi-fication. **Range:** all India; south of Himalayan foothills to 1400m. **Habitat:** forests, clearings, orchards, light habitation.

Forest Wagtail

FOREST WAGTAIL
Dendronanthus indicus 17cm. Sexes alike. Olive-brown above, dark-brown wings with yellow-spotted bands; dark tail with white outer feathers; dull buffy-white below; two black bands across lower throat and breast diagnostic. Solitary or in pairs on forest-paths and below trees; characteristic sideways movement of tail and rear part of body as it runs on ground; spends considerable time up in branches also, either when disturbed or sometimes resting during day; also runs on horizontal branches, picking insects. **Food:** insects, small snails, worms. **Voice:** *pink...* or *tsif..* call note. **Range:** breeds in Assam; winters in NE India, E and W Ghats, Sri I.anka; to about 2000m. **Habitat:** forests, clearings and cultivation, stream-sides.

WHITE WAGTAIL (Pied)

Motacilla alba 18cm. Ashy back, rump; white forehead, ear-coverts, large wing-patch and outer-tail feathers; black hind-crown, nape, continuous with throat and upper-breast; white below. The grey or black back and rump, white or black ear-coverts and absence of black eye-streak identify the various races. The **Masked Wagtail** *M personata* has black ear-coverts. Usually in pairs or small bands, often two races mixing freely; prefers damp areas; runs on ground, wagging tail constantly. **Food:** insects. **Voice:** sharp *cheet-sik* or *chizzit..,* uttered on the wing. **Range:** winter visitor over most of India; *personata* breeds sporadically in parts of NW and W Himalaya. **Habitat:** open damp areas, riverbanks, cultivation, roadside ditches, canals.

White Wagtail

WHITE-BROWED WAGTAIL (Large Pied)

Motacilla maderaspatensis 21cm. Black above; prominent white supercilium, large wing-band and outer tail feathers; black throat, breast; white below. Female is usually browner where male is black. The black-backed races of **White Wagtail** *M alba* have conspicuous white forehead. Mostly in pairs, though small parties may feed together in winter; a bird of flowing waters, being especially fond of rock-strewn rivers; feeds at edge of water wagging tail frequently. **Food:** insects. **Voice:** sharp *tzizit* or *cheezit..* call; pleasant whistling song of breeding male. **Range:** most of India south of Himalayan foothills to about 1200m; only resident wagtail in the Indian plains, breeding up to 2000m in peninsula mountains. **Habitat:** rocky streams, rivers, ponds, tanks, wet cultivation.

White-Browed Wagtail

CITRINE WAGTAIL (Yellow-Headed)

Motacilla citreola 17cm. Grey back; diagnostic yellow head, sides of face, complete underbody; white in dark wings. The Black-backed **Yellow-Headed Wagtail** *M c calcarata* has deep-black back and rump; yellow of head may be paler in female; plumage of races often confusing. Sociable, often with other wagtails; shows marked preference for damp areas, sometimes moves on floating vegetation on pond surfaces; either walks cautiously or makes short dashes. **Food:** insects, small snails. **Voice:** ordinary call note is a wheezy *tzzeep*, quite similar in-tone to Yellow Wagtail. **Range:** winter visitor over most of India; the black-backed race breeds in Ladakh, Lahaul and Spiti and Kashmir, between 1500-4600m. **Habitat:** marshes, wet cultivation, jheel-edges.

Citrine Wagtail

Tim Loseby

Yellow Wagtail

YELLOW WAGTAIL

Motacilla flava 17cm. Sexes almost alike. Olive back; slaty-grey head, ear-coverts; faint white supercilium; bright yellow below. Duller in winter. The commonest races are the Grey-headed Wagtail described above and the Blue-headed Yellow Wagtail *M f beema* with blue-grey head and clear white supercilium and malar streak. Small necks on marshy ground; moves gently or in short runs; very active, wags tail frequently; often huge congregations, in paddy cultivation and prior to departure to breeding grounds. **Food:** insects. **Voice:** high-pitched *weeezie...* and *tssreep...* notes, uttered mostly on wing. **Range:** winter visitor throughout India, including in Himalayan valleys. **Habitat:** marshy areas, cultivation, mangroves.

Joanna Van Grusien

Grey Wagtail

GREY WAGTAIL

Motacilla cinerea 17cm. **Br Male:** grey above; white supercilium; brownish wings, with yellow-white band; yellow-green at base of tail crump); blackish tail with white outer-feathers; black throat and white malar stripe; yellow below. **Wr Male and Female:** whitish-throat (sometimes mottled black in breeding female); paler-yellow below. Mostly solitary or in pairs; typical wagtail, feeding on ground, incessantly wagging tail; settles on house roofs and overhead wires. **Food:** insects, small molluscs. **Voice:** sharp *tzitsi..* calls, uttered on the wing; pleasant song and display flight of breeding male. **Range:** breeds in Himalaya, from N Baluchistan east to Nepal,1200-4300m; winters from foothills south throughout India. **Habitat:** rocky mountain streams in summer; open areas, forest clearings, waterside in winter.

M.K. Kuppuraj

Paddyfield Pipit

PADDYFIELD PIPIT

Anthus rufulus 15cm. Sexes alike. Fulvous-brown above, with dark-brown centres of feathers, giving a distinctive appearance; dark brown tail, with white outer-feathers, easily seen in flight; dull-fulvous below, streaked dark-brown on sides of throat, neck and entire breast. The winter-visiting **Tawny Pipit** *A campestris* usually lacks streaks on underbody while the **Blyth's Pipit** *A godlewskii* is indistinguishable in field, except by its harsher call-note, pairs or several scattered on ground; run in short spurts; singing males perch on grass-tufts. **Food:** insects, seeds, spiders. **Voice:** thin *tsip, tseep* and *tsip..tseep..* calls; trilling song of breeding male. **Range:** south of Himalaya. **Habitat:** grassland, marshy ground, cultivation.

OLIVE-BACKED PIPIT (Indian Tree Pipit)

Anthus hodgsoni 15cm. Sexes alike. Olive-brown above, streaked dark-brown; dull-white supercilium, two wing-bars and in outer tail-feathers; pale buff-white below, profusely streaked dark-brown on entire breast, flanks. The **Tree Pipit** *A trivialis* is brown above, without olive wash. Gregarious in winter; spends most time on ground, running briskly; if approached close, flies with *tseep..* call into trees. **Food:** insects, grass and other seeds. **Voice:** faint *tseep..* call; lark-like song of breeding male. **Range:** breeds in the Himalaya; winters in foothills and almost all over India, except arid NW, Kutch; *trivialis* breeds only in NW Himalaya and is commoner in winter over C India, but sporadically over range of *hodgsoni*. **Habitat:** forests, grassy slopes.

Olive-Backed Pipit

BROWN ACCENTOR

Prunella collaris 17cm. Sexes alike. Grey-brown above, streaked brown/rufous-brown on back; dark-brown wings with two pale-white wing bars; blackish-brown tail, with narrow buffy tip to feathers; whitish chin, throat, spotted black; grey throat-sides, breast, belly; flanks broadly-streaked chestnut. Pairs or up to half-dozen birds together; moves on ground, hops silently, often very close to observer; also settles on boulders, bush-tops. The **Brown Accentor** *P fulvescens* (15cm) has a diagnostic long white supercilium. **Food:** small insects, seeds. **Voice:** silent on ground, but utters a trilling *tchirrr..ip..* when flushed; sweet-sounding, warbling song (June-July), either from ground or during short display-flight. **Range:** high-mountain bird found in the Himalaya. **Habitat:** rocky areas, mountain slopes, stony meadows.

Brown Accentor

ROBIN ACCENTOR

Prunella rubeculoides 17cm. Sexes alike. Pale-brown above, streaked darker on back; grey head, throat; two whitish wing-bars; rufous breast and creamy-white belly; streaks on flanks. The **Rufous-Breasted Accentor** *P strophiata* (15cm) has heavily streaked throat and conspicuous rufous supercilium. Flocks in winter, occasionally along with other accentors, pipits and sparrows; rather tame; hops on ground, flies into bushes if intruded upon beyond a point. **Food:** insects, small seeds. **Voice:** a sharp trilling note; also a *tszi...tszi..;* short, chirping song. **Range:** high Himalaya; breeds 3200-5300m; descends in winter to about 2000m, rarely below 1500m. **Habitat:** Tibetan facies; damp grass, scrub.

Robin Accentor

R.K. Gaur

Streaked Weaver

Sunjoy Monga

Baya Weaver

Krupakar Senani

Red Avadavat

STREAKED WEAVER

Ploceus manyar 15cm. **Br Male:** yellow crown; blackish head-sides; fulvous streaks on dark brown back; heavily streaked lower throat, breast. **Female and Non br Male**: streaked above; yellow stripe over eye continues to behind ear-coverts; very pale below, boldly streaked on throat, breast. The **Black-Breasted Weaver** *P benghalensis* male has dark breast-band. Gregarious; prefers tall grass, reed beds in well-watered areas; active, as a rule not flying into trees; often nests close to other weavers. **Food:** seeds, grain, insects. **Voice:** high-pitched chirping, wheezy notes and chatter, much like Baya's. **Range:** south of the Himalaya; rare in Rajasthan and NW; the eastern race *peguensis* is darker, much more rufous above. **Habitat:** reed beds, tall grass in well-watered areas, marshes.

BAYA WEAVER

Ploceus philippinus 15cm. **Br Male:** bright yellow crown; dark brown above, streaked yellow; dark-brown ear-coverts, throat; yellow breast. **Female:** buffy-yellow above, streaked darker; pale supercilium, throat, turning buffy-yellow on breast, streaked on sides. **Non br Male:** bolder streaking than female; male of eastern race *burmanicus* has yellow restricted to crown. Gregarious; one of the most familiar and common birds of India, best known for its nest; keeps to cultivated areas, interspersed with trees; feeds on ground and in standing crop. **Food:** grain, seeds, insects, nectar. **Voice:** chirping and high-pitched wheezy notes of breeding male; very noisy at nest-colony (monsoons). **Range:** most of India from about 1000m in outer Himalaya; evidently absent in Kashmir. **Habitat:** open country, tree and palms.

RED AVADAVAT (Munia)

Amandava amandava 10cm. **Br Male:** crimson and brown, spotted white on wings, flanks; white-tipped tail. **Female:** brown above, spotted on wings; crimson rump; dull white throat; buffy grey breast, yellow-brown below. **Non br Male:** like female, but greyer throat, upper breast distinctive. Small flocks, often with other munias; partial to tall grass and scrub, preferably around well-watered areas; active and vibrant birds, rather confiding also; large numbers captured for bird markets. **Food:** grass seeds; also insects when breeding. **Voice:** shrill and high-pitched notes, uttered in flight also. **Range:** all India, south of Himalayan foothills. **Habitat:** tall grass, reeds, sugarcane, scrub, gardens.

GREEN AVADAVAT (Munia)

Amandava formosa 10cm. **Male:** olive-green above, with blackish tail; yellow below, paler on throat; prominent dark and white-barrings on flanks diagnostic. **Female:** more brown above, paler below, with fewer barrings on flanks. Small flocks, sometimes gathering into several dozen birds; does not usually associate with other munias; like others of family, feeds on ground, picking up grass seeds; sometimes raids standing crops; when disturbed, the flock flies off into grass or bush, occasionally uttering faint *scheep..* calls. **Food:** mostly small seeds. **Voice:** faint *swee...swee...* notes; when disturbed, a variation on this note. **Range:** broad belt across C India, from around Mt Abu to C Orissa and south to N Andhra Pradesh and around Mahabaleshwar; evidently absent in the coastal regions. **Habitat:** sugarcane, scrub and grass.

Green Avadavat

INDIAN SILVERBILL (White-Throated Munia)

Lonchura malabarica 10cm. Sexes alike. Dull-brown above, with white rump; very dark, almost black, wings, pointed tail; pale buffy-white below, with some brown on flanks; thick, grey-blue or slaty beak striking. Gregarious, mostly keeps to scrub in open country; feeds on ground and on standing crop, especially millet; overall a rather 'dull' bird, both in colour and demeanour. **Food:** small seeds, millet. **Voice:** faint *tee..tee..* notes; sometimes also a whistling note. **Range:** all India; to about 1500m in Himalaya, chiefly the outer ranges. **Habitat:** prefers dry areas; cultivation, scrub and grass; sometimes light, open forests.

Indian Silverbill

WHITE-RUMPED MUNIA (White-Backed)

Lonchura striata 10cm. Sexes alike. Blackish-brown above, with conspicuous white rump; at close range, pale (shaft) streaks visible on back; dark wings and pointed tail; dark-brown throat; whitish-cream below. The race *acuticauda* of Himalayan foothills and NE regions has a grey belly with fine streaks. Small to medium-sized flocks, often seen along with other munias; quite active, feeds on ground and also on standing crops and grasses, sometimes large, mixed gatherings can cause damage to standing crops. **Food:** grass seeds, crops; also feeds on insects, especially when breeding (chiefly during rains). **Range:** peninsular India, south of line from S Gujarat, across C Madhya Pradesh to S Bihar and Orissa. **Habitat:** scrub, cultivation, grass; forests and orchards.

White-Rumped Munia

Scaly-Breasted Munia

SCALY-BREASTED MUNIA (Spotted)

Lonchura punctulata 10cm. Sexes alike. Choco-brown above; olivish-yellow, pointed tail; white bars on rump; chestnut sides of face, chin, throat; white below, thickly speckled with very dark brown on breast, flanks and part of belly (speckles may be absent during winter and much of summer). Sociable, moving in flocks of six to several dozen birds, often with other munias, weaver birds; feeds on ground and low bush, but rests in trees. **Food:** seeds, small berries; also insects. **Voice:** common call a double-noted *ki.tee....ki.tee.* **Range:** most of India, to about 1500m in parts of the Himalaya; absent in much of Punjab, NW regions and W Rajasthan. **Habitat:** open scrub, cultivation, especially where interspersed with trees; also gardens.

Black-Headed Munia

BLACK-HEADED MUNIA

Lonchura malacca 10cm. Sexes alike. Black head, throat, breast, belly centre and thighs; rufous-chestnut back, deeper chestnut on rump; white upper belly, sides of underbody. The races *rubroniger* and *atricapilla* of N and NE India have white of lower parts replaced by chestnut. Gregarious, except when breeding, as in other munias; prefers reed beds and cultivation, especially where flooded; during breeding season (rains), often seen along with Streaked Weaver birds; feeds on ground. **Food:** grass seeds, paddy; occasionally insects. **Voice:** faint, *pee...pee...* calls. **Range:** foothills and terai from SE Punjab eastwards; most of NE, N Orissa; peninsular India south of line from Bombay to S Madhya Pradesh. **Habitat:** reed beds, paddy, grass and scrub.

Fire-Fronted Serin

FIRE-FRONTED SERIN (Gold-Fronted Finch)

Serinus pusillus 12cm. Sexes alike. Scarlet-orange forehead; blackish-grey crown; buffy back, streaked dark; yellow-orange rump, shoulder; yellow wing-edges and whitish wing-bars; sooty-brown below, with grey and buff; dull yellow-buff belly and flanks, streaked brown. Gregarious; quite active and on the move; feeds on flower-heads and on ground; drinks and bathes often; spends considerable time in bushes and low trees. **Food:** flower and grass seeds; small berries. **Voice:** pleasant twittering *chrr..chrr*; a faint *tree...tree...* call-note. **Range:** W Himalaya, extreme west to Garhwal; 750-4500m; breeds mostly at 2400-4000m. **Habitat:** rocky, bush-covered mountainsides.

YELLOW-BREASTED GREENFINCH (Himalayan)

Carduelis spinoides 14cm. **Male:** blackish-brown crown, ear-coverts, malar stripe; yellow forehead, supercilium, sides of neck; greenish-brown back, streaked dark; wings have yellow, black-brown and some white; yellow rump, sides of tail; yellow below. **Female:** duller, with less yellow in wings. The male **Tibetan Siskin** *C thibetana* (12cm) of NE lacks dark-brown above. Usually small flocks; keeps to low growth, feeding on flower-heads; moves considerably. **Food:** flower and other seeds; also insects. **Voice:** twittering *dwit.it.it..* notes; also a long-drawn *weeeee.chu* call, rather Iora-like; liquid song. **Range:** the Himalaya; foothills to about 4400m; breeds mostly about 1800-3000m. **Habitat:** forest slopes, meadows, gardens, scrub.

Yellow-Breasted Greenfinch

EUROPEAN GOLDFINCH

Carduelis carduelis 14cm. Sexes alike. Crimson forehead; greyish-brown above, with large, white rump-patch and black and white; black and yellow wings striking, at rest and in flight. Young birds have streaked upperparts. Sociable; forages on ground; also attends to flower-heads; undulating, somewhat dancing flight. **Food:** seeds of flowers, especially thistle and sunflowers. **Voice:** ordinary call-note a somewhat liquid *witwit..witwit..* ; pleasant, twittering song; also a *chhrrilk* call. **Range:** the Himalaya, extreme west to around C Nepal; breeds mostly 2000-4000m, ascending somewhat more; descends into foothills in winter. **Habitat:** open coniferous forests, orchards, cultivation, scrub.

European Goldfinch

PLAIN MOUNTAIN FINCH (Hodgson's)

Leucosticte nemoricola 15cm. Sexes alike. Grey-brown above, streaked dark-brown; greyer on rump; pale buffy bar and markings in dark-brown wings; dull grey-brown below, streaked browner on breast-sides and flanks. The **Brandt's Mountain Finch** *L brandti* (18cm) is darker above, with rosy-pink rump and white in outer-tail. Finches with plenty of white in wings, and found in the high Tibetan country of the Himalaya are snow finches. Gregarious; good-sized flocks on ground, amidst stones; calls often when feeding. **Food:** grass and other seeds; small insects. **Voice:** twittering and chattering notes, rather sparrowlike in tone; call frequently. **Range:** high Himalaya, breeds about 3200-4800m (above timber-line); descends in winter, occasionally to as low as 1000m. **Habitat:** open meadows, dwarf scrub, cultivation.

Plain Mountain Finch

DARK-BREASTED ROSEFINCH (Nepal)

Carpodacus nipalensis 15cm. **Male:** crimson-rose forehead; rose-red supercilium and dark, broad eye-stripe; deep crimson-brown above; pinkish throat and dark crimson-maroon breast-band. **Female:** buff-brown above; two buffy wing-bars; unstreaked below. Absence of crimson on rump identifies male from Common and Blanford's; female Blanford's is unstreaked below, but grey belly and white undertail distinctive. Small parties, sometimes with others; feeds on ground and bush. **Food:** seeds, berries. **Voice:** plaintive, two-note whistle. **Range:** the Himalaya, east of W Nepal; breeds about 3000-4400m; descends in winter. **Habitat:** rhododendron, fir forests; bushy, rocky slopes; clearings.

COMMON ROSEFINCH

Carpodacus erythrinus 15cm. **Male:** crimson above, tinged brown; dark eye-stripe; crimson rump, underbody, fading into dull rose-white belly. **Female:** buff-brown above, streaked dark; two pale wing-bars; dull-buff below, streaked, except on belly. The male **Blanford's Rosefinch** *C rubescens* lacks dark eye-stripe and has two crimson wing-bars. Small flocks; feeds in bush, on crops and ground; associates with other birds. **Food:** crop seeds, fruit, buds, nectar. **Voice:** rather quiet in winter; pleasant song of up to eight notes; may sing before departure from wintering grounds; also a double-noted, questioning, *twee..ee* call. **Range:** breeds in the Himalaya, 2700-4000m; winters over most of India. **Habitat:** cultivation, open forests, gardens, bushes.

Common Rosefinch

PINK-BROWED ROSEFINCH

Carpodacus rodochrous 15cm. **Male:** rosy-pink forehead, broad supercilium; crimson-brown, unstreaked crown, eye-stripe; streaked back and pinkish rump, underbody. **Female:** streaked throughout; pale yellowish supercilium. The **Red-mantled Rosefinch** *C rhodochlamys* (18cm) is similar, but larger. The **Beautiful Rosefinch** *C pulcherrimus* has streaked crown. Usually small flocks, sometimes with others; feeds on ground, on paths and clearings; perches on trees and in bush; undergoes considerable altitudinal movement. **Food:** seeds, berries. **Voice:** single-noted, *sweet..* call; song of breeding male. **Range:** the Himalaya, less common in E Himalaya; breeds about 2800-4000m; winters low, sometimes to 600m. **Habitat:** open forests, dwarf junipers, upland habitation.

Pink-Browed Rosefinch

Joanna Van Gruisen

Otto Pfister

STREAKED ROSEFINCH (Eastern Great)

Carpodacus rubicilloides 19cm. **Male:** crimson-red head, sides, underbody spotted white; grey-brown back washed pink and streaked brown; pinkish rump. **Female:** grey-brown, streaked; pale-buff below, streaked dark. The **Great Rose-finch** *C rubicilla* is paler, with fewer streaks on back. The **Red-fronted Rosefinch** *C puniceus* (20cm) is more scarlet. Small parties, occasionally several dozens together; may associate with others, feeds on ground and in bushes; a bird of higher regions, even in winter. **Food:** seeds, berries. **Voice:** loud, single-note call. **Range:** high Himalaya, Ladakh to Bhutan; breeds above 3500m, to about 4800m; usually does not descend below 2000m in winter. **Habitat:** high-altitude barren areas, scrub.

Streaked Rosefinch

RED CROSSBILL

Loxia curvirostra 15cm. **Male:** dull-red above, lightly marked brown; dark stripe through eyes; blackish wings, short, forked tail; unmarked dull-red below. **Female:** olivish above, lightly marked brown; yellower on rump, dark brown wings, tail; olive-yellow below. The crossed mandibles are seen at close range. Small, active parties; keep to conifer-tops; unique beak helps feed on conifer seeds; clings sideways and upside-down to extract seeds from cones; also descends on ground. **Food:** chiefly conifer seeds. **Voice:** fairly loud *chip..chip..chip..* call, both when feeding and during flight; creaky, trilling song. **Range:** the Himalaya, east of Himachal; 2700-4000m; may descend in winter. **Habitat:** coniferous forests.

Red Crossbill

RED-HEADED BULLFINCH

Pyrrhula erythrocephala 17cm. **Male:** black around base of beak, eyes; brick-red crown; grey back: white rump; glossy purple black wings, forked tail; black chin; rust-red below; ashy white belly. **Female:** like male, but olive-yellow on crown; grey brown back, underbody. The male **Orange Bullfinch** *P aurantiaca* (14cm) of W Himalaya has orange-yellow back and underbody; female is yellow-brown. Small parties, occasionally with other birds; feed in low bushes, sometimes on ground; a bird of cover, rather quiet and secretive. **Food:** seeds, buds, berries; also flower-nectar. **Voice:** single or double-noted *pheu..pheu..* call. **Range:** the Himalaya, Kashmir to extreme east; breeds 2400-4000m; descends in winter to about 1200m. **Habitat:** forests, bushes.

Red-Headed Bullfinch

Joanna Van Gruisan

Black-and-Yellow Grosbeak

BLACK-AND-YELLOW GROSBEAK

Mycerobas icterioides 22cm. **Male:** black head, throat, wings, tail and thighs; yellow collar, back, underbody below breast; thick, finchbill. **Female:** grey above; buffy rump, belly. The very similar male **Collared Grosbeak** *M affinis* is brighter yellow (often with orangish wash), with yellow thighs. Small parties in tall coniferous forest also feeds on ground and bushes, but spends much time in higher branches, where difficult to see; rather noisy. **Food:** conifer seeds, shoots; also berries and insects. **Voice:** loud two- or three-noted whistle is familiar birdcall of W Himalaya; loud *chuck...chuck* note when feeding; rich song of male. **Range:** the Himalaya. **Habitat:** mountain forests.

Tim Inskipp

White-Winged Grosbeak

WHITE-WINGED GROSBEAK

Mycerobas carnipes 22cm. **Male:** black above, on throat and breast; olive-yellow rump, belly and wing-spots; larger, white wing-patch. **Female:** brownish-grey where male is black; streaks on ear-coverts. The **Spot-Winged Grosbeak** *M melanozanthos* male is uniformly black above, with more white in wings; less black below, more bright yellow; female is boldly streaked black and yellow. Small flocks, often with other grosbeaks; active and noisy; mostly feeds in higher branches. **Food:** chiefly seeds of juniper; also other seeds, fruit; insects, especially when breeding. **Voice:** loud three- or four-noted calls, usually from treetop; sometimes a harsh note. **Range:** the Himalaya, extreme west to east; 1500-4000m, but mostly above 2500m, even in winter. *M melanozanthos* descends much lower in winter. **Habitat:** dwarf juniper above timberline; high forest; may be seen in bamboo and pine during winter.

Tim Inskipp

Gold-Naped Finch

GOLD-NAPED FINCH (Gold-Headed Black)

Pyrrhoplectes epauletta 15cm. **Male:** orange-yellow hindcrown, nape; blackish plumage; white on tertiaries seen as conspicuous 'V' on wing/lower-back. **Female:** greenish crown, grey nape; rufous-brown above; grey-black wing-tips, tail; dull-brown below; white wing-lining as in male. Small parties of eight to ten birds; feeds mostly on ground and low bushes. **Food:** seeds, berries. **Voice:** high-pitched *pew..pew..* call. **Range:** the Himalaya: Himachal eastwards; breeds about 2800-4000m; descends in winter to 1400m. **Habitat:** rhododendron and ringal bamboo in summer; dense bushes; scrub in winter.

CRESTED BUNTING

Melophus lathami 15cm. **Male:** striking glossy blade plumage, with long, pointed crest and chestnut wings, tail. **Female:** crested; olive-brown above, streaked darker; rufous in wings distinctive; buffy-yellow below, streaked dark on breast; darkish moustachial stripe. Small flocks; feeds on ground and mountainsides, perches on ruins, walls, stones and low bushes; on ground, an active and upright bird. **Food:** grass seeds; presumably also insects. **Voice:** faint *chip..* call; pleasant, though somewhat monotonous song of breeding male (May-August). **Range:** resident over wide part of India, from outer Himalaya to about 1800m south to SW Maharashtra and N Andhra; appears to move considerably after the rains. **Habitat:** open, bush and rock-covered mountainsides, open country: also cultivation.

Crested Bunting

ROCK BUNTING

Emberiza cia 15cm. **Male:** blue-grey head with black coronal stripe, eye-stripe, malar stripe, the latter curled and meeting eye-stripe diagnostic; whitish supercilium, cheeks; pale chestnut-brown back, streaked dark; unmarked rump; white outersides of dark tail distinctive; blue-grey throat, breast; rufous-chestnut below. **Female:** slightly duller. The male **Chestnut-Eared Bunting** *E fucata* has black-streaked grey head, white throat, breast and chestnut ear-coverts. Solitary or in small parties; active and restless; nicks tail often; regularly settles on bushes and trees. **Food:** seeds, small insects. **Voice:** squeaky *tsip...tsip..* note, calls often; common bird-call of W Himalaya; has squeaky song of several notes. **Range:** the Himalaya; winters in foothills and plains of N India. **Habitat:** grassy, rocky hillsides in open forests; cultivation, scrub.

Rock Bunting

GREY-NECKED BUNTING

Emberiza buchanani 15cm. **Male:** grey head with white eye-ring; brown-back, with faint rufous wash and dark streaks; white edges of dark tail; whitish throat, mottled rufous; dark moustachial stripe, not easily visible; pale rufous-chestnut below. **Female:** somewhat duller than male; more prominent moustachial stripe. Winter visitor; small flocks, feeds mostly on ground, sometimes along with other birds; quite active. **Food:** grass seeds, sometimes grain. **Voice:** a faint single note. **Range:** winter visitor; quite common over W and C India. **Habitat:** open rocky grassy country, scrub.

Grey-Necked Bunting

White-Capped Bunting

WHITE-CAPPED BUNTING (Chestnut-Breasted)

Emberiza stewarti 15cm. **Male:** grey-white top of head; black eye-stripe, whitish cheeks, black chin, upper-throat distinctive; chestnut back, rump; white outer-tail; white breast with chestnut gorget below; dull-fulvous below, chestnut flanks. **Female:** lacks black and white head pattern of male; brown above, streaked; rufous-chestnut rump; fulvous-buff below, with rufous breast. The male **House Bunting** *E striolata* (14cm), with more or less overlapping range, has grey-white head, completely streaked black. Small flocks, often with other buntings, finches; feeds on ground; rests in bushes, trees. **Food:** chiefly grass seeds. **Voice:** faint but sharp *tsit..* or *chit..* note. **Range:** breeds in W Himalaya, extreme west to Garhwal, 1500-3500m; winters in W Himalayan foothills, and over extensive parts of W and C India, south to Maharashtra. **Habitat:** open, grass-covered, rocky hillsides, scrub.

Yellow-Breasted Bunting

YELLOW-BREASTED BUNTING

Emberiza aureola 15cm. **Br Male:** blackish forehead, sides of face, chin, throat; deep chestnut above; yellow throat, neck-sides; chestnut upper-breast-band; yellow below, streaked flanks. Black mask absent in winter, when dark ear-coverts and yellow supercilium distinctive. **Female:** brown above, streaked; pale crown stripe, supercilium, edged by dark stripes; pale-chestnut rump; yellow below; streaked flanks. Winter visitor; small flocks, up to forty birds; associates with other buntings, finches; mostly feeds on ground. **Food:** seeds, grain; catches insects. **Voice:** a *tzip...tzip...* note; also a soft *trrssit.* **Range:** quite common in winter from Nepal eastwards, in plains and terai. **Habitat:** cultivation, scrub; habitation, gardens.

Black-Headed Bunting

BLACK-HEADED BUNTING

Emberiza melanocephala 18cm. **Male:** black head; thin yellow collar and rufous-chestnut back: unmarked yellow below, with some rufous on breast-sides; wing-bars. **Female:** dull fulvous-brown above, streaked; yellowish rump; pale buff-yellow below; very similar to female Red-Headed Bunting. Gregarious; winter visitor, often great numbers with other buntings, notably the Red-headed; feeds on crops and ground; does considerable damage to standing crop; bold, not easily driven away from croplands; in most areas, the yellow males are in greater numbers. **Food:** seeds, grain. **Voice:** musical *tzeett..* call-note; a faint *chip...* occasionally. **Range:** common in winter (mid-September to April) over wide part in W and C India; Gujarat, Rajasthan, W and C Madhya Pradesh, Maharashtra, parts of Karnataka. **Habitat:** open cultivation.

RED-HEADED BUNTING
Emberiza bruniceps 17cm. **Male:** rufous-chestnut crown, throat, breast; olive-yellow back, streaked blackish; unmarked yellow rump; whitish wing-bars; yellow neck-sides, under-body below breast. **Female:** pale-brown above, streaked; yellowish rump. The male **Chestnut Bunting** *E rutila* (14cm) is completely chestnut above and on throat. Highly gregarious winter visitor; huge numbers, frequently along with Black-headed; cause considerable damage to crops. **Food:** seeds, grain. **Voice:** high-pitched *tzeett..* call. **Range:** common winter visitor over most of country south of the Himalaya; absent in extreme south and along eastern coastal regions. **Habitat:** open cultivated areas.

Red-Headed Bunting

WHITE-BROWED ROSEFINCH
Carpodacus thura 17cm. **Male:** brown above, streaked blackish; pink and white forehead, su-percilium; dark eye-stripe; rose-pink rump and double wing-bar. **Female:** streaked brown; broad, whitish supercilium and single wing-bar; yellow rump; buffy below, streaked. The white in supercilium easily iden-tifies this species. Small flocks, either by themselves or with other finches; mostly feeds on ground, but settles on bushes and small trees. **Food:** seeds, berries. **Voice:** calls often when feeding on ground, a fairly loud *pupuepipi* call. **Range:** the Himalaya, breeds 3000-4000m; winters to about 1800m. **Habitat:** tree-line forests, fir, juniper, rhododendron; open mountainsides and bushes in winter.

White-Browed Rosefinch

Glossary

adult	Mature, capable of breeding. Final plumage.
aquatic	Living on or in water.
altitudinal migrant	Moving between low valleys and high mountains.
arboreal	Living in trees.
banyan	A fig tree (*Ficus bengalensis*).
biotope	An area of uniform environment, flora and fauna.
bund	Man-made embankment.
cap	Upper head.
carpal	The forward pointing area on a closed wing.
casque	Growth above bill of hornbills.
cere	Patch of bare skin at base of bill of raptors.
colonial	Nesting in close colonies.
crepuscular	Active at dusk.
crown	Upper part of head.
culmen	Ridge on the upper bill.
deciduous	Forests that shed leaves seasonally.
dimorphic	Having more than one form of plumage.
diurnal	Active during daytime.
duars	Forested areas, south of eastern Himalaya.
eclipse	Changed plumage after breeding seasons.
endemic	Indigenous and confined.
evergreen	Forests that retain their leaves.
family	Specific group of genera.
fledglings	Phase in chicks.
flight feathers	Primaries, secondaries and tail feathers.
frugivorous	Fruit eating.
fulvous	Brownish-yellow.
genus	Group of related species.
ghats	Hills parallel to the east and west coasts of India.
gorget	Band across upper chest.
granivorous:	Grain eating.
gregarious	Living in communities or flocks.
hackles	Long and pointed neck feathers.
hawking	Capturing phases prior to adult.
immature	Plumage phases prior to adult.
iris	Coloured eye membrane surrounding pupil.
jheel	Shallow lake or wetland.
juvenile	Immature bird immediately after leaving nest.

leading edge	Front edge of forewing.
lores	Area in front of eye.
mandible	Bill or beak.
malar	Stripe on side of throat.
mantle	Back and adjoining areas.
mask	Dark plumage round eye and ear-coverts.
migration	Seasonal movement.
morph	One of several distinct types of plumage in the same species.
monsoon	Rainy season.
moult	Seasonal shedding of plumage.
nape	Back of neck.
nocturnal	Active at night.
nomadic	Species without specific territory except when breeding.
nullah	Ditch or stream bed.
orbital ring	Narrow ring of skin or feathers round the eye.
passerines	Perching and song birds.
pectoral	The breast area.
pipal	A tree of the fig family (*Ficus religiosa*).
primaries	Main flight feathers.
raptors	Birds of prey, excluding owls.
resident	Non-migratory.
rump	Lower back and base of tail.
secondaries	Lesser tail feathers.
sholas	Small forests in valleys.
speculum	Area of colour on wings.
submontane	Low foothills.
subterminal band	Broad band on outer part of feather.
supercilium	Streak above eye.
terai	Alluvial stretch of land, south of Himalaya.
terminal band	Broad band on tip of tail.
terrestial	Ground living.
trailing edge	Rear edge of wing.
vinaceous	Red wine coloured.
Wattle	Bare skin, often coloured on part of head.

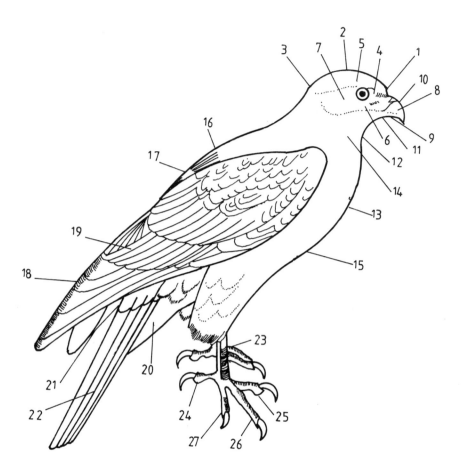

1. **Forehead**
2. **Crown**
3. **Nape**
4. **Nores**
5. **Supercilium**
6. **Cheeks**
7. **Bar-coverts**
8. **Upper mandible**
9. **Lower mandible**
10. **Culmen or bill ridge**
11. **Chin**
12. **Throat**
13. **Breast**
14. **Neck**
15. **Belly**
16. **Back**
17. **Wing coverts**
18. **Primaries**
19. **Secondaries**
20. **Under tail coverts**
21. **Upper tail coverts**
22. **Tail feathers**
23. **Tarsus**
24. **Hind toe**
25. **Inner toe**
26. **Middle toe**
28. **Outer toe**

Bibliography

Anon. (1891) *List of Bird's Eggs in the Indian Museum.* Calcutta: Indian Museum.

Anon. (1987) *Checklist of Birds of Kaziranga & Manas Sanctuaries.* Bombay: IIT.

Anon. (1988) *Rare Birds of India.*Calcutta: Botanical Survey of India.

Anon. (1990) *Wealth of India; Birds.* New Delhi: CSIR.

Anon. (1991) *Pitti Island, Lakshadweep: An Ornithological Study.* Madras; Madras Naturalists' Society.

Anon. (1992) *India's Wetlands, Mangroves and Coral Reefs.* New Delhi: WWF.

Anon. (1993) *Directory of Indian Wetlands.* New Delhi: WWF.

Anon. (1994) *Sri Lanka Avifaunal List (in Sinhala-English).* Colombo: The Wildlife & Nature Protection Society of Sri Lanka.

Anon. (1995) *Fauna of Tiger Reserves.* Calcutta: ZSI.

Anon. (1997) *Pocket Guide to Common Birds of South Gujarat.* Surat: Nature Club.

Anon. (undated) *Birds of Pachmari Wildlife Sanctuary.*

Anon. *Endemic Birds of Sri Lanka.* Sri Lanka: Dept. of Wildlife Conservation.

Anon. *Breeding Waterbirds Sanctuary, Keoladeo Ghana, Bharatpur.* Bombay: BNHS.

Anon. (undated) *Birds of Delhi & District.*

Anon. (undated) *Glimpses of Glorious Bharatpur. A Conspectus.* New Delhi: Oxford Printing Works.

Abdulali, H. (1973) *Checklist of the Birds of Maharashtra with Notes on Their Status Around Bombay.* Bombay: BHNS.

Abdulali, H. & Panday, J.D. (1978) *Checklist of the Birds of Delhi, Agra and Bharatpur.* New Delhi: published by the author.

Abdulali, H. (1981) *Checklist of the Birds of Borivali National Park with Notes on Their Status.* Bombay: BNHS.

Agarwal, R. & Bhatnagar, R. (eds.) (1982) *Management of Problem Birds in Aviation and Agriculture.* New Delhi : IARI.

Ahimaz, P. (1990) *Birds of Madras.* Madras: CPR Environmental Education Centre.

Ali, S. & Abdulali, H. (1941) *The Birds of Bombay and Salsette.* Bombay: Prince of Wales Museum.

Ali, S. (1941) *The Book of Indian Birds.* Bombay: BNHS.

Ali, S. (1945) *The Birds of Kutch.* London: OUP.

Ali, S. (1949) *Indian Hill Birds.* Bombay: OUP.

Ali, S. (1953) *The Birds of Travancore and Cochin.* Bombay: OUP.

Ali, S. (1956) *The Birds of Gujarat.* Bombay: Gujarat Research Society.

Ali, S. (1960) *A Picture Book of Sikkim Birds.* Gangtok: Government of Sikkim.

Ali, S. (1962) *The Birds of Sikkim.* Delhi: OUP.

Ali, S. & Ripley, D. (1964-74*) Handbook of the Birds of India & Pakistan* (Vols. 1-10). Bombay: OUP.

Ali, S. & Futehally, L. (1967) *Common Birds.* New Delhi: NBT.

Ali, S. (1968) *Common Indian Birds, A Picture Album.* New Delhi: NBT.

Ali, S. (1969) *Birds of Kerala.* Madras: OUP.

Ali, S. & Futehally, L .(1969) *Hamare Parichat Pakshee (in Hindi).* New Delhi: NBT.

Ali, S. (1977) *Field Guide to the Birds of the Eastern Himalayas.* Bombay: OUP.

Ali, S. (1979) *Bird Study in India: Its History and its Importance.* New Delhi: ICCR.

Ali, S. & Hussain, S.A. (1980-86) *Studies on the Movement and Population of Indian Avifauna. Annual Reports I-4.* Bombay: BNHS

Ali, S. (1980) *Ecological Reconnaissance of Vedaranyam Swamp, Thanjavur District, Tamil Nadu.* Bombay: BNHS.

Ali, S. *et al.* (1981) *Harike Lake Avifauna Project.* Bombay: BNHS.

Ali, S. & Grubh, R. (1981-89) *Ecological Study of Bird Hazard at Indian Aerodromes* (Vols. I & 2). Bombay: BNHS.

Ali, S. & Grubh, R. *Potential Problem Birds at Indian Aerodromes*. Bombay: BNHS.

Ali, S. & Rahmani, A. (1982-89) *The Great Indian Bustard* (Vols.1-2). Bombay: BNHS.

Ali, S. & Ripley, D. (1983) *A Pictorial Guide to the Birds of the Indian Subcontinent*. Bombay: OUP.

Ali, S., Rahmani *et al.* (1984) *The Lesser Florican in Sailana*. Bombay: BNHS.

Ali, S. *et al.* (1984) *Strategy for Conservation of Bustards in Maharashtra*. Bombay: BNHS.

Ali, S . (1985) *Fall of a Sparrow*. Bombay: OUP.

Ali, S. *et al.* (1985) *The Great Indian Bustard in Gujarat*. Bombay: BNHS.

Ali, S.& Vijayan, S. (1986) *Keoladeo National Park Ecology Study*. Bombay: BNHS.

Ali, S., Daniel J.C. & Rahmani, A. (1986) *Study of Ecology of Some Endangered Species of Wildlife and Their Habitat. The Floricans*. Bombay: BNHS.

Ali, S. & Ripley, D. (1987) *Handbook of the Birds of India & Pakistan*. Compact Ed. Bombay: OUP.

Ali, S. (1990) *Status and Ecology of the Lesser and Bengal Floricans with Reports on Jerdon's Courser and Mountain Quail*. Bombay: BNHS.

Ali, S. (1996) *The Book of Indian Birds*. (12th and enlarged centenary ed.) New Delhi: BNHS & OUP.

Ali, S., Biswas, B. & Ripley, D. (1996) *Birds of Bhutan*. Calcutta: ZSI.

Ambedkar, V.C. (1964) *Some Indian Weaver Birds*. Bombay: Univ. of Bombay.

Ara, J. (1970) *Watching Birds*. New Delhi: NBT.

BNHS (1996) *Dr. Salim Ali Centenary Issue Vol . 93, No.3*. Bombay: BNHS.

Babault, G. (1920) *Mission Guy Babault dans les Provinces Centrales de l'Inde dans la Region Occidentale de l'Himalaya et Ceylon 1914. Resultats Scientifiques*. Oiseaux. Impimerie Generale Lahure, Paris. (French)

Badshah, M.A. (1968) *Checklist of the Birds of Tamil Nadu*. Madras: Forest Department.

Baker, E.C.S. (1908) *The Indian Ducks and Their Allies*. Bombay: BNHS.

Baker, E.C.S. (1913) *Indian Pigeons and Doves*. London: Witherby & Co.

Baker, E.C.S. (1921-30) *Game-Birds of India, Burma & Ceylon*. (Vols. I-3). London: John Bale.

Baker, E.C.S. (1922-31) *Fauna of British India. BIRDS* (Vols. I-8). London: Taylor and Francis.

Baker, E.C.S. (1923) *A Handlist of the Genera and Species of Birds of the Indian Empire*. Bombay: BNHS.

Baker, E.C.S. (1923) *Handlist of the Birds of the Indian Empire*. Bombay: RO Spence.

Baker, E.C.S. (1932-35) *The Nidification of Birds of the Indian Empire*. (Vols.1-4) London: Taylor and Francis.

Baker, E.C.S. (1942) *Cuckoo Problems*. London: H.F. & G. Witherby.

Baker, H.R. & Inglis, C.M. (1930) *The Birds of Southern India: Madras, Malabar, Travancore, Cochin, Coorg and Mysore*. Madras: Govt. Press.

Banks, J. (1980) *A Selection of the Birds of Sri Lanka*. London: Authors Publication.

Baral, H.S. (undated) *Birds of Chitwan*. Kathmandu: Victoria Travels.

Barnes, H.E. (1885) *Handbook to the Birds of the Bombay Presidency*. Calcutta: Calcutta Central Press.

Bates, R.S.P. (1931) *Bird Life in India*. Madras: Madras Diocesan Press.

Bates, R.S.P. & Lowther, E.H.N. (1952) *Breeding Birds of Kashmir*. Bombay: OUP.

Beebe, W. (1927,1994) *Pheasant Jungles*. Reading: WPA.

Bhamburkar, P.M. & Desai, N. (1993) *Study Report of Mansingh Deo Wildlife Sanctuary*. Nagpur: WWF.

Bhushan, B. (1993) *Jerdon's or Double-banded Courser—a Preliminary Survey*. Bombay: BNHS.

Blyth, E. (1849-52) *Catalogue of the Birds in the Museum of Asiatic Society*. Calcutta: J. Thomas Baptist Mission Press.

Biswas, B. (1953) *A Checklist of Genera of Indian Birds*.

Buckton, S. (1995) *Indian Birding Itineraries*. Sandy UK: OBC.

Burg, G. *et al.* (1994) *Ornithology of the Indian Subcontinent 1872-1992. An Annotated Bibliography*. Washington DC: Smithsonian Institution.

Butler, E.A. (1879) *A Catalogue of the Birds of Sind, Katiawar, North Gujarat and Mount Aboo.* Bombay

Butler, E.A .(1880) *A Catalogue of the Birds of the Southern Portion of the Bombay Presidency.* Bombay.

Bump, G. (1964) *A Study and Review of the Black Francolin and the Gray Francolin.*

Chakravarthy, A.K. & Tejasvi, K.P.C.C. (1992) *Birds of Hill Region of Karnataka.* Bangalore: Navbharath Enterprises.

Chatrath, K.J.S. (1992) *Wetlands of India.* New Delhi: Ashish Pub. House.

Chaudhari, A.B. & Chakrabarti (undated) *Wildlife Biology of the Sundarbans Forests, A Study of the Breeding Biology of Birds.* Calcutta: Office of the Divisional Forest Officer.

Christensen, G.C. *et al.* (1964) *A Study and Review of the Common Indian Sandgrouse and the Imperial Sandgrouse.*

Chopra, U.C. (1984) *Our Feathered Friends.* New Delhi: CBT.

Choudhury , A . (1990) *Checklist of the Birds of Assam.* Guwahati: Sofia Press.

Choudhury, A. (993) *A Naturalist in Karbi-Anglong.* Guwahati: Sofia Press.

Choudhury, A. (1995) *Wildlife Surveys in Bherjan, Borajan, and Podumani Reserve Forests of Tinsukia Dist. Assam.* Guwahati: Rhino Foundation.

Choudhury, A. (1996) *Surveys of the White-winged Duck and the Bengal Florican in Tinsukia District and Adjacent Areas of Assam and Arunachal Pradesh.* Guwahati: The Rhino Foundation.

Cocker, Mark & Inskipp, C. (1988) *Hodgson: A Himalayan Ornithologist.* London: OUP.

Cox, J. (1985) *Observation on Falconry and Pakistan.*

Cunningham, Lt.-Col. D.D. (1903*) Some Indian Friends and Acquaintances.* London: John Murray.

Curson, J. *Birding in Southern India and the Andamans. A Guide to Selected Sites.*

Dani, C.S. (1992) *A Checklist of the Birds of Orissa.* Government of Orissa: Wildlife Wing, Forest Dept.

Daniel, J.C. *et al.* (1986-87) *Blacknecked Crane in Ladakh.* Parts I-2. Bombay: BNHS.

Daniel, J.C. *et al.* (1991-95) *Ecology and Behavior of Resident Raptors with Special Reference to Endangered Species.* Parts I-3. Bombay: BNHS.

Daniel, J.C. & Rao Y.N. (1991) *Ecology of Point Calimere Sanctuary.* Bombay: BNHS.

Daniels, R. (1983) *Birds of Madurai Campus.* Madurai: ACRI.

Daniels, R. (1992). *Birds of Urban South India.* Bangalore: Indian Institute of Science.

Daniels, R. (1996) *Fieldguide to the Birds of Southwest India.* New Delhi: OUP.

Das, A.K. & Dev Roy, M.K. (1989) *A General Account of Mangrove Fauna of Andaman and Nicobar Islands.* Calcutta: ZSI.

Datta, S. (1995) *Birds of the Dhubri District.* Guwahati: Nature's Beckon.

Dave, K.N. (1985) *Birds in Sanskrit Literature.* Delhi: Motilal Banarsidass.

De, R.N. (1990) *The Sundarbans.* Calcutta: OUP.

Department of Forests, Punjab (1993) *Punjabi Names of the Birds of Punjab.* Chandigarh.

Department of Forests, Punjab (1992) *Water birds of Harike Sanctuary.* Chandigarh.

Dewar, D. (1906) *Bombay Duck.* London. John Lane: The Bodley Head.

Dewar, D. (1909) *Birds of the Plains.* London: John Lanc.

Dewar, D. (1911) *The Indian Crow; His Book.* Madras: Higginbotham & Co. London: Luzac & Co.

Dewar, D. (1913) *Glimpses of Indian Birds.* London:John Lane.

Dewar, D. (1915) *Birds of the Indian Hills.* London: The Bodley Head.

Dewar, D. (1916) *A Bird Calendar for Northern India.* London: Thacker.

Dewar, D. (1923) *Himalayan and Kashimiri Birds.* London: J. Lane.

Dewar, D. (1923) *Indian Birds.* London: John Lane the Bodley Head.

Dewar, D. (1923) *Birds at the Nest.* London: John Lane.

Dewar, D. (1923-25) *The Common Birds of India.* Vols.I-2. Calcutta and Simla: Thacker and Spink.

Dewar, D. (1924) *Birds of an Indian Village.* Bombay: OUP.

Dewar, D. (1925) *Indian Bird Life.* London: John Lane The Bodley Head Limited.

Dewar, D. (1928) *Game Birds.* London: Chapman & Hall.

Dewar, D. (1929) *Indian Birds' Nests.* Bombay: Thacker Spink.

Dewar, D. (undated) *Animals of No Importance.* Calcutta: Thacker, Spink & Co.

de Zoysa, N. & Raheem, R. (1990) *Sinharaja. A Rainforest in Sri Lanka.* Colombo: March for Conservation.

de Zylva, T.S.U. (1984) *Birds of Sri Lanka: A Selection of Fifty Six Colour Pictures.* Colombo: Trumpet Publishers.

de Zylva, T.S.U. (1996) *Wings in the Wetlands.* Sri Lanka: The Victor Hasselblad Wildlife Trust.

Dharmakumarsinhji, R.S. (1954) *Birds of Saurashtra.* Bombay:TOI Press.

Dharmakumarsinhji, R.S. & Lavkumar, K.S. (1972) *Sixty Indian Birds.* New Delhi: Ministry of Information and Broadcasting.

Dhiman, D.K. (1988) *Bird Hit Prevention Programme in IAAI Airports.* New Delhi: Institute of Aviation Management.

Easa, P.S. (1991) *Birds of Peechi Vazhani Wildlife Sanctuary: A Survey Report.* Trichur: Nature Education Society.

EHA (E.H. Aitken) (1923) *A Naturalist on the Prowl: Or in the Jungle.* London: W. Thacker & Co.

EHA Introduction by Ali, S. (1947) *The Common Birds of India.* Bombay: Thacker & Co. Ltd.

EHA (undated) *The Common Birds of Bombay.* Bombay: Thacker, Spink & Co.

EHA. *Concerning Animals and Other Matters.*

Ewans, M. (1989) *Bharatpur, Bird Paradise.* London: H.F. & G. Witherby.

Fairbank, Rev. H .(1921) *Birds of Mahableshwar.* Ahmadnager: Published by the author.

Fairbank, Rev. H. (1921) *The Waterfowl of India & Asia.* Published by the author.

Felsinger, C.G.A. (1934) *Birds in the Garden in the Low Country Wet-Zone of Ceylon.* Colombo: Privately published.

Felsinger, C.G.A. (1972) *It was the Babbler's Nest.* Colombo: Lake House Investments Ltd.

Ferguson, W. (1887) *List of the Birds of Ceylon:* Colombo: Ceylon Observer Press.

Finn, F. (1901) *How to Know the Indian Ducks.* Calcutta: Thacker, Spinks & Co.

Finn, F. (1901) *Lists of Birds in the Indian Museum.* Calcutta: Indian Museum.

Finn, F. (1916) *Game Birds of India & Asia.* Calcutta: Thacker, Spink & Co.

Finn, F. (1917) *The Birds of Calcutta.* Calcutta: Thacker, Spink & Co.

Finn, F. (1920) *How to Know the Indian Waders.* Calcutta: Thacker, Spink & Co.

Finn, F. (1920) *Indian Sporting Birds.* London: F. Edwards.

Finn, F. (1921) *The Water Fowl of India & Asia.* Calcutta & Simla: Thacker, Spink & Co.

Finn, F. (1950) *Garden & Aviary Birds of India.* Calcutta: Thacker, Spink & Co.

Fleming, R.L. Sr & Fleming, R. Jr (1970) *Birds of Kathmandu and Surrounding Hills.* Kathmandu: Jore Ganesh Press.

Fleming, R.L. (1977) *Comments on the Endemic Birds of Sri Lanka.* Colombo: Ceylon Bird Club.

Fleming, R.L. (1979) *Birds of the Sagarmatha National Park.* Avalok. Kathmandu.

Fleming, R.L. Sr. *et al.* (1984) *Birds of Nepal: With reference to Kashmir and Sikkim.* Nepal: Nature Himalayas.

Fletcher, T. & Bainbridge (1924) *Birds of an Indian Garden.* Calcutta & Simla: Thacker, Spink & Co.

Futehally, L. (1959) *About Indian Birds.* India: Blackie & Son (India) Ltd.

Gandhi, M.& Husain, O. (1993) *Bird Quiz.* New Delhi: Rupa & Co.

Ganguli, U. (1975) *A Guide to the Birds of the Delhi Area.* New Delhi: ICHR.

Gaur, R.K. (1994) *Indian Birds.* New Delhi: Brijbasi Printers.

Gee, B. *South India, Sri Lanka and the Andaman Islands.*

George, J. (ed.) (1994) *Annotated Checklist of the Birds of Bangalore.* Bangalore: Birdwatchers' Field Club.

Gogoi, C. (1995) *Birds of Greater Guwahati,* Guwahati: Assam Science Society.

Gole, P. (1996) *Environment & Ornithology in India.* Jaipur: Rawat Publications.

Gole, P. *A Guide to the Cranes of India.* Bombay: BNHS.

Gould, J. (1832) *A Century of Birds from the Himalayan Mountains.* London: Published by the author.

Gould, J. (1850-73) *Birds of Asia*. Vols. I-6. London: Published by the author.

Green, A.J. (1992) *The Status and Conservation of the White-winged Wood Duck*. Slimbridge: IWRB.

Grewal, B. (ed) (1988) *Insight Guide to Indian Wildlife*. Singapore: APA Publication.

Grewal, B. (1995) *Birds of the Indian Subcontinent*. Hong Kong: The Guidebook Company Limited.

Grewal, B. (1995) *Birds of the India & Nepal*. London: New Holland.

Grewal, B. (1995) *Threatened Birds of India*. New Delhi.

Grewal, B. & Sahgal, B. (1995) *Birds of the Corbett Tiger Reserve and its Environs* . New Delhi.

Grewal, B.(ed) (1995) *The Avifauna of the Indian Subcontinent* Part 1. Bombay: Sanctuary Vol XV No 5.

Grewal, B. (ed) (1995) *The Avifauna of the Indian Subcontinent* Part 2. Bombay: Sanctuary Vol. XV No 6.

Grewal, B. (1997) *Bharatvarsh ke Sankatgrast Pakshee*. (in Hindi) New Delhi.

Grewal, B. (1997) *Report of the 6th Birdwatching Camp, Sitabani*. Ramnagar: Corbett Birdwatching Programme.

Grewal, B. (1998) *A Photographic Guide to the Birds of the Himalayas*. London: New Holland.

Haly, A. (1887) *First Report on the Collection of Birds in the Colombo Museum*. Colombo.

Haroun er Rashid. (1967) *Systematic List of the Birds of East Pakistan*. Dacca: Asiatic Society of Pakistan.

Harris, P. (1996) *The Birds of Goa, A Complete Checklist*. Lowestoft UK. Eastern Publications.

Harris, P. (1996) *Goa, The Independent Birder's Guide*. Lowestoft UK. Eastern Publications.

Harvey, W.G. (1990) *Birds in Bangladesh*. Dhaka: University Press Limited.

Henderson, G. & Hume A.O. (1873) *Lahore to Yarkhand*.

Henry, G.M. (1927) *Birds of Ceylon*. London: The Ceylon Government.

Henry, G.M. & Wait, W.E. (1927-35) *Coloured Plates of the Birds of Ceylon*. Colombo: Ceylon Govt.

Henry, G.M. (1953) *A Picture Book of Ceylon Birds*. Dept. of Information. Ceylon.

Henry, G.M. (1955) *A Guide to the Birds of Ceylon*. London: OUP.

Hodgson, B.H. (1846) *Catalogue of the Specimens and Drawings of Mammalia and Birds of Nepal & Tibet*. London: British Museum.

Hoffman, T. (1984) *National Red Data List of Endangered and Rare Birds of Sri Lanka*. Colombo: Ceylon Bird Club.

Holmer, M.R.N. (1923) *Indian Bird life*. London: OUP.

Holmer, M.R.N. (1926) *Bird Study in India*. London: OUP.

Horsfield, T. & Moore, F. (1854-58) *Catalogue of the Birds in the Museum of the Hon. East India Company*. Vol. 1&2. London: W.H. Allen.

Hume, A.O. (1869) *My Scrap Book: or Rough Notes on Indian Oology and Ornithology*. Calcutta: C.B. Lewis, Baptist Mission Press.

Hume, A.O. (1873) *Contributions to Indian Ornithology. With 32 hand coloured plates by Keulemans*. London: L. Reeve & Co.

Hume A.O. *Indian Ornithological Collector's Vade-Mecum*. Calcutta: Central Press.

Hume, A.O. (ed) (1873-83) *Stray Feathers* (Vols. 1-12) Published by the Editor.

Hume, A.O. & Marshall (1879-81) *The Game Birds of India, Burmah, and Ceylon*. Vols. I-3. London: John Bale.

Hume, A.O. & Oates (1889) *Hume's Nests & Eggs of Indian Birds*. (Vol. I-3) London: R. H. Porter.

Hunter, W.W. (1896) *Life of Brian Houghton Hodgson*. London: John Murray.

Hussain, S.A. *et al* . (1984) *Avifaunal Profile of Chilika Lake*. Bombay: BNHS.

Hussain, S.A. (1987-91) *Bird Migration Project*. Parts I-3. Bombay: BNHS.

Hussain, S.A .& D'Silva, C. (1987) *Waterfowl Indicator*. Bombay: BNHS.

Hutson, Major-General H.P.W. (1954) *The Birds About Delhi*. The Delhi Bird Watching Society.

Inglis, C.M. (undated) *Sixty-eight Indian Birds*. Darjeeling: Natural History Museum.

Inskipp, C. (1988) *A Birdwatchers' Guide To Nepal*. England: Prion.

Inskipp, C. (1989) *A Popular Guide to the Birds and Mammals of The Annapurna Conservation Area*.

Nepal: Annapurna Conservation Area Project (ACAP).

Inskipp, C. & Inskipp, T. (1983) *Report on a Survey of Bengal Floricans*. Cambridge: ICPB.

Inskipp, C. (1989) *Nepal's Forest Birds: Their Status and Conservation*. Cambridge, UK.

Inskipp, T. & Inskipp, C. (1991) *A Guide to The Birds of Nepal*. London: Christopher Helm.

Inskipp, C. & Inskipp, T. *An Introduction to Birdwatching in Bhutan*. Thimpu, Bhutan: WWF.

Inskipp, T. *et al.* (1996) *An Annotated Checklist of the Birds of the Oriental Region*. Sandy, UK: OBC.

Inskipp, T., Inskipp, C. & Grimmet, R. (in prep) *Birds of the Indian Subcontinent*. UK: A&C Black.

Jerath, N. (1993) *Harike Wetland—An Avian Paradise*. Punjab State Council for Science & Technology.

Jerdon, T.C. (1845-1847) *Illustrations of Indian Ornithology, Containing Fifty Figures of New, Unfigured or Interesting Species of Birds, Chiefly from the South of India*. Madras.

Jerdon, T.C. (1862-64) *The Birds of India: A Natural History*. Vols. I-3. Calcutta: The Military Orphan Press.

Jerdon, T.C. (1864) *The Game Birds and Wildfowl of India*. London: Military Orphan Press.

Jonathan, J.K. & Kulkarni (1989) *Beginners' Guide to Field Ornithology*. Calcutta: ZSI.

Jones, A.E. (undated) *The Common Birds of Simla*. Simla: Liddells Printing Works.

Kalpavriksh (1991) *What's That Bird? A Guide to Birdwatching, with Special Reference to Delhi*. New Delhi: Kalpavrksh.

Kalpavriksh (1991) *The Delhi Ridge Forest, Decline and Conservation*. New Delhi: Kalpavriksh.

Kalpavriksh (1996) *Small & Beautiful: Sultanpur National Park*. New Delhi: Kalpavriksh.

Karoor, J.J. (1986) *List of Birds That May be Found in Periyar Wildlife Sanctuary*. Peermade Wildlife Preservation Society.

Kaul, S.C. (1939) *Birds of Kashmir*. Srinagar: The Normal Press.

Kazmierczak, K. (1996) *A Checklist of Indian Birds*. UK: Published by the author.

Kazmierczak, K. & Singh, R. *A Bird Watchers Guide to India*. UK: Prion Ltd.

Kelaart, E.F. (1853) *Prodromus Faunae Zeylanicae*. Colombo: Observer Press.

Kershaw, C. (1925) *Familiar Birds of Ceylon*. Colombo: H.W. Cave & Co.

Kershaw, C. (1949) *Bird Life in Ceylon*.

Khacher, L. (undated) *Birds of the Indian Wetland*. New Delhi: Department of Environment.

King, B. *et al.* (1991) A *Field Guide to the Birds of South East Asia*. London: Collins.

Kotagama, S. (1986) *Kurullan Narambamu*. (in Sinhala) Colombo: Pubudu Publishers.

Kotagama, S. & Fernando, P. (1994) *A Field Guide to the Birds of Sri Lanka*. Colombo: The Wildlife Heritage Trust of Sri Lanka.

Kothari, A. & Chhapgar, B.F. (eds.) (1996) *Salim Ali's India*. New Delhi: OUP & BNHS.

Krishnan, M. (1986) *Vedanthangal Water-Bird Sanctuary*. Chennai: Govt. of Tamil Nadu.

Kumar, G. & Lamba, B. (1985) *Studies on Migratory Birds and their Behavior in Corbett National Park*. Calcutta : ZSI.

Kumar, K. (1992) *Keoladeo National Park, Bharatpur: Flora & Fauna*. Bharatpur.

Lamba, B. (1987*)* *Fauna of Corbett National Park*. Calcutta: ZSI.

Lamba, B. (1987) *Status Survey of Fauna, Nanda Devi National Park*. Calcutta: ZSI.

Lamfuss, G. (1994) *The Birds of Sri Lanka, A Complete Birdwatcher's Checklist*. Colombo: Ceylon Bird Club.

Law, S.C. (1923) *Pet Birds of Bengal*. Calcutta & Simla: Thacker, Spink & Co.

Law, S.C. (1934) *Kalidaser Pakhi (in Bengali)*. Calcutta: Gurudas Chattopadhayay & Sons.

Law, S.C. (1935) *Jalachari (in Bengali)*. Calcutta: Gurudas Chattopadhyay & Sons.

Legge, W.V.A. (1867) *History of the Birds of Ceylon*. London: Taylor & Francis.

Lester, C.D. *The Birds of Kutch*.

Lowther, E.H.N. (1949) *A Bird Photographer in India*. London: OUP.

Lister, M.D. (1954) *A Contribution to the Ornithology of the Darjeeling Area*. Bombay: BNHS .

Lushington, C. (1949) *Bird Life in Ceylon*. Colombo: Times of Ceylon Ltd.

MacDonald, M. (1960) *Birds in My Indian Garden*. London: Jonathan Cape.

MacDonald, M. (1962) *Birds in The Sun: Some Beautiful Birds of India*. London: D.B. Taraporevala Sons & Co. Pvt. Ltd.

Mackintosh, L.J. (1915) *Birds of Darjeeling and India: Part I*. Calcutta: J.N. Banerjee & Son.

Mahabal, A .& Lamba, B. (1987) *On the Birds of Poona and Vicinity*. Calcutta: ZSI.

Majumdar, N. (1977) *Bird Migration*. New Delhi: NCERT.

Majumdar, N. (1984) *On a Collection of Birds from Bastar District*. Calcutta: ZSI.

Majumdar, N. (1984) *On a Collection of Birds from Adilabad District. Andhra Pradesh*. Calcutta; ZSI.

Majumdar, N. (1988) *On a Collection of Birds from Koraput District. Orissa*. Calcutta: ZSI.

Malik, D. & Malik, M.S. (1992) *Checklist of Birds of Zainabad*. Gujarat: Desert Courser Camp.

Mandal, A.K. & Nandi, N.C. (1989) *Fauna of the Sundarban Mangrove Eco-system*. Calcutta: ZSI.

Marshall, G.F. (1877) *Birds Nesting in India*. Calcutta: Central Press.

Martens, J. (1980) *Vocalization, Relationships and Distributional History of the Asian Phylloscopine Warblers*. Berlin: Verlag Paul Parey.

Mason, C.W. & Maxwell-Lefroy, H. (1912) *The Food of Birds in India*. Calcutta: Thacker, Spink & Co.

Mathews, W.H. & Edwards, V.S. (1944) *A List of Birds of Darjeeling*. Published by the authors.

Mathur, H.N. *et al.* (1993) *Birds of Tripura—A Checklist*. Agartala: Tripura State Council for Science and Technology.

Mehrotra, K.N. & Bhatnagar R.K. (1979) *Status of Economic Ornithology in India*. New Delhi: ICAR.

Messurier, Colonel A. Le (1904) *Game, Shore and Water Birds of India*. London: W. Thacker and Co.

Mierow, D. (1988). *Birds of the Central Himalayas*. Bangkok: Craftsman Press.

Mookherjee, K. (1995) *Birds and Trees of Tolly*. Calcutta: Tollygunge Club.

Mukherjee, A.K. (1979) *Peacock, Our National Bird*. New Delhi: Publications Div.

Mukherjee, A.K. & Dasgupta, J.M. (1986) *Catalogue of Birds in the Zoological Survey of India*. Calcutta: ZSI.

Mukherjee, A.K. (1992) *Birds of Goa*. Calcutta: ZSI.

Mukherjee, A.K. (1995) *Birds of Arid & Semi Arid Tracts*. Calcutta: ZSI.

Mukherjee, K. (1994) *Narendrapur Wildlife Sanctuary*. Calcutta: K Dey.

*Murray, J.A. (1888) *Indian Birds or the Avifauna of British India*. Vols. I-2. London: Trubner & Co.

Murray, J.A. (1889) *The Edible and Game Birds of British India with its Dependencies and Ceylon*. London: Trubner.

Murray, J.A. (1890) *The Avifauna of the Island of Ceylon*. Bombay: Educational Society Press.

Musavi, A.H. & Urfi, A.J. (1987) *Avifauna of the Aligarh Region*. Nature Conservation Society of India.

Nair, S.M. (1992) *Endangered Animals of India and Their Conservation*. New Delhi: NBT.

Nameer, P.O. (1992/93) *Birds of Kole Wetlands*. Parts 1&2. Trichur: FRI & Kerala Forest Department.

Nameer, P.O. (1992) *Birds of Chimmoni Wildlife Sanctuary*. Trichur: Kerala FRI & Forest Department.

Neelakantan, K.K. (1958) *Keralathile Pakshikal*. (in Malayalam). Trichur: Kerala Sahitya Academy.

Neelakantan, K.K., Sashikumar & Venugopalan (1993) *A Book of Kerala Birds*. Trivandrum: WWF.

Nugent, R. (1991) *The Search for the Pink-headed Duck* .Boston: Houghton Mifflin.

Oates, E.W. (1883) *Handbook of the Birds of British Burma*. Vols.1-2. London: RH Porter.

Oates, E.W. & Blandford (1889-98) *Fauna of British India Birds*. Vols.1-4. London: Taylor & Francis.

Oates, E.W. (1898) *A Manual of the Game Birds of India: Part I-Land Birds*. Bombay: Messrs. A.J. Combridge.

Oates, E.W. (1899) *A Manual of the Game Birds of India: Part 2-Game Birds*. Bombay: A.J. Combridge.

Oriental Bird Club (1995) *Bulletin 22 Special India Issue*. Sandy: OBC.

Osman, S.M. (1991) *Hunters of the Air, A Falconers Notes* . New Delhi: WWF.

Osmaston, B.B. & Sale, J.B. (1989) *Wildlife of Dehra Dun and Adjacent Hills*. Dehra Dun: Natraj Publishers.

Palin, H. & Lester, C.D. (1904) *The Birds of Cutch*. Bombay: Times Press.

Panani, D. (1996) *Rethinking Wetland Laws: A Case Study of Pulicat Bird Sanctuary*. New Delhi: WWF.

Perera, D.G.A. & Kotagama, S. (1983) *A Systematic Nomenclature for the Birds of Sri Lanka*. Dehiwela: Tisara Prakashana.

Phillips, W.W.A. (1949-1961) *Birds of Ceylon*: Vols.1-4. Colombo: Ceylon Daily News Press, Lake House.

Phillips, W.W.A. (1953) *Revised Checklist of the Birds of Ceylon*. National Museums of Ceylon.

Phillips, W.W.A. (1978) *Annotated Checklist of the Birds of Ceylon*. Colombo: Ceylon Bird Club.

Phukan, H.P. (1987) *Death at Jatinga: An Enquiry into the Jatinga Bird Mystery*. Guwahati: Forest Dept. Assam.

Pinn, F. (1985) *L. Mandelli- Darjeeling Ornithologist*. London.

Pittie, A. & Robertson, A. (1993) A *Nomenclature of Birds of the Indian Subcontinent*. Bangalore: Ornithological Society of India.

Pittie, A. (1995) *A Bibliographic Index to the Orinthology of the Indian Region*. Part 1. Hyderabad: Published by the author

Rahmani, A. *et al.* (1985) *Threats to the Karera Bustard Sanctuary*. Bombay: BNHS.

Rahmani, A. *et al.* (1985,89) *The Floricans*. Annual Report 1984-85, 88-89. Bombay: BNHS.

Rahmani, A. (1986) *Status of the Great Indian Bustard in Rajasthan*. Bombay: BNHS.

Rahmani, A. & Sankaran, R. (1986) *The Lesser Florican*. Bombay: BNHS.

Rahmani, A. (1987) *The Great Indian Bustard*. Bombay: BNHS.

Rahmani, A. (1987) *Dihaila Jheel: Conservation Strategies*. Bombay: BNHS.

Rahmani, A. & Manakadan, R. (1988) *Bustard Sanctuaries in India*. Bombay: BNHS.

Rahmani, A. *et al.* (1988) *The Bengal Florican*. Bombay: BNHS.

Rahmani, A. *et al.* (1996) *A Study of the Ecology of the Grasslands of the Indian Plains with Particular Reference to their Endangered Fauna*. Bombay: BNHS.

Rai, Y.M. (1983) *Birds of the Meerut Region*. Meerut: Vardhaman Printers.

Raju, K. (1985)*A Checklist of Birds of Vishakapatnam Region*. Vishakapatnam: APNHS.

Ranasinghe, D. (1976) *Asirimath Kurulu Lokaya (in Sinhala)* Colombo: Wildlife and Nature Society.

Ranasinghe, D. (1977) *A Guide to Bird Watching in Sri Lanka*. Colombo.

Ranasinghe, D. & De Zylva, T.S.U. (1978) *Sri Lanka Avifaunal List*. Colombo: Ceylon Bird Club.

Rangaswami, S. & Sridhar, S. (1993) *Birds of Rishi Valley*. Andhra Pradesh.

Reid, G. (1886) *Catalogue of the Birds in the Provincial Museum, N-W.P and Oudh, Lucknow*. Calcutta.

Ripley, D. (1952) *Search for the Spiny Babbler*. Boston: Houghton Mifflin.

Ripley, D. (1978) *A Bundle of Feathers*. London: OUP.

Ripley, D. (1982) *A Synopsis of the Birds of India and Pakistan*. Bombay: BNHS.

Roberts, T.J. (1991-92) *The Birds of Pakista*. Vols. I-2. Karachi: OUP.

Roberts ,T.J. *et al.* *A Checklist of Birds of Karachi & Lower Sindh*. Pakistan: WWF.

Robertson, A. & Jackson, M. (1992) *Birds of Periyar: An Aid to Birdwatching in the Periyar Sanctuary*. Jaipur.

Saha, B & Dasgupta, J. (1992) *Birds of Goa*. Calcutta: ZSI.

Samsad, P. (1984) *Chilika; A Report*. Calcutta: Prakriti Samsad.

Sankaran, R. (1993) *The Status and Conservation of the Nicobar Scrubfowl*. Coimbatore: Sacon.

Sankaran, R. (1995) *Impact Assessment of Nest Collection on the Edible Swiftlet in the Nicobar Islands*. Coimbatore: Sacon.

Sankaran, R. (1995) *The Nicobar Megapode and other Endemic Avifauna of the Nicobar Islands*. Coimbatore: Sacon.

Sankala, K. (1990) *Gardens of Eden; The Waterbird Sanctuary of Bharatpur*. New Delhi: Vikas.

Sargeant, D. (1994) *A Birders' Checklist of the Birds of Nepal*. UK: Norfolk, private publication.

Sarmah, N.C. (1996) *Checklist, Dibru-Saikhowa Wildlife Sanctuary*. Tinsukia: Muniruddin Ahmed.

Satyamurti, S.T (1970) *Catalogue of the Bird Gallery Museum*. Madras.

Satyamurti, S.T. (1979) *Bird's Eggs and Nests.* Madras.

Sawhney, J.C. *The Cranes.* Bombay: WWF.

Saxena, V.S. (1969) *Birds of Bharatpur, A Field Checklist.* Jaipur: Govt. Central Press.

Saxena, V.S. (1975) *A Study of the Flora and Fauna of Bharatpur Bird Sanctuary.* Rajasthan: Department of Tourism.

Sen Gupta, P.K. (1955) *Birds Around Shantiniketan.* West Bengal.

Sharma, B. (1991) *The Book of Indian Birds.* New Delhi: Harper Collins.

Sharma, S.C. (1985) *Birds of Sultanpur Bird Sanctuary—A Checklist.* New Delhi: WWF.

Sharma, S.C. (1989) *Ten Thousand Ducks in Five Acres.* New Delhi: Kalpavrikish.

Sharma, S.C. & Kothari, A. (1991) *Save the Bhindawas Lake Bird Sanctuary.* New Delhi: Kalpavrikish.

Sharma, S.K. *Ornithology of Indian Weaver Birds.* Delhi: Himanshu Publishers.

Sharma, S.K. (1995) *Ornithobotany.* Delhi: Himanshu Publishers.

Sharpe, R.B. (1891) *Scientific Results of the Second Yarkhand Mission.* London: Taylor and Francis.

Shepard, M. (1978) *Let's Look at Sri Lanka. An Orintholidays' Guide.* UK.

Shepard, M. (1987) *Let's look at North India. An Orintholidays' Guide.* UK.

Singh, A. & Singh, N. (1985) *Birds of Dudhwa National Park.* Uttar Pradesh.

Singh, B. (1996) *Siberian Cranes.* New Delhi: WWF.

Singh, G. (1993) *A Checklist of Birds of Punjab.* Punjab: Govt. Press.

Singh, K.R. (1994) *Birds of Rajasthan.* Jaipur: Rajasthan Tourism.

Singh, R. & Singh, K.S. *A Pocket-book of Indian Pheasants.* Dehradun: WII.

Singh, R. & Singh, K.S. (1995) *Pheasants of India and their Aviculture.* New Delhi: WWF.

Singh, Raj. *Bird and Wildlife Sanctuaries of India, Nepal & Bhutan.* New Delhi.

Singh, R.N.(1962) *Harmare Jal Pakshi.* (in Hindi) New Delhi: Publications Division.

Singh, R.N. (1977) *Our Birds.* New Delhi: Publications Division.

Siromoney, G. (1971) *Birds of Tambaram Area and Water-birds of Vedanthangal.* Madras: Madras Christian College.

Smetackek, F. (undated) *Birds of the Lake Region, Nainital-Naukotchia Tal.* Bhimtal: Society of Appeal for Vanishing Environments.

Smith, C.W. & Doyly, Sir C. (1828) *The Feathered Game of Hindostan.* Patna: Behar Amateur Lithographic Press.

Smith, C.W. & Doyly, Sir C. (1829) *Oriental Ornithology.* Patna: Behar Amateur Lithographic Press.

Smythies, B.E. (1953) *The Birds of Burma.* London: Oliver and Boyd.

Snilloc. (1945) *Mystery Birds of India.* Bombay: Thacker & Company Limited.

Sonobe, K. (ed) (1993) *A Field Guide to the Waterbirds of Asia.* Tokyo.

Soni, V.C. (1988) *Ecology and Behavior of the Indian Black Ibis.* Gujarat: University of Saurasthra.

Stanford, J.K. & Mayr, E. (1940) *The Vernay-Cutting Expedition to Southern Burma.*

Stefee, N.D. (1981) *Field Checklist of the Birds of Peninsular India.* Russ Mason's Natural History Tours.

Stefee, N.D. (1981) *Field Checklist of the Birds of Nepal, Kashmir, Garwal and Sikkim.* Russ Mason's Natural History Tours.

Sugathan, R. *et al.* (1985) *Studies on the Movement and Population Structure of Indian Avifauna.* Bombay: BNHS.

Taher, S. & Pittie, A. (1989) *A Checklist of the Birds of Andhra Pradesh.* Published by the author.

Talukdar, B.N. & Mahanta, R. (1991) *Pabitora Wildlife Sanctuary* (Checklist of Birds) Assam.

Talukdar, B.N. & Sharma, P. (1995) *Checklist of Birds of Orang Wildlife Sanctuary.* Assam.

Tennent, J.E. (1861) *Sketches of the Natural History of Ceylon.* London: Longman Green.

Tikader, B.K. (1983) *Threatened Animals of India.* Calcutta: ZSI.

Tikader, B.K. (1984) *Birds of Andaman & Nicobar Islands.* Calcutta: ZSI.

Tikader, B.K. & Das, A.K. (1984) *Glimpses of Animal Life of Andaman & Nicobar Islands.* Calcutta: ZSI.

Toor, H.S. & Sandhu, P.S. (1981) *Harmful Birds and their Control.* Ludhiana: Punjab Agriculture University.

Torfrida. (1944) *Nurseries of Heaven: More Birds.* Nilgiris: Mrs May Dart, Wellington.

Torfrida (1944) *Nurseries of Heaven: Birds.* Nilgiris: Mrs May Dart, Kotagiri.

Tyabji, H. (1994) *The Birds of Bandavgarh National Park.* New Delhi.

Tyagi, A.K. & Lamba, B.S. (1984) *A Contribution to the Breeding Biology of Two Indian Mynas.* Calcutta: ZSI.

Vagrant'. (1868) *Random Notes on Indian and Burman Ornithology.* Bangalore: Regimental Press.

Vaurie, Charles. (1972) *Tibet and its Birds.* London: H.F. & G. Witherby Ltd.

Verghese, *et al.* (1995) *Bird Diversity & Conservation Thrusts for the Nineties and Beyond.* Bangalore: OSI.

Verghese, *et al.* (1993) *Bird Conservation—Strategies for the Nineties and Beyond.* Bangalore: OSI.

Vijayan, L. (ed) (1995) *Avian Conservation In India.* Coimbatore: SACON.

Vira, R. & Dave, K.N. (1943) *Scientific Nomenclature of Birds of India, Burma and Ceylon.* Nagpur: Indian Academy of Indian Culture.

Wait, W.E. (1925) *Birds of Ceylon.* London: Dualu & Co.

Wan Tho, Loke. (1958) *A Company of Birds.* London: Michael Joseph.

Ward, Geoff. (1994) *Islamabad Birds.* Islamabad: Asian Study Group.

Wedderburn, Sir William. (1912) *Allan Octavian Hume.* London: T. Fisher Unwin.

Whistler, H., Kinnear, N., Ali, S. *The Vernay Scientific Survey of the Eastern Ghat; Ornithological Section—Together with The Hyderabad State Ornithological Survey 1930-38.*

Whistler, Hugh. (1928) *Popular Handbook of Indian Birds.* London: Gurney and Jackson.

Wijesinghe, D.P. (1994) *Checklist of the Birds of Sri Lanka.* Colombo: Ceylon Bird Club.

Wikramanayake, E.B. (1997) *Go to the Birds.* Colombo: Ceylon Bird Club.

Willoughby, Paul. *Goa: A Birder's Guide*

Woodcock, Martin. (1980) *Collins Handguide to the Birds of the Indian Subcontinent.* London: Collins.

Wright, R.C and Dewar, D. (1925) *The Ducks of India.* London: H.F. & G. Witherby.

WWF India (1994) Ramsar Sites; *Chilika, Sambhar Lake, Keoladeo National Park, Loktak Lake, Wular Lake, Harike Lake.* (Six Booklets). WWF.

Ziddi, S. & Bhagava, S. (1995) *Bharatpur.* New Delhi: Indus.

ZSI. (1992) *Fauna of West Bengal Part 1.* Calcutta: ZSI.

Sound Guides:

Connop, S. (1993) *Birdsongs of Nepal.* New York: Turaco.

Connop, S. (1995) *Birdsongs of the Himalayas.* Toronto: Turaco.

*Sivaprasad P.S. (1994) *An Audio Guide to the Birds of South India.* London: OBC.

White T. (1984)*A Field Guide to the Bird Songs of South East Asia.* London: British Library.

Forthcoming Books:

Grewal, B. & Mahajan, J. (in prep) *Indian Bird Paintings.* Hong Kong: Local Colour.

Kazmierczak, K. & van Perlo, B. (in prep) *A Pocket Guide to the Birds of the Indian Subcontinent.* UK: Pica Press.

Pittie, A. (in prep) *A Bibliographic Index to the Ornithology of the Indian Region.* Part 2. Hyderabad.

Ripley, S.D., Rasmussen, P. & Anderton, J. (in prep) *Field Guide to the Birds of South Asia.* USA: Univ. of Texas Press.

Systematic Index of Families and Species

R	=	widespread resident
r	=	very local resident
W	=	widespread winter visitor
w	=	sparse winter visitor
P	=	widespread migrant
p	=	sparse migrant
V	=	vagrant
?	=	status uncertain
rl	=	introduced resident

(ex) = extinct

ORDER: CRACIFORMES
Family: Megapodiidae

Nicobar Scrubfowl (Spurfowl)	r	*Megapodius nicobariensis*

ORDER: GALLIFORMES
Family: Phasianidae

Snow Partridge	r	*Lerwa lerwa*
Tibetan Snowcock	r	*Tetraogallus tibetanus*
Himalayan Snowcock	r	*Tetraogallus himalayensis*
Buff-throated Partridge	r	*Tetraophasis szechenyii*
Chukar	R	*Alectoris chukar*
Black Francolin (Black Partridge)	R	*Francolinus francolinus*
Painted Francolin (Painted Partridge)	R	*Francolinus pictus*
Chinese Francolin	r	*Francolinus pintadeanus*
Grey Francolin (Grey Partridge)	R	*Francolinus pondicerianus*
Swamp Francolin (Swamp Partridge)	r	*Francolinus gularis*
Tibetan Partridge	r	*Perdix hodgsoniae*
Common Quail	RW	*Coturnix coturnix*
Japanese Quail	w	*Coturnix japonica*
Rain Quail (Black-breasted Quail)	R	*Coturnix coromandelica*
Blue-breasted Quail	R	*Coturnix chinensis*
Jungle Bush Quail	R	*Perdicula asiatica*
Rock Bush Quail	R	*Perdicula argoondah*
Painted Bush Quail	R	*Perdicula erythrorhyncha*
Manipur Bush Quail	r	*Perdicula manipurensis*
Hill Partridge	r	*Arborophila torqueola*
Rufous-throated Partridge	r	*Arborophila rufogularis*
White-cheeked Partridge (White-cheeked Hill Partridge)	r	*Arborophila atrogularis*
Chestnut-breasted Partridge (Red-breasted Hill Partridge)	r	*Arborophila mandellii*
Mountain Bamboo Partridge	r	*Bambusicola fytchii*
Red Spurfowl	R	*Galloperdix spadicea*
Painted Spurfowl	R	*Galloperdix lunulata*
Sri Lanka Spurfowl	r	*Galloperdix bicalcarata*

Himalayan Quail (Mountain Quail)	(ex)	*Ophrysia superciliosa*
Blood Pheasant	r	*Ithaginis cruentus*
Western Tragopan	r	*Tragopan melanocephalus*
Satyr Tragopan	r	*Tragopan satyra*
Blyth's Tragopan	r	*Tragopan blythii*
Temminck's Tragopan	r	*Tragopan temminckii*
Koklass Pheasant	r	*Pucrasia macrolopha*
Himalayan Monal	r	*Lophophorus impejanus*
Sclater's Monal	r	*Lophophorus sclateri*
Red Junglefowl	R	*Gallus gallus*
Grey Junglefowl	R	*Gallus sonneratii*
Sri Lanka Junglefowl	R	*Gallus lafayetiir*
Kalij Pheasant	r	*Lophura leucomelanos*
Tibetan Eared Pheasant	r?	*Crossoptilon harmani*
Cheer Pheasant	r	*Catreus wallichii*
Mrs Hume's Pheasant	r	*Syrmaticus humiae*
Common Pheasant	rl	*Phasianus colchicus*
Grey Peacock Pheasant	r	*Polyplectron bicalcaratum*
Indian Peafowl	R	*Pavo cristatus*
Green Peafowl (Burmese Peafowl)	r	*Pavo muticus*

ORDER: ANSERIFORMES
Family: Dendrocygndiae

Fulvous Whistling-duck (Large Whistling-teal)	r	*Dendrocygna bicolor*
Lesser Whistling-duck (Lesser Whistling-teal)	R	*Dendrocygna javanica*

Family: Anatidae
Oxyurinae

White-headed Duck (White-headed Stiff-tailed Duck)	w	*Oxyura leucocephala*

Cygninae

Mute Swan	V	*Cygnus olor*
Whooper Swan	V	*Cygnus cygnus*
Tundra Swan	V	*Cygnus columbianus*

Anatinae

Anserini

Bean Goose	V	*Anser fabalis*
Greater White-fronted Goose	w	*Anser albifrons*
Lesser White-fronted Goose	V	*Anser erythropus*
Greylag Goose	W	*Anser anser*
Bar-headed Goose	rW	*Anser indicus*

Snow Goose	V	*Anser caerulescens*
Red-breasted Goose	V	*Branta ruficollis*
Ruddy Shelduck (Ruddy Sheldrake)	rW	*Tadorna ferruginea*
Common Shelduck	W	*Tadorna tadorna*
White-winged Duck	r	*Cairina scutulata*
Comb Duck	R	*Sarkidiornis melanotos*
Cotton Pygmy-goose (Cotton Teal)	R	*Nettapus coromandelianus*

Anatini

Mandarin Duck	V	*Aix galericulata*
Gadwall	W	*Anas strepera*
Falcated Duck	w	*Anas falcata*
Eurasian Wigeon	W	*Anas penelope*
Mallard	rW	*Anas platyrhynchos*
Spot-billed Duck	R	*Anas poecilorhyncha*
Northern Shoveler	W	*Anas clypeata*
Sunda Teal	r	*Anas gibberifrons*
Northern Pintail	W	*Anas acuta*
Garganey	W	*Anas querquedula*
Baikal Teal	V	*Anas formosa*
Common Teal	W	*Anas crecca*
Marbled Duck	w	*Marmaronetta angustirostris*
Pink-headed Duck	(ex)	*Rhodonessa caryophyllacea*
Red-crested Pochard	W	*Rhodonessa rufina*
Common Pochard	W	*Aythya ferina*
Ferruginous Pochard	rW	*Aythya nyroca*
Baer's Pochard	w	*Aythya baeri*
Tufted Duck	W	*Aythya fuligula*
Greater Scaup	w	*Aythya marila*
Long-tailed Duck	V	*Clangula hyemalis*
Common Goldeneye	w	*Bucephala clangula*
Smew	w	*Mergellus albellus*
Red-breasted Merganser	V	*Mergus serrator*
Common Merganser (Goosander)	rW	*Mergus merganser*

ORDER: TURNICIFORMES
Family: Turnicidae

Small Buttonquail (Little Bustardquail)	R	*Turnix sylvatica*
Yellow-legged Buttonquail	R	*Turnix tanki*
Barred Buttonquail (Common Bustardquail)	R	*Turnix suscitator*

ORDER: PICIFORMES
Family: Indicatoridae

Yellow-rumped Honeyguide	r	*Indicator xanthonotus*

Family: Picidae

Eurasian Wryneck	rW	*Jynx torquilla*
Speckled Piculet	r	*Picumnus innominatus*
White-browed Piculet (Rufous Piculet)	r	*Sasia ochracea*
Brown-capped Pygmy Woodpecker	R	*Dendrocopos nanus*
Grey-capped Pygmy Woodpecker	r	*Dendrocopos canicapillus*
Brown-fronted Woodpecker	r	*Dendrocopos auriceps*
Fulvous-breasted Woodpecker	R	*Dendrocopos macei*
Stripe-breasted Woodpecker	r	*Dendrocopos atratus*
Yellow-crowned Woodpecker (Yellow-fronted Pied Woodpecker)	R	*Dendrocopos mahrattensis*
Rufous-bellied Woodpecker	r	*Dendrocopos hyperythrus*
Crimson-breasted Woodpecker	r	*Dendrocopos cathpharius*
Darjeeling Woodpecker	r	*Dendrocopos darjellensis*
Great Spotted Woodpecker	r	*Dendrocopos major*
Sind Woodpecker	r	*Dendrocopos assimilis*
Himalayan Woodpecker	r	*Dendrocopos himalayensis*
Rufous Woodpecker	R	*Celeus brachyurus*
White-bellied Woodpecker (Indian Great Black Woodpecker)	r	*Dryocopus javensis*
Andaman Woodpecker	r	*Dryocopus hodgei*
Lesser Yellownape (Small Yellow-naped Woodpecker)	R	*Picus chlorolophus*
Greater Yellownape (Large Yellow-naped Woodpecker)	R	*Picus flavinucha*
Laced Woodpecker	r	*Picus vittatus*
Streak-throated Woodpecker (Little Scaly-bellied Green Woodpecker)	R	*Picus xanthopygaeus*
Scaly-bellied Woodpecker	r	*Picus squamatus*
Grey-headed Woodpecker (Black-naped Green Woodpecker)	R	*Picus canus*
Himalayan Flameback (Himalayan Golden-backed Three-toed Woodpecker)	r	*Dinopium shorii*
Common Flameback (Indian Golden-backed Three-toed Woodpecker)	r	*Dinopium javanense*
Black-rumped Flameback (Lesser Golden-backed Woodpecker)	R	*Dinopium benghalense*
Greater Flameback (Larger Golden-backed Woodpecker)	R	*Chrysocolaptes lucidus*
White-naped Woodpecker (Black-backed Woodpecker)	r	*.Chrysocolaptes festivus*
Pale-headed Woodpecker	r	*Gecinulus grantia*
Bay Woodpecker (Red-eared)	r	*Blythipicus pyrrhotis*
Heart-spotted Woodpecker	r	*Hemicircus canente*
Great Slaty Woodpecker	r	*Mulleripicus pulverulentus*

Family: Megalaimidae

Great Barbet (Great Hill Barbet)	r	*Megalaima virens*

Brown-headed Barbet (Green Barbet)	R	*Megalaima zeylanica*
Lineated Barbet	R	*Megalaima lineata*
White-cheeked Barbet (Small Green)	R	*Megalaima viridis*
Yellow-fronted Barbet	r	*Megalima flavifrons*
Golden-throated Barbet	r	*Megalaima franklinii*
Blue-throated Barbet	R	*Megalaima asiatica*
Blue-eared Barbet	r	*Megalaima australis*
Crimson-fronted Barbet	r	*Megalaima rubricapilla*
Coppersmith Barbet (Crimson-breasted Barbet)	R	*Megalaima haemacephala*

ORDER: BUCEROTIFORMES
Family: Bucerotidae

Malabar Grey Hornbill	R	*Ocyceros griseus*
Sri Lanka Grey Hornbill	R	*Ocyceros gingalensis*
Indian Grey Hornbill	R	*Ocyceros birostris*
Malabar Pied Hornbill	R	*Anthracoceros coronatus*
Oriental Pied Hornbill (Indian Pied Hornbill)	R	*Anthracoceros albirostris*
Great Hornbill (Great Pied Hornbill)	R	*Buceros bicornis*
Brown Hornbill (White-throated Brown Hornbill)	r	*Anorrhinus tickelli*
Rufous-necked Hornbill	r	*Aceros nipalensis*
Wreathed Hornbill	R	*Aceros undulatus*
Narcondam Hornbill	r	*Aceros narcondami*
Plain-pouched Hornbill	r/V	*Aceros subruficollis*

ORDER: UPUPIFORMES
Family: Upupidae

Common Hoopoe	RW	*Upupa epops*

ORDER: TROGONIFORMES
Family: Trogonidae

Malabar Trogon	R	*Harpactes fasciatus*
Red-headed Trogon	R	*Harpactes erythrocephalus*
Ward's Trogon	r	*Harpactes wardi*

ORDER: CORACIIFORMES
Family: Coraciidae

European Roller	rp	*Coracias garrulus*
Indian Roller	R	*Coracias benghalensis*
Dollarbird (Broad-billed Roller)	r	*Eurystomus orientalis*

Family: Alcedinidae

Blyth's Kingfisher (Great Blue)	r	*Alcedo hercules*

Common Kingfisher (Small Blue)	R	*Alcedo atthis*
Blue-eared Kingfisher	r	*Alcedo meninting*
Oriental Dwarf Kingfisher (Three-toed Kingfisher)	r	*Ceyx erithacus*

Family: Halcyonidae

Brown-winged Kingfisher	r	*Halcyon amauroptera*
Stork-billed Kingfisher	R	*Halcyon capensis*
Ruddy Kingfisher	r	*Halcyon coromanda*
White-throated Kingfisher (White-breasted Kingfisher)	R	*Halcyon smyrnensis*
Black-capped Kingfisher	R	*Halcyon pileata*
Collared Kingfisher (White-collared Kingfisher)	r	*Todiramphus chloris*

Family: Cerylidae

Crested Kingfisher (Greater Pied)	R	*Megaceryle lugubris*
Pied Kingfisher (Lesser Pied)	R	*Ceryle rudis*

Family: Meropidae

Blue-bearded Bee-eater	r	*Nyctyornis athertoni*
Green Bee-eater	R	*Merops orientalis*
Blue-cheeked Bee-eater	rS	*Merops persicus*
Blue-tailed Bee-eater	R	*Merops philippinus*
European Bee-eater	sP	*Merops apiaster*
Chestnut-headed Bee-eater	R	*Merops leschenaulti*

ORDER: CUCULIFORMES
Family: Cuculidae

Pied Cuckoo (Pied Crested)	P	*Clamator jacobinus*
Chestnut-winged Cuckoo (Red-winged Creasted Cuckoo)	r	*Clamator coromandus*
Large Hawk Cuckoo	r	*Hierococcyx sparverioides*
Common Hawk Cuckoo	R	*Hierococcyx varius*
Hodgson's Hawk Cuckoo	r	*Hierococcyx fugax*
Indian Cuckoo	R	*Cuculus micropterus*
Eurasian Cuckoo	r	*Cuculus canorus*
Oriental Cuckoo (Himalayan)	r	*Cuculus saturatus*
Lesser Cuckoo (Small Cuckoo)	r	*Cuculus poliocephalus*
Banded Bay Cuckoo	r	*Cacomantis sonneratii*
Grey-bellied Cuckoo (Indian Plaintive Cuckoo)	r	*Cacomantis passerinus*
Plaintive Cuckoo (Rufous-bellied Plaintive Cuckoo)	r	*Cacomantis merulinus*
Asian Emerald Cuckoo	r	*Chrysococcyx maculatus*
Violet Cuckoo	r	*Chrysococcyx* xanthorhynchus
Drongo Cuckoo	r	*Surniculus lugubris*

Asian Koel	R	*Eudynamys scolopacea*
Green-billed Malkoha	r	*Phaenicophaeus tristis*
Blue-faced Malkoha	r	*Phaenicophaeus viridirostris*
Sirkeer Malkoha	r	*Phaenicophaeus* leschenaultii
Red-faced Malkoha	r	*Phaenicophaeus* pyrrhocephalus

Family: Centropodidae

Greater Coucal (Crow-pheasant)	R	*Centropus sinensis*
Brown Coucal		
(Andaman Coucal)	r	*Centropus andamanensis*
Lesser Coucal	r	*Centropus bengalensis*
Green-billed Coucal (Ceylon)	r	*Centropus chlororhynchus*

ORDER: PSITTACIFORMES
Family: Psittacidae

Vernal Hanging Parrot		
(Indian Lorikeet)	R	*Loriculus vernalis*
Sri Lanka Hanging Parrot		
(Ceylon Lorikeet)	R	*Loriculus beryllinus*
Alexandrine Parakeet		
(Large Indian Parakeet)	R	*Psittacula eupatria*
Rose-ringed Parakeet	R	*Psittacula krameri*
Slaty-headed Parakeet	r	*Psittacula himalayana*
Grey-headed Parakeet		
(Eastern Slaty-headed Parakeet)	r	*Psittacula finschii*
Intermediate Parakeet		
(Rothschild's Parakeet)	r?	*Psittacula intermedia*
Plum-headed Parakeet		
(Blossom-headed Parakeet)	R	*Psittacula cyanocephala*
Blossom-headed Parakeet		
(Eastern Blossom-headed)	r	*Psittacula roseata*
Malabar Parakeet		
(Blue-winged Parakeet)	R	*Psittacula columboides*
Layard's Parakeet	r	*Psittacula calthropae*
Derbyan Parakeet		
(Lord Derby's Parakeet)	r	*Psittacula derbiana*
Red-breasted Parakeet		*Psittacula alexandri*
Nicobar Parakeet	r	*Psittacula caniceps*
Long-tailed Parakeet		
(Red-cheeked Parakeet)	r	*Psittacula longicauda*

ORDER: APODIFORMES
Family: Apodidae

Glossy Swiftlet		
(White-bellied Swiftlet)	r	*Collocalia esculenta*
Indian Swiftlet		
(Indian Edible-nest Swiftlet)	r	*Collocalia unicolor*

Himalayan Swiftlet	r	*Collocalia brevirostris*
Edible-nest Swiftlet		
(Andaman Grey-rumped Swiftlet)	r	*Collocalia fuciphaga*
White-rumped Needletail		
(White-rumped Spinetail)	R	*Zoonavena sylvatica*
White-throated Needletail	s	*Hirundapus caudacutus*
Silver-backed Needletail		
(Cochinchina Spinetail Swift)	r	*Hirundapus* cochinchinensis
Brown-backed Needletail		
(Large Brown-throated Spinetail)	R	*Hirundapus giganteus*
Asian Palm Swift	R	*Cypsiurus balasiensis*
Alpine Swift	R	*Tachymarptis melba*
Common Swift	r	*Apus apus*
Fork-tailed Swift		
(Large White-rumped Swift)	R	*Apus pacificus*
Dark-rumped Swift		
(Dark-backed Swift)	r	*Apus acuticauda*
House Swift	R	*Apus affinis*

Family: Hemiprocnidae

Crested Treeswift	R	*Hemiprocne coronata*

ORDER: STRIGIFORMES
Family: Tytonidae

Barn Owl	R	*Tyto alba*
Grass Owl	r	*Tyto capensis*
Oriental Bay Owl	r	*Phodilus badius*

Family: Strigidae

Andaman Scops Owl	r	*Otus balli*
Mountain Scops Owl		
(Spotted Scops Owl)	r	*Otus spilocephalus*
Pallid Scops Owl	V	*Otus brucei*
Eurasian Scops Owl	w	*Otus scops*
Oriental Scops Owl	R	*Otus sunia*
Collared Scops Owl	R	*Otus bakkamoena*
Eurasian Eagle Owl		
(Great Horned Owl)	R	*Bubo bubo*
Spot-bellied Eagle Owl		
(Forest Eagle Owl)	r	*Bubo nipalensis*
Dusky Eagle Owl		
(Dusky Horned Owl)	r	*Bubo coromandus*
Brown Fish Owl	R	*Ketupa zeylonensis*
Tawny Fish Owl	r	*Ketupa flavipes*
Buffy Fish Owl	r?	*Ketupa ketupu*
Mottled Wood Owl	R	*Strix ocellata*

Brown Wood Owl	R	*Strix leptogrammica*
Tawny Owl	r	*Strix aluco*
Collared Owlet (Collared Pygmy)	r	*Glaucidium brodiei*
Asian Barred Owlet	r	*Glaucidium cuculoides*
Jungle Owlet		
(Barred)	R	*Glaucidium radiatum*
Chestnut-backed Owlet	r	*Glaucidium castanonotum*
Little Owl	r	*Athene noctua*
Spotted Owlet	R	*Athene brama*
Forest Owlet	(ex)	*Athene blewitti*
Boreal Owl	V	*Aegolius funereus*
Brown Hawk Owl	r	*Ninox scutulata*
Andaman Hawk Owl	r	*Ninox affinis*
Long-eared Owl	rw	*Asio otus*
Short-eared Owl	w	*Asio flammeus*

Family: Batrachostomidae

Sri Lanka Frogmouth	r	*Batrachostomus moniliger*
Hodgson's Frogmouth	r	*Batrachostomus hodgsoni*

Family: Eurostopodidae

Great Eared Nightjar	r	*Eurostopodus macrotis*

Family: Caprimulgidae

Grey Nightjar (Indian Jungle)	R	*Caprimulgus indicus*
Eurasian Nightjar (European)	p	*Caprimulgus europaeus*
Sykes's Nightjar	sw	*Caprimulgus mahrattensis*
Large-tailed Nightjar (Long-tailed)	R	*Caprimulgus macrurus*
Jerdon's Nightjar (Indian Long-tailed)	R	*Caprimulgus atripennis*
Indian Nightjar	R	*Caprimulgus asiaticus*
Savanna Nightjar (Franklin's)	R	*Caprimulgus affinis*

ORDER:COLUMBIFORMES
Family:Columbidae

Rock Pigeon (Blue Rock Pigeon)	R	*Columba livia*
Hill Pigeon	r	*Columba rupestris*
Snow Pigeon	r	*Columba leuconota*
Yellow-eyed Pigeon		
(Eastern Stock Pigeon)	w	*Columba eversmanni*
Common Wood Pigeon	w	*Columba palumbus*
Speckled Wood Pigeon	r	*Columba hodgsonii*
Ashy Wood Pigeon	r	*Columba pulchricollis*
Nilgiri Wood Pigeon	R	*Columba elphinstonii*
Sri Lanka Wood Pigeon	r	*Columba torringtoni*
Pale-capped Pigeon (Purple Wood)	w	*Columba puniceadi*
Andaman Wood Pigeon	r	*Columba palumboides*

European Turtle Dove	V	*Streptopelia turtur*
Oriental Turtle Dove (Rufous Turtle)	RW	*Streptopelia orientalis*
Laughing Dove (Little Brown)	R	*Streptopelia senegalensis*
Spotted Dove	R	*Streptopelia chinensis*
Red Collared Dove (Red Turtle)	R	*Streptopelia tranquebarica*
Eurasian Collared Dove (Indian Ring)	R	*Streptopelia decaocto*
Barred Cuckoo Dove (Bar-tailed)	r	*Macropygia unchall*
Andaman Cuckoo Dove	r	*Macropygia rufipennis*
Emerald Dove	R	*Chalcophaps indica*
Nicobar Pigeon	r	*Caloenas nicobarica*
Orange-breasted Green Pigeon	r	*Treron bicincta*
Pompadour Green Pigeon	r	*Treron pompadora*
Thick-billed Green Pigeon	r	*Treron curvirostra*
Yellow-footed Green Pigeon		
(Yellow-legged Green or Bengal)	R	*Treron phoenicoptera*
Pin-tailed Green Pigeon	r	*Treron apicauda*
Wedge-tailed Green Pigeon	r	*Treron sphenura*
Green Imperial Pigeon	r	*Ducula aenea*
Mountain Imperial Pigeon (Imperial)	r	*Ducula badia*
Pied Imperial Pigeon	r	*Ducula bicolor*

ORDER: GRUIFORMES
Family: Otididae

Little Bustard	V	*Tetrax tetrax*
Indian Bustard (Great Indian)	r	*Ardeotis nigriceps*
McQueen's Bustard (Houbara)	w	*Chlamydotis macqueeni*
Bengal Florican	r	*Houbaropsis bengalensis*
Lesser Florican (Likh)	r	*Sypheotides indica*

Family: Gruidae

Siberian Crane	w	*Grus leucogeranus*
Sarus Crane	r	*Grus antigone*
Demoiselle Crane	W	*Grus virgo*
Common Crane	W	*Grus grus*
Hooded Crane	V	*Grus monacha*
Black-necked Crane	sw	*Grus nigricollis*

Family: Heliornithidae

Masked Finfoot	r	*Heliopais personata*

Family: Rallidae

Andaman Crake	r	*Rallina canningi*
Red-legged Crake	V?	*Rallina fasciata*
Slaty-legged Crake	R	*Rallina eurizonoides*
Slaty-breasted Rail	R	*Gallirallus striatus*

Water Rail	rW	*Rallus aquaticus*
Corn Crake	V	*Crex crex*
Brown Crake	R	*Amaurornis akool*
White-breasted Waterhen	R	*Amaurornis phoenicurus*
Black-tailed Crake	r	*Porzana bicolor*
Little Crake	V	*Porzana parva*
Baillon's Crake	rW	*Porzana pusilla*
Spotted Crake	W	*Porzana porzana*
Ruddy-breasted Crake (Ruddy)	R	*Porzana fusca*
Watercock	R	*Gallicrex cinerea*
Purple Swamphen (Purple Moorhen)	R	*Porphyrio porphyrio*
Common Moorhen	R	*Gallinula chloropus*
Common Coot	RW	*Fulica atra*

ORDER: CICONIIFORMES
Family: Pteroclidae

Tibetan Sandgrouse	r	*Syrrhaptes tibetanus*
Pallas's Sandgrouse	V	*Syrrhaptes paradoxus*
Pin-tailed Sandgrouse	V?	*Pterocles alchata*
Chestnut-bellied Sandgrouse (Indian Sandgrouse)	R	*Pterocles exustus*
Spotted Sandgrouse	w	*Pterocles senegallus*
Black-bellied Sandgrouse (Imperial Sandgrouse)	r?W	*Pterocles orientalis*
Painted Sandgrouse (Close-barred)	R	*Pterocles indicus*

Family: Scolopacidae

Scolopacinae

Eurasian Woodcock	rW	*Scolopax rusticola*
Solitary Snipe	r	*Gallinago solitaria*
Wood Snipe	r	*Gallinago nemoricola*
Pintail Snipe	W	*Gallinago stenura*
Swinhoe's Snipe	w	*Gallinago megala*
Great Snipe	V	*Gallinago media*
Common Snipe (Fantail)	rW	*Gallinago gallinago*
Jack Snipe	w	*Lymnocryptes minimus*

Tringinae

Black-tailed Godwit	W	*Limosa limosa*
Bar-tailed Godwit	W	*Limosa lapponica*
Whimbrel	W	*Numenius phaeopus*
Eurasian Curlew	W	*Numenius arquata*
Spotted Redshank	W	*Tringa erythropus*
Common Redshank	sW	*Tringa totanus*
Marsh Sandpiper	W	*Tringa stagnatilis*

Common Greenshank	W	*Tringa nebularia*
Nordmann's Greenshank		
(Spotted Greenshank)	V	*Tringa guttifer*
Green Sandpiper	W	*Tringa ochropus*
Wood Sandpiper	W	*Tringa glareola*
Terek Sandpiper	W	*Xenus cinereus*
Common Sandpiper	sW	*Actitis hypoleucos*
Ruddy Turnstone	W	*Arenaria interpres*
Asian Dowitcher	w	*Limnodromus semipalmatus*
Great Knot	w	*Calidris tenuirostris*
Red Knot	V	*Calidris canutus*
Sanderling	W	*Calidris alba*
Spoon-billed Sandpiper	w	*Calidris pygmeus*
Little Stint	W	*Calidris minuta*
Red-necked Stint	w	*Calidris ruficollis*
Temminck's Stint	W	*Calidris temminckii*
Long-toed Stint	w	*Calidris subminuta*
Sharp-tailed Sandpiper	V	*Calidris acuminata*
Dunlin	w	*Calidris alpina*
Curlew Sandpiper	W	*Calidris ferruginea*
Broad-billed Sandpiper	w	*Limicola falcinellus*
Ruff	W	*Philomachus pugnax*
Red-necked Phalarope	w	*Phalaropus lobatus*
Red Phalarope	V	*Phalaropus fulicaria*

Family: Rostratulidae

Greater Painted-snipe	R	*Rostratula benghalensis*

Family: Jacanidae

Pheasant-tailed Jacana	R	*Hydrophasianus chirurgus*
Bronze-winged Jacana	R	*Metopidius indicus*

Family: Burhinidae

Eurasian Thick-knee (Stone-curlew)	R	*Burhinus oedicnemus*
Great Thick-knee (Great Stone Plover)	r	*Esacus recurvirostris*
Beach Thick-knee	r?	*Esacus neglectus*

Family: Charadriidae

Recurvirostrinae

Haematopodini

Eurasian Oystercatcher	w	*Haematopus ostralegus*

Recurvirostrini

Ibisbill	r	*Ibidorhyncha struthersii*
Black-winged Stilt	R	*Himantopus himantopus*
Pied Avocet	rW	*Recurvirostra avosetta*

Charadriinae

European Golden Plover (Golden)	V	*Pluvialis apricaria*
Pacific Golden Plover		
(Eastern Golden Plover)	W	*Pluvialis fulva*
Grey Plover	w	*Pluvialis squatarola*
Common Ringed Plover	V	*Charadrius hiaticula*
Long-billed Plover	w	*Charadrius placidus*
Little Ringed Plover	RW	*Charadrius dubius*
Kentish Plover	RW	*Charadrius alexandrinus*
Lesser Sand Plover	sW	*Charadrius mongolus*
Greater Sand Plover	W	*Charadrius leschenaultii*
Caspian Plover	V	*Charadrius asiaticus*
Oriental Plover (Sand Plover)	V	*Charadrius veredus*
Black-fronted Dotterel	V	*Elseyornis melanops*
Northern Lapwing (Eurasian Lapwing)	W	*Vanellus vanellus*
Yellow-wattled Lapwing	R	*Vanellus malabaricus*
River Lapwing (Spur-winged)	R	*Vanellus duvaucelii*
Grey-headed Lapwing	w	*Vanellus cinereus*
Red-wattled Lapwing	R	*Vanellus indicus*
Sociable Lapwing	w	*Vanellus gregarius*
White-tailed Lapwing	W	*Vanellus leucurus*

Family: Glareolidae

Dromadinae

Crab-plover	w	*Dromas ardeola*

Glareolinae

Jerdon's Courser	r	*Rhinoptilus bitorquatus*
Cream-colored Courser	rw	*Cursorius cursor*
Indian Courser	R	*Cursorius coromandelicus*
Collared Pratincole (Common)	w	*Glareola pratincola*
Oriental Pratincole (Indian)	R	*Glareola maldivarum*
Small Pratincole	R	*Glareola lactea*

Family: Laridae

Larinae

Stercorariini

Brown Skua (Antarctic Skua)	V	*Catharacta antarctica*
South-Polar Skua (MacCormick's)	V	*Catharacta maccormicki*
Pomarine Jaeger (Pomatorhine)	V	*Stercorarius pomarinus*
Parasitic Jaegar	V	*Stercorarius parasiticus*

Rynchopini

Indian Skimmer	r	*Rynchops albicollis*

Larini

Sooty Gull	V	*Larus hemprichii*
Mew Gull	V	*Larus canus*
Heuglin's Gull (Herring)	w	*Larus heuglini*
Yellow-legged Gull (Herring)	w	*Larus cachinnans*
Pallas's Gull (Great Black-headed)	W	*Larus ichthyaetus*
Brown-headed Gull	sW	*Larus brunnicephalus*
Black-headed Gull	W	*Larus ridibundus*
Slender-billed Gull	W	*Larus genei*
Little Gull	V	*Larus minutus*

Sternini

Gull-billed Tern	rW	*Gelochelidon nilotica*
Caspian Tern	W	*Sterna caspia*
River Tern	R	*Sterna aurantia*
Lesser Crested Tern	R	*Sterna bengalensis*
Great Crested Tern	R	*Sterna bergii*
Sandwich Tern	w	*Sterna sandvicensis*
Roseate Tern	r	*Sterna dougallii*
Black-naped Tern	r	*Sterna sumatrana*
Common Tern	sW	*Sterna hirundo*
Arctic Tern	V	*Sterna paradisaea*
Little Tern	R	*Sterna albifrons*
Saunders's Tern	s?	*Sterna saundersi*
White-cheeked Tern	s	*Sterna repressa*
Black-bellied Tern	r	*Sterna acuticauda*
Bridled Tern (Brown-winged)	s	*Sterna anaethetus*
Sooty Tern	s	*Sterna fuscata*
Whiskered Tern	RW	*Chlidonias hybridus*
White-winged Tern (White-winged Black)	w	*Chlidonias leucopterus*
Black Tern	V	*Chlidonias niger*
Brown Noddy (Noddy Tern)	V	*Anous stolidus*
Black Noddy (White-capped Noddy)	V?	*Anous minutus*
White Tern (Indian Ocean White)	r	*Gygis alba*

Family: Accipitridae

Pandioninae

Osprey	rW	*Pandion haliaetus*

Accipitrinae

Jerdon's Baza	r	*Aviceda jerdoni*
Black Baza (Indian Black-crested)	r	*Aviceda leuphotes*
Oriental Honey-buzzard	RW	*Pernis ptilorhyncus*
Black-shouldered Kite		
(Black-winged Kite)	R	*Elanus caeruleus*
Red Kite	V	*Milvus milvus*
Black Kite (Pariah Kite)	R	*Milvus migrans*
Brahminy Kite	R	*Haliastur indus*
White-bellied Sea Eagle	R	*Haliaeetus leucogaster*
Pallas's Fish Eagle	R	*Haliaeetus leucoryphus*
White-tailed Eagle	w	*Haliaeetus albicilla*
Lesser Fish Eagle		
(Himalyan Grey-headed Fishing)	R	*Ichthyophaga humilis*
Grey-headed Fish Eagle		
(Himalayan)	R	*Ichthyophaga ichthyaetus*
Lammergeier	R	*Gypaetus barbatus*
Egyptian Vulture		
	R	*Neophron percnopterus*
(Small White Scavenger)		
White-rumped Vulture		
(Indian White-backed Vulture)	R	*Gyps bengalensis*
Long-billed Vulture		
(Indian Long-billed)	R	*Gyps indicus*
Himalayan Griffon	R	*Gyps himalayensis*
Eurasian Griffon	R	*Gyps fulvus*
Cinereous Vulture	rW	*Aegypius monachus*
Red-headed Vulture (King Vulture)	R	*Sarcogyps calvus*
Short-toed Snake Eagle	R	*Circaetus gallicus*
Crested Serpent Eagle	R	*Spilornis cheela*
Nicobar Serpent Eagle	r	*Spilornis minimus*
Andaman Serpent Eagle	r	*Spilornis elgini*
Eurasian Marsh Harrier	W	*Circus aeruginosus*
Hen Harrier	w	*Circus cyaneus*
Pallid Harrier	W	*Circus macrourus*
Pied Harrier	rw	*Circus melanoleucos*
Montagu's Harrier	W	*Circus pygargus*
Crested Goshawk	R	*Accipiter trivirgatus*
Shikra	R	*Accipiter badius*
Nicobar Sparrowhawk	r	*Accipiter butleri*
Chinese Sparrowhawk	V	*Accipiter soloensis*

Japanese Sparrowhawk	w	*Accipiter gularis*
Besra	r	*Accipiter virgatus*
Eurasian Sparrowhawk	RW	*Accipiter nisus*
Northern Goshawk	rw	*Accipiter gentilis*
White-eyed Buzzard	R	*Butastur teesa*
Common Buzzard	rW	*Buteo buteo*
Long-legged Buzzard	rW	*Buteo rufinus*
Upland Buzzard	w	*Buteo hemilasius*
Black Eagle	R	*Ictinaetus malayensis*
Lesser Spotted Eagle	R	*Aquila pomarina*
Greater Spotted Eagle	RW	*Aquila clanga*
Tawny Eagle	R	*Aquila rapax*
Steppe Eagle	W	*Aquila nipalensis*
Imperial Eagle	W	*Aquila heliaca*
Golden Eagle	r	*Aquila chrysaetos*
Bonelli's Eagle	r	*Hieraaetus fasciatus*
Booted Eagle		
(Booted Hawk Eagle)	rW	*Hieraaetus pennatus*
Rufous-bellied Eagle	r	*Hieraaetus kienerii*
Changeable Hawk Eagle	R	*Spizaetus cirrhatus*
Mountain Hawk Eagle (Hodgson's)	r	*Spizaetus nipalensis*

Family: Falconidae

Collared Falconet (Red-breasted)	r	*Microhierax caerulescens*
Pied Falconet (White-legged)	r	*Microhierax melanoleucus*
Lesser Kestrel	w?p	*Falco naumanni*
Common Kestrel	RW	*Falco tinnunculus*
Red-necked Falcon	R	*Falco chicquera*
Amur Falcon (Red-legged)	s?p	*Falco amurensis*
Merlin	wp	*Falco columbarius*
Eurasian Hobby	rW	*Falco subbuteo*
Oriental Hobby	r	*Falco severus*
Laggar Falcon	R	*Falco jugger*
Saker Falcon (Lanner)	w	*Falco cherrug*
Peregrine Falcon	rw	*Falco peregrinus*

Family: Podicipedidae

Little Grebe	R	*Tachybaptus ruficollis*
Red-necked Grebe	V	*Podiceps grisegena*
Great Crested Grebe	rw	*Podiceps cristatus*
Horned Grebe	V	*Podiceps auritus*
Black-necked Grebe	w	*Podiceps nigricollis*

Family: Phaethontidae

Red-billed Tropicbird	Vs?	*Phaethon aethereus*
Red-tailed Tropicbird	r	*Phaethon rubricauda*
White-tailed Tropicbird	V	*Phaethon lepturus*

Family: Sulidae

Masked Booby	V	*Sula dactylatra*
Red-footed Booby	V	*Sula sula*
Brown Booby	V	*Sula leucogaster*

Family: Anhingidae

Darter (Snakebird)	R	*Anhinga melanogaster*

Family: Phalacrocoracidae

Little Cormorant	R	*Phalacrocorax niger*
Indian Cormorant (Shag)	R	*Phalacrocorax fuscicollis*
Great Cormorant	RW	*Phalacrocorax carbo*

Family: Ardeidae

Little Egret	R	*Egretta garzetta*
Western Reef Egret (Indian Reef Heron)	R	*Egretta gularis*
Pacific Reef Egret	r	*Egretta sacra*
Grey Heron	RW	*Ardea cinerea*
Goliath Heron (Giant Heron)	r?V	*Ardea goliath*
White-bellied Heron	r	*Ardea insignis*
Great-billed Heron	V	*Ardea sumatrana*
Purple Heron	R	*Ardea purpurea*
Great Egret (Large Egret)	Rw	*Casmerodius albus*
Intermediate Egret (Smaller Egret)	R	*Mesophoyx intermedia*
Cattle Egret	R	*Bubulcus ibis*
Indian Pond Heron	R	*Ardeola grayii*
Chinese Pond Heron	r	*Ardeola bacchus*
Little Heron (Little Green Heron)	r	*Butorides striatus*
Black-crowned Night Heron	R	*Nycticorax nycticorax*
Malayan Night Heron	R	*Gorsachius melanolophus*
Little Bittern	r	*Ixobrychus minutus*
Yellow Bittern	r	*Ixobrychus sinensis*
Cinnamon Bittern (Chestnut Bittern)	r	*Ixobrychus cinnamomeus*
Black Bittern	r	*Dupetor flavicollis*
Great Bittern (Bittern)	w	*Botaurus stellaris*

Family: Phoenicopteridae

Greater Flamingo	rW	*Phoenicopterus ruber*
Lesser Flamingo	r	*Phoenicopterus minor*

Family: Threskiornithidae

Glossy Ibis	RW	*Plegadis falcinellus*
Black-headed Ibis (White Ibis)	R	*Threskiornis melanocephalus*

Black Ibis	R	*Pseudibis papillosa*
Eurasian Spoonbill	RW	*Platalea leucorodia*

Family: Pelecanidae

Great White Pelican (Rosy Pelican)	rW	*Pelecanus onocrotalus*
Dalmatian Pelican	w	*Pelecanus crispus*
Spot-billed Pelican (Grey Pelican)	r	*Pelecanus philippensis*

Family: Ciconiidae

Painted Stork	R	*Mycteria leucocephala*
Asian Openbill	R	*Anastomus oscitans*
Black Stork	w	*Ciconia nigra*
Woolly-necked Stork (White-necked)	R	*Ciconia episcopus*
White Stork	W	*Ciconia ciconia*
Oriental Stork	V	*Ciconia boyciana*
Black-necked Stork	r	*Ephippiorhynchus asiaticus*
Lesser Adjutant	r	*Leptoptilos javanicus*
Greater Adjutant	r	*Leptoptilos dubius*

Family: Fregatidae

Great Frigatebird (Lesser)	V	*Fregata minor*
Lesser Frigatebird (Least)	V	*Fregata ariel*

Family: Gaviidae

Black-throated Loon (Diver)	V	*Gavia arctica*

Family: Procellariidae

Procellariinae

Barau's Petrel	p?	*Pterodroma baraui*
Bulwer's Petrel	V	*Bulweria bulwerii*
Jouanin's Petrel	p	*Bulweria fallax*
Wedge-tailed Shearwater	p	*Puffinus pacificus*
Flesh-footed Shearwater (Pink-footed)	p	*Puffinus carneipes*
Persian Shearwater	p?	*Puffinus persicus*

Hydrobatinae

Wilson's Storm-petrel	p	*Oceanites oceanicus*
White-faced Storm-petrel	V	*Pelagodroma marina*
Black-bellied Storm-petrel		
(Dusky-vented Storm-petrel)	V	*Fregetta tropica*
White-bellied Storm-petrel	V	*Fregetta grallaria*
Swinhoe's Storm-petrel	p?	*Oceanodroma monorhis*

ORDER: PASSERIFORMES

Family: Pittidae

Blue-naped Pitta	r	*Pitta nipalensis*
Blue Pitta	r	*Pitta cyanea*
Hooded Pitta	r	*Pitta sordida*
Indian Pitta	R	*Pitta brachyura*

Family: Eurylaimidae

Silver-breasted Broadbill (Collared)	r	*Serilophus lunatus*
Long-tailed Broadbill	r	*Psarisomus dalhousiae*

Family: Irenidae

Asian Fairy Bluebird	r	*Irena puella*
Blue-winged Leafbird		
(Gold-mantled Chloropsis)	R	*Chloropsis cochinchinensis*
Golden-fronted Leafbird (Chloropsis)	R	*Chloropsis aurifrons*
Orange-bellied Leafbird (Chloropsis)	r	*Chloropsis hardwickii*

Family: Laniidae

Red-backed Shrike	p	*Lanius collurio*
Rufous-tailed Shrike (Isabelline)	W	*Lanius isabellinus*
Brown Shrike	w	*Lanius cristatus*
Burmese Shrike	p	*Lanius collurioides*
Bay-backed Shrike	R	*Lanius vittatus*
Long-tailed Shrike (Rufous-backed)	R	*Lanius schach*
Grey-backed Shrike (Tibetan)	rW	*Lanius tephronotus*
Great Grey Shrike	R	*Lanius excubitor*

Family: Corvidae

Pachycephalinae

Mangrove Whistler (Grey Thickhead)	r	*Pachycephala grisola*

Corvinae

Corvini

Eurasian Jay	r	*Garrulus glandarius*
Black-headed Jay (Black-throated)	r	*Garrulus lanceolatus*
Sri Lanka Blue Magpie	r	*Urocissa ornata*
Yellow-billed Blue Magpie	R	*Urocissa flavirostris*
Red-billed Blue Magpie	R	*Urocissa erythrorhyncha*

Common Green Magpie	r	*Cissa chinensis*
Rufous Treepie (Indian Treepie)	R	*Dendrocitta Vagabunda*
Grey Treepie (Himalyan Treepie)	r	*Dendrocitta formosae*
White-bellied Treepie	r	*Dendrocitta leucogastra*
Collared Treepie	r	*Dendrocitta frontalis*
Andaman Treepie	r	*Dendrocitta bayleyi*
Black-billed Magpie (Eurasian)	r	*Pica pica*
Hume's Groundpecker		
(Hume's Ground-chough)	r	*Pseudopodoces humilis*
Spotted Nutcracker (Nutcracker)	r	*Nucifraga caryocatactes*
Red-billed Chough	r	*Pyrrhocorax pyrrhocorax*
Yellow-billed Chough (Alpine)	r	*Pyrrhocorax graculus*
Eurasian Jackdaw	rw	*Corvus monedula*
House Crow	R	*Corvus splendens*
Rook	wp	*Corvus frugilegus*
Carrion Crow	rw	*Corvus corone*
Large-billed Crow (Jungle Crow)	R	*Corvus macrorhynchos*
Common Raven	r	*Corvus corax*

Artamini

Ashy Wood		
(Ashy Swallow-shrike)	R	*Artamus fuscus*
White-breasted Woodswallow		
(White-rumped Woodswallow)	r	*Artamus leucorynchus*

Oriolini

Eurasian Golden Oriole	R	*Oriolus oriolus*
Black-naped Oriole	rw	*Oriolus chinensis*
Slender-billed Oriole	r	*Oriolus tenuirostris*
Black-hooded Oriole (Black-headed)	R	*Oriolus xanthornus*
Maroon Oriole	r	*Oriolus traillii*
Large Cuckooshrike	R	*Coracina macei*
Bar-bellied Cuckooshrike (Barred)	r	*Coracina striata*
Black-winged Cuckooshrike		
(Smaller Grey Cuckooshrike)	R	*Coracina melaschistos*
Black-headed Cuckooshrike	R	*Coracina melanoptera*
Pied Triller (Pied Cuckooshrike)	r	*Lalage nigra*
Rosy Minivet	rw	*Pericrocotus roseus*
Ashy Minivet	V	*Pericrocotus divaricatus*
Small Minivet	R	*Pericrocotus cinnamomeus*
White-bellied Minivet	r	*Pericrocotus erythropygius*
Grey-chinned Minivet	r	*Pericrocotus solaris*
Long-tailed Minivet	R	*Pericrocotus ethologus*
Short-billed Minivet	r	*Pericrocotus brevirostris*
Scarlet Minivet	R	*Pericrocotus flammeus*
Bar-winged Flycatcher-shrike		
(Pied Flycatcher-shrike)	R	*Hemipus picatus*

Dicrurinae

Rhipidurini

Yellow-bellied Fantail (Flycatcher)	r	*Rhipidura hypoxantha*
White-throated Fantail (Flycatcher)	R	*Rhipidura albicollis*
White-browed Fantail (Flycatcher)	R	*Rhipidura aureola*

Dicrurini

Black Drongo	R	*Dicrurus macrocercus*
Ashy Drongo	R	*Dicrurus leucophaeus*
White-bellied Drongo	R	*Dicrurus caerulescens*
Crow-billed Drongo	r	*Dicrurus annectans*
Bronzed Drongo	R	*Dicrurus aeneus*
Lesser Racket-tailed Drongo	r	*Dicrurus remifer*
Spangled Drongo (Hair-crested)	r	*Dicrurus hottentottus*
Andaman Drongo	r	*Dicrurus andamanensis*
Greater Racket-tailed Drongo	R	*Dicrurus paradiseus*

Monarchini

Black-naped Monarch (Flycatcher)	r	*Hypothymis azurea*
Asian Paradise-flycatcher	R	*Terpsiphone paradisi*

Aegithininae

Common Iora	R	*Aegithina tiphia*
Marshall's Iora	r	*Aegithina nigrolutea*

Malaconotinae

Large Woodshrike	R	*Tephrodornis gularis*
Common Woodshrike	R	*Tephrodornis pondicerianus*

Family: Bombycillidae

Bohemian Waxwing	V	*Bombycilla garrulus*

Family: Cinclidae

White-throated Dipper	r	*Cinclus cinclus*
Brown Dipper	r	*Cinclus pallasii*

Family: Muscicapidae

Turdinae

Rufous-tailed Rock Thrush (Rock Thrush)	p	*Monticola saxatilis*
Blue-capped Rock Thrush		

(Blue-headed Rock Thrush)	r	*Monticola cinclorhynchus*
Chestnut-bellied Rock Thrush	r	*Monticola rufiventris*
Blue Rock Thrush	rW	*Monticola solitarius*
Sri Lanka Whistling Thrush	R	*Myophonus blighi*
Malabar Whistling Thrush	R	*Myophonus horsfieldii*
Blue Whistling Thrush	R	*Myophonus caeruleus*
Pied Thrush (Pied Ground Thrush)	sp	*Zoothera wardii*
Orange-headed Thrush	R	*Zoothera citrina*
Siberian Thrush	w	*Zoothera sibirica*
Spot-winged Thrush	r	*Zoothera spiloptera*
Plain-backed Thrush	r	*Zoothera mollissima*
Long-tailed Thrush	r	*Zoothera dixoni*
Scaly Thrush		
(Speckled Mountain Thrush)	R	*Zoothera dauma*
Long-billed Thrush		
(Large Brown Thrush)	r	*Zoothera monticola*
Dark-sided Thrush		
(Lesser Brown Thrush)	r	*Zoothera marginata*
Tickell's Thrush	R	*Turdus unicolor*
Black-breasted Thrush	w	*Turdus dissimilis*
White-collared Blackbird	r	*Turdus albocinctus*
Grey-winged Blackbird	r	*Turdus boulboul*
Eurasian Blackbird	R	*Turdus merula*
Chestnut Thrush		
(Grey-headed Thrush)	r	*Turdus rubrocanus*
Kessler's Thrush	V	*Turdus kessleri*
Grey-sided Thrush (Fea's Thrush)	w	*Turdus feae*
Eyebrowed Thrush (Dark Thrush)	w	*Turdus obscurus*
Dark-throated Thrush	W	*Turdus ruficollis*
Dusky Thrush (Red Throated)	w	*Turdus naumanni*
Fieldfare	V	*Turdus pilaris*
Song Thrush	V	*Turdus philomelos*
Mistle Thrush	r	*Turdus viscivorus*
Gould's Shortwing	r	*Brachypteryx stellata*
Rusty-bellied Shortwing	r	*Brachypteryx hyperythra*
White-bellied Shortwing		
(Rufous-bellied Shortwing)	r	*Brachypteryx major*
Lesser Shortwing	r	*Brachypteryx leucophrys*
White-browed Shortwing	r	*Brachypteryx montana*

Muscicapinae

Muscicapini

Brown-chested Jungle Flycatcher		
(Olive Flycatcher)	wr?	*Rhinomyias brunneata*
Spotted Flycatcher	p	*Muscicapa striata*
Dark-sided Flycatcher (Sooty)	r	*Muscicapa sibirica*
Asian Brown Flycatcher	rW	*Muscicapa dauurica*
Rusty-tailed Flycatcher		

(Rufous-tailed Flycatcher)	r	*Muscicapa ruficauda*
Brown-breasted Flycatcher	r	*Muscicapa muttui*
Ferruginous Flycatcher	r	*Muscicapa ferruginea*
Yellow-rumped Flycatcher	V	*Ficedula zanthopygia*
Slaty-backed Flycatcher		
(Rusty-breasted Blue Flycatcher)	r	*Ficedula hodgsonii*
Rufous-gorgeted Flycatcher		
(Orange-gorgeted Flycatcher)	r	*Ficedula strophiata*
Red-throated Flycatcher		
(Red-breasted Flycatcher)	W	*Ficedula parva*
Kashmir Flycatcher		
(Kashmir Red-breasted Flycatcher)	sw	*Ficedula subrubra*
White-gorgeted Flycatcher	r	*Ficedula monileger*
Snowy-browed Flycatcher		
(Rufous-breasted Blue Flycatcher)	r	*Ficedula hyperythra*
Little Pied Flycatcher	r	*Ficedula westermanni*
Ultramarine Flycatcher		
(White-browed Blue Flycatcher)	r	*Ficedula superciliaris*
Slaty-blue Flycatcher	r	*Ficedula tricolor*
Sapphire Flycatcher	r	*Ficedula sapphira*
Black-and-orange Flycatcher	r	*Ficedula nigrorufa*
Verditer Flycatcher	R	*Eumyias thalassina*
Dull-blue Flycatcher		
(Dusky Blue Flycatcher)	r	*Eumyias sordida*
Nilgiri Flycatcher	r	*Eumyias albicaudata*
Large Niltava	r	*Niltava grandis*
Small Niltava	r	*Niltava macgrigoriae*
Rufous-bellied Niltava	r	*Niltava sundara*
Vivid Niltava		
(Rufous-bellied Blue Flycatcher)	r	*Niltava vivida*
White-tailed Flycatcher	r	*Cyornis concretus*
White-bellied Blue Flycatcher	r	*Cyornis pallipes*
Pale-chinned Flycatcher		
(Brook's Flycatcher)	r	*Cyornis poliogenys*
Pale Blue Flycatcher	r	*Cyornis unicolor*
Blue-throated Flycatcher	r	*Cyornis rubeculoides*
Hill Blue Flycatcher		
(Large-billed Blue Flycatcher)	r	*Cyornis banyumas*
Tickell's Blue Flycatcher	R	*Cyornis tickelliae*
Pygmy Blue Flycatcher	r	*Muscicapella hodgsoni*
Grey-headed Canary Flycatcher	r	*Culicicapa ceylonensis*

Saxicolini

Common Nightingale	V	*Luscinia megarhynchos*
Siberian Rubythroat	W	*Luscinia calliope*
White-tailed Rubythroat (Himalayan)	r	*Luscinia pectoralis*
Bluethroat	sW	*Luscinia svecica*
Firethroat	V	*Luscinia pectardens*
Indian Blue Robin (Blue Chat)	r	*Luscinia brunnea*

Siberian Blue Robin	V	*Luscinia cyane*
Orange-flanked Bush Robin	r	*Tarsiger cyanurus*
Golden Bush Robin	r	*Tarsiger chrysaeus*
White-browed Bush Robin	r	*Tarsiger indicus*
Rufous-breasted Bush Robin (Rufous-bellied Bush Robin)	r	*Tarsiger hyperythrus*
Rufous-tailed Scrub Robin (Rufous Chat)	p	*Cercotrichas galactotes*
Oriental Magpie Robin	R	*Copsychus saularis*
White-rumped Shama	r	*Copsychus malabaricus*
Indian Robin	R	*Saxicoloides fulicata*
Rufous-backed Redstart (Eversmann's Redstart)	w	*Phoenicurus erythronota*
Blue-capped Redstart (Blue-headed Redstart)	r	*Phoenicurus coeruleocephalus*
Black Redstart	rW	*Phoenicurus ochruros*
Common Redstart	V	*Phoenicurus phoenicurus*
Hodgson's Redstart	w	*Phoenicurus hodgsoni*
White-throated Redstart	r	*Phoenicurus schisticeps*
Daurian Redstart	rw	*Phoenicurus auroreus*
White-winged Redstart (Guldenstadt's Redstart)	r	*Phoenicurus erythrogaster*
Blue-fronted Redstart	r	*Phoenicurus frontalis*
White-capped Water Redstart	r	*Chaimarrornis leucocephalus*
Plumbeous Water Redstart	r	*Rhyacornis fuliginosus*
White-bellied Redstart (Hodgson's Shortwing)	r	*Hodgsonius phaenicuroides*
White-tailed Robin	r	*Myiomela leucura*
Blue-fronted Robin	r	*Cinclidium frontale*
Grandala	r	*Grandala coelicolor*
Little Forktail	r	*Enicurus scouleri*
Black-backed Forktail	r	*Enicurus immaculatus*
Slaty-backed Forktail	r	*Enicurus schistaceus*
White-crowned Forktail (Leschenault's Forktail)	r	*Enicurus leschenaulti*
Spotted Forktail	r	*Enicurus maculatus*
Purple Cochoa	r	*Cochoa purpurea*
Green Cochoa	r	*Cochoa viridis*
Stoliczka's Bushchat	r	*Saxicola macrorhyncha*
Hodgson's Bushchat	w	*Saxicola insignis*
Common Stonechat (Collared Bushchat)	R	*Saxicola torquata*
White-tailed Stonechat	r	*Saxicola leucura*
Pied Bushchat	R	*Saxicola caprata*
Jerdon's Bushchat	r	*Saxicola jerdoni*
Grey Bushchat (Dark-grey Bushchat)	R	*Saxicola ferrea*
Hume's Wheatear (Chat)	?	*Oenanthe alboniger*

Northern Wheatear	V	*Oenanthe oenanthe*
Variable Wheatear (Pied Chat)	W	*Oenanthe picata*
Pied Wheatear (Pleschanka's Pied Chat)	?	*Oenanthe pleschanka*
Rufous-tailed Wheatear (Red-tailed Chat)	w	*Oenanthe xanthoprymna*
Desert Wheatear	r	*Oenanthe deserti*
Isabelline Wheatear (Chat)	W	*Oenanthe isabellina*
Brown Rock-chat	R	*Cercomela fusca*

Family: Sturnidae

Asian Glossy Starling	r	*Aplonis panayensis*
Spot-winged Starling (Spotted-winged Stare)	r	*Saroglossa spiloptera*
White-faced Starling (Ceylon White-headed Myna)	r	*Sturnus senex*
Chestnut-tailed Starling (Grey-headed Myna)	R	*Sturnus malabaricus*
White-headed Starling (Myna)	r	*Sturnus erythropygius*
Brahminy Starling (Black-headed Myna)	R	*Sturnus pagodarum*
Purple-backed Starling	V	*Sturnus sturninus*
White-shouldered Starling	V	*Sturnus sinensis*
Rosy Starling (Rosy Pastor)	WP	*Sturnus roseus*
Common Starling	WP	*Sturnus vulgaris*
Asian Pied Starling	R	*Sturnus contra*
Common Myna	R	*Acridotheres tristis*
Bank Myna	R	*Acridotheres ginginianus*
Jungle Myna	R	*Acridotheres fuscus*
White-Vented Myna (Orange-billed Jungle Myna)	r	*Acridotheres cinereus*
Collared Myna	r	*Acridotheres albocinctus*
Golden-crested Myna	r	*Ampeliceps coronatus*
Sri Lanka Myna	r	*Gracula ptilogenys*
Hill Myna (Grackle)	R	*Gracula religiosa*

Family: Sittidae

Sittinae

Chestnut-vented Nuthatch	r	*Sitta nagaensis*
Kashmir Nuthatch (European)	r	*Sitta cashmirensis*
Chestnut-bellied Nuthatch	R	*Sitta castanea*
White-tailed Nuthatch	r	*Sitta himalayensis*
White-cheeked Nuthatch	r	*Sitta leucopsis*
Velvet-fronted Nuthatch	R	*Sitta frontalis*
Beautiful Nuthatch	r	*Sitta formosa*

Tichodrominae

Wallcreeper	rW	*Tichodroma muraria*

Family: Certhiidae

Certhiinae

Certhinii

Eurasian Treecreeper	r	*Certhia familiaris*
Bar-tailed Treecreeper (Himalayan Treecreeper)	r	*Certhia himalayana*
Rusty-flanked Treecreeper (Nepal Treecreeper)	r	*Certhia nipalensis*
Brown-throated Treecreeper (Sikkim Treecreeper)	r	*Certhia discolor*

Salpornithini

Spotted Creeper (Grey)	r	*Salpornis spilonotus*

Troglodytinae

Winter Wren	r	*Troglodytes troglodytes*

Family: Paridae

Remizinae

White-crowned Penduline Tit	r	*Remiz coronatus*
Fire-capped Tit	r	*Cephalopyrus flammiceps*

Parinae

Rufous-naped Tit (Simla Black Tit)	r	*Parus rufonuchalis*
Rufous-vented Tit (Rufous-bellied Crested Tit)	r	*Parus rubidiventris*
Spot-winged Tit (Crested Black Tit)	r	*Parus melanolophus*
Coal Tit	r	*Parus ater*
Grey-crested Tit (Brown Crested Tit)	r	*Parus dichrous*
Great Tit (Grey Tit)	R	*Parus major*
Green-backed Tit	r	*Parus monticolus*
White-naped Tit (White-winged Black Tit)	r	*Parus nuchalis*
Black-lored Tit (Yellow-cheeked Tit)	r	*Parus xanthogenys*

Yellow-cheeked Tit		
(Black-spotted Yellow Tit)	r	*Parus spilonotus*
Yellow-browed Tit	r	*Sylviparus modestus*
Sultan Tit	r	*Melanochlora sultanea*

Family: Aegithalidae

White-cheeked Tit	r	*Aegithalos leucogenys*
Black-throated Tit		
(Red-headed Tit)	r	*Aegithalos concinnus*
White-throated Tit	r	*Aegithalos niveogularis*
Rufous-fronted Tit	r	*Aegithalos iouschistos*

Family: Hirundinidae

Sand Martin (Collared Sand Martin)	R	*Riparia riparia*
Pale Martin	V?	*Riparia diluta*
Plain Martin (Plain Sand Martin)	R	*Riparia paludicola*
Eurasian Crag Martin	r	*Hirundo rupestris*
Rock Martin		
(Pale Crag Martin)	V?	*Hirundo fuligula*
Dusky Crag Martin	R	*Hirundo concolor*
Barn Swallow	RW	*Hirundo rustica*
Pacific Swallow (House)	r	*Hirundo tahitica*
Wire-tailed Swallow	R	*Hirundo smithii*
Red-rumped Swallow	RW	*Hirundo daurica*
Striated Swallow (Larger Striated)	r	*Hirundo striolata*
Streak-throated Swallow		
(Indian Cliff Swallow)	R	*Hirundo fluvicola*
Northern House Martin	rW	*Delichon urbica*
Asian House Martin	r	*Delichon dasypus*
Nepal House Martin	r	*Delichon nipalensis*

Family: Regulidae

Goldcrest	r	*Regulus regulus*

Family: Pycnonotidae

Crested Finchbill		
(Finch-billed Bulbul)	r	*Spizixos canifrons*
Striated Bulbul	r	*Pycnonotus striatus*
Grey-headed Bulbul	r	*Pycnonotus priocephalus*
Black-headed Bulbul	r	*Pycnonotus atriceps*
Black-crested Bulbul		
(Black-headed Yellow Bulbul)	R	*Pycnonotus melanicterus*
Red-whiskered Bulbul	R	*Pycnonotus jocosus*
White-eared Bulbul		
(White-cheeked Bulbul)	R	*Pycnonotus leucotis*
Himalayan Bulbul		

(White-cheeked Bulbul)	R	*Pycnonotus leucogenys*
Red-vented Bulbul	R	*Pycnonotus cafer*
Yellow-throated Bulbul	r	*Pycnonotus xantholaemus*
Yellow-eared Bulbul	r	*Pynconotus penicillatus*
Flavescent Bulbul		
(Blyth's Bulbul)	r	*Pycnonotus flavescens*
White-browed Bulbul	r	*Pycnonotus luteolus*
White-throated Bulbul	r	*Alophoixus flaveolus*
Olive Bulbul	r	*Iole virescens*
Yellow-browed Bulbul	r	*Iole indica*
Ashy Bulbul		
(Brown-eared Bulbul)	r	*Hemixos flavala*
Mountain Bulbul		
(Rufous-bellied Bulbul)	r	*Hypsipetes mcclellandii*
Black Bulbul	R	*Hypsipetes leucocephalus*
Nicobar Bulbul	r	*Hypsipetes nicobariensis*

Family Hypocoliidae

Grey Hypocolius	w	*Hypocolius ampelinus*

Family: Cisticolidae

Zitting Cisticola		
(Streaked Fantail Warbler)	R	*Cisticola juncidis*
Bright-headed Cisticola		
(Fantail Warbler)	R	*Cisticola exilis*
Rufous-vented Prinia		
(Long-tailed Grass Warbler)	r	*Prinia burnesii*
Striated Prinia		
(Brown Hill Warbler)	r	*Prinia criniger*
Hill Prinia		
(Black-throated Hill Warbler)	r	*Prinia atrogularis*
Grey-crowned Prinia		
(Hodgson's Wren Warbler)	r	*Prinia cinereocapilla*
Rufous-fronted Prinia (Wren Warbler)	R	*Prinia buchanani*
Rufescent Prinia		
(Beavan's Wren Warbler)	r	*Prinia rufescens*
Grey-breasted Prinia		
(Franklin's Wren Warbler)	R	*Prinia hodgsonii*
Graceful Prinia		
(Streaked Wren Warbler)	R	*Prinia gracilis*
Jungle Prinia	R	*Prinia sylvatica*
Yellow-bellied Prinia	R	*Prinia flaviventris*
Ashy Prinia	R	*Prinia socialis*
Plain Prinia	R	*Prinia inornata*

Family: Zosteropidae

Sri Lanka White-eye	R	*Zosterops ceylonensis*

Oriental White-eye	R	*Zosterops palpebrosus*

Family: Sylviidae

Acrocephalinae

Chestnut-headed Tesia		
(Chestnut-headed Ground Warbler)	r	*Tesia castaneocoronata*
Slaty-bellied Tesia	r	*Tesia olivea*
Grey-bellied Tesia		
(Dull Slaty-bellied Ground Warbler)	r	*Tesia cyaniventer*
Pale-footed Bush Warbler	r	*Cettia pallidipes*
Japanese Bush Warbler	?	*Cettia diphone*
Brownish-flanked Bush Warbler		
(Strong-footed Bush Warbler)	r	*Cettia fortipes*
Chestnut-crowned Bush Warbler		
(Large Bush Warbler)	r	*Cettia major*
Aberrant Bush Warbler	r	*Cettia flavolivacea*
Yellowish-bellied Bush Warbler		
(Verreaux's Bush Warbler)	r	*Cettia acanthizoides*
Grey-sided Bush Warbler		
(Rufous-capped Bush Warbler)	r	*Cettia brunnifrons*
Cetti's Bush Warbler		
(Cetti's Warbler)	w	*Cettia cetti*
Spotted Bush Warbler	r	*Bradypterus thoracicus*
Long-billed Bush Warbler	r	*Bradypterus major*
Chinese Bush Warbler	V	*Bradypterus tacsanowskius*
Brown Bush Warbler	r	*Bradypterus luteoventris*
Russet Bush Warbler	?	*Bradypterus seebohmi*
Sri Lanka Bush Warbler	?	*Bradypterus palliseri*
Lanceolated Warbler		
(Streaked Grasshopper Warbler)	w	*Locustella lanceolata*
Grasshopper Warbler	w	*Locustella naevia*
Rusty-rumped Warbler		
(Pallas's Warbler)	w	*Locustella certhiola*
Moustached Warbler	rw	*Acrocephalus melanopogon*
Sedge Warbler	V	*Acrocephalus schoenobaenus*
Black-browed Reed Warbler	w	*Acrocephalus bistrigiceps*
Paddyfield Warbler	W	*Acrocephalus agricola*
Blunt-winged Warbler	r	*Acrocephalus concinens*
Blyth's Reed Warbler	W	*Acrocephalus dumetorum*
Great Reed Warbler	w	*Acrocephalus arundinaceus*
Oriental Reed Warbler	?	*Acrocephalus orientalis*
Clamorous Reed Warbler		
(Indian Great Reed Warbler)	R	*Acrocephalus stentoreus*
Thick-billed Warbler	w	*Acrocephalus aedon*
Booted Warbler	W	*Hippolais caligata*
Mountain Tailorbird		
(Golden-headed Tailorbird)	r	*Orthotomus cuculatus*

Common Tailorbird	R	*Orthotomus sutorius*
Dark-necked Tailorbird		
(Black-necked Tailorbird)	r	*Orthotomus atrogularis*
White-browed Tit Warbler		
(Stoliczka's Tit Warbler)	r	*Leptopoecile sophiae*
Common Chiffchaff		
(Brown Leaf Warbler)	sW	*Phylloscopus collybita*
Mountain Chiffchaff	?	*Phylloscopus sindianus*
Plain Leaf Warbler	w	*Phylloscopus neglectus*
Dusky Warbler	W	*Phylloscopus fuscatus*
Smoky Warbler	sw	*Phylloscopus fuligiventer*
Tickell's Leaf Warbler	sW	*Phylloscopus affinis*
Buff-throated Warbler	?	*Phylloscopus subaffinis*
Sulphur-bellied Warbler		
(Olivaceous Leaf Warbler)	sW	*Phylloscopus griseolus*
Radde's Warbler	V	*Phylloscopus schwarzi*
Buff-barred Warbler		
(Orange-barred Leaf Warbler)	r	*Phylloscopus pulcher*
Ashy-throated Warbler		
(Grey-faced Leaf Warbler)	r	*Phylloscopus maculipennis*
Lemon-rumped Warbler		
(Pallas's Warbler)	r	*Phylloscopus chloronotus*
Brooks's Leaf Warbler	W	*Phylloscopus subviridis*
Yellow-browed Warbler		
	rW	*Phylloscopus inornatus*
(Inornate Leaf Warbler)		
Hume's Warbler	W	*Phylloscopus humei*
Arctic Warbler	V	*Phylloscopus borealis*
Greenish Warbler		
(Dull Green Leaf Warbler)	rW	*Phylloscopus trochiloides*
Pale-legged Leaf Warbler	V	*Phylloscopus tenellipes*
Large-billed Leaf Warbler	rW	*Phylloscopus magnirostris*
Tytler's Leaf Warbler	r	*Phylloscopus tytleri*
Western Crowned Warbler		
(Large Crowned Leaf Warbler)	r	*Phylloscopus occipitalis*
Eastern Crowned Warbler	V	*Phylloscopus coronatus*
Blyth's Leaf Warbler	r	*Phylloscopus reguloides*
Yellow-vented Warbler		
(Black-browed Leaf Warbler)	r	*Phylloscopus cantator*
Golden-spectacled Warbler		
(Black-browed Flycatcher Warbler)	r	*Seicercus burkii*
Grey-hooded Warbler		
(Grey-headed Flycatcher Warbler)	r	*Seicercus xanthoschistos*
White-spectacled Warbler		
(Allied Flycatcher Warbler)	r	*Seicercus affinis*
Grey-cheeked Warbler	r	*Seicercus poliogenys*
Chestnut-crowned Warbler	r	*Seicercus castaniceps*
Broad-billed Warbler	r	*Tickellia hodgsoni*
Rufous-faced Warbler		
(White-throated Flycatcher Warbler)	r	*Abroscopus albogularis*

Black-faced Warbler r *Abroscopus schisticeps*
Yellow-bellied Warbler r *Abroscopus superciliaris*

Megalurinae

Striated Grassbird r *Megalurus palustris*
(Striated Marsh Warbler)
Bristled Grassbird
(Bristled Grass Warbler) r *Chaetornis striatus*
Rufous-rumped Grassbird
(Large Grass Warbler) r *Graminicola bengalensis*
Broad-tailed Grassbird r *Schoenicola platyura*

Garrulacinae

Ashy-headed Laughingthrush
(Ashy-headed Babbler) r *Garrulax cinereifrons*
White-throated Laughingthrush r *Garrulax albogularis*
White-crested Laughingthrush r *Garrulax leucolophus*
Lesser Necklaced Laughingthrush r *Garrulax monileger*
Greater Necklaced Laughingthrush
(Black-gorgeted Laughingthrush) r *Garrulax pectoralis*
Striated Laughingthrush r *Garrulax striatus*
Rufous-necked Laughingthrush r *Garrulax ruficollis*
Chesnut-backed Laughingthrush r *Garrulax nuchalis*
Yellow-throated Laughingthrush r *Garrulax galbanus*
Wynaad Laughingthrush r *Garrulax delesserti*
Rufous-vented Laughingthrush r *Garrulax gularis*
Moustached Laughingthrush
(Ashy Laughingthrush) r *Garrulax cineraceus*
Rufous-chinned Laughingthrush r *Garrulax rufogularis*
Spotted Laughingthrush
(White-spotted Laughingthrush) r *Garrulax ocellatus*
Grey-sided Laughingthrush r *Garrulax caerulatus*
Spot-breasted Laughingthrush r *Garrulax merulinus*
White-browed Laughingthrush r *Garrulax sannio*
Nilgiri Laughingthrush r *Garrulax cachinnans*
Grey-breasted Laughingthrush
(White-breasted Laughingthrush) r *Garrulax jerdoni*
Streaked Laughingthrush r *Garrulax lineatus*
Striped Laughingthrush
(Manipur Streaked Laughingthrush) r *Garrulax virgatus*
Brown-capped Laughingthrush r *Garrulax austeni*
Blue-winged Laughingthrush r *Garrulax squamatus*
Scaly Laughingthrush
(Plain-colored Laughingthrush) r *Garrulax subunicolor*
Elliot's Laughingthrush r *Garrulax elliotii*
Variegated Laughingthrush r *Garrulax variegatus*
Brown-cheeked Laughingthrush

(Prince Henri's Laughingthrush)	r	*Garrulax henrici*
Black-faced Laughingthrush	r	*Garrulax affinis*
Chestnut-crowned Laughingthrush		
(Red-headed Laughingthrush)	r	*Garrulax erythrocephalus*
Red-faced Liocichla		
(Crimson-winged Laughingthrush)	r	*Liocichla phoenicea*

Sylviinae

Timaliini

Abbott's Babbler	r	*Malacocincla abbotti*
Buff-breasted Babbler		
(Tickell's Babbler)	r	*Pellorneum tickelli*
Spot-throated Babbler		
(Brown Babbler)	r	*Pellorneum albiventre*
Marsh Babbler	r	*Pellorneum palustre*
Puff-throated Babbler		
(Spotted Babbler)	R	*Pellorneum ruficeps*
Brown-capped Babbler	r	*Pellorneum fuscocapillum*
Large Scimitar Babbler		
(Long-billed Scimitar Babbler)	r	*Pomatorhinus hypoleucos*
Spot-breasted Scimitar Babbler	r	*Pomatorhinus erythrocnemis*
Rusty-cheeked Scimitar Babbler	r	*Pomatorhinus erythrogenys*
Indian Scimitar Babbler	R	*Pomatorhinus horsfieldii*
White-browed Scimitar Babbler		
(Slaty-headed Scimitar Babbler)	r	*Pomatorhinus schisticeps*
Streak-breasted Scimitar Babbler		
(Rufous-necked Scimitar Babbler)	r	*Pomatorhinus ruficollis*
Red-billed Scimitar Babbler		
(Lloyd's Scimitar Babbler)	r	*Pomatorhinus ochraciceps*
Coral-billed Scimitar Babbler	r	*Pomatorhinus ferruginosus*
Slender-billed Scimitar Babbler	r	*Xiphirhynchus superciliaris*
Long-billed Wren Babbler	r	*Rimator malacoptilus*
Streaked Wren Babbler		
(Short-tailed Wren Babbler)	r	*Napothera brevicaudata*
Eyebrowed Wren Babbler		
(Small Wren Babbler)	r	*Napothera epilepidota*
Scaly-breasted Wren Babbler	r	*Pnoepyga albiventer*
Pygmy Wren Babbler		
(Brown Wren Babbler)	r	*Pnoepyga pusilla*
Nepal Wren Babbler	r	*Pnoepyga immaculata*
Rufous-throated Wren Babbler		
(Tailed Wren Babbler)	r	*Spelaeornis caudatus*
Rusty-throated Wren Babbler		
(Mishmi Wren Babbler)	r	*Spelaeornis badeigularis*
Bar-winged Wren Babbler		
(Long-tailed Spotted Wren Babbler)	r	*Spelaeornis troglodytoides*
Spotted Wren Babbler	r	*Spelaeornis formosus*
Long-tailed Wren Babbler		

(Streaked Long-tailed Wren babbler)	r	*Spelaeornis chocolatinus*
Tawny-breasted Wren Babbler		
(Long-tailed Wren Babbler)	r	*Spelaeornis longicaudatus*
Wedge-billed Wren Babbler		
(Wedge-billed Wren)	r	*Sphenocichla humei*
Rufous-fronted Babbler		
(Red-fronted Babbler)	r	*Stachyris rufifrons*
Rufous-capped Babbler		
(Red-headed Babbler)	r	*Stachyris ruficeps*
Black-chinned Babbler		
(Red-billed Babbler)	r	*Stachyris pyrrhops*
Golden Babbler		
(Gold-headed Babbler)	r	*Stachyris chrysaea*
Grey-throated Babbler		
(Black-throated Babbler)	r	*Stachyris nigriceps*
Snowy-throated Babbler		
(Austen's Spotted Babbler)	r	*Stachyris oglei*
Tawny-bellied Babbler		
(Rufous-bellied Babbler)	R	*Dumetia hyperythra*
Dark-fronted Babbler		
(Black-headed Babbler)	r	*Rhopocichla atriceps*
Striped Tit Babbler		
(Yellow-breasted Babbler)	R	*Macronous gularis*
Chestnut-capped Babbler		
(Red-capped Babbler)	R	*Timalia pileata*
Yellow-eyed Babbler	R	*Chrysomma sinense*
Jerdon's Babbler	r	*Chrysomma altirostre*
Spiny Babbler	r	*Turdoides nipalensis*
Common Babbler	R	*Turdoides caudatus*
Striated Babbler	r	*Turdoides earlei*
Slender-billed Babbler	r	*Turdoides longirostris*
Large Grey Babbler	R	*Turdoides malcolmi*
Rufous Babbler	R	*Turdoides subrufus*
Jungle Babbler	R	*Turdoides striatus*
Orange-billed Babbler		
(Ceylon Rufous Babbler)	r	*Turdoides rufescens*
Yellow-billed Babbler		
(White-headed Babbler)	R	*Turdoides affinis*
Giant Babax		
(Giant Tibetan Babax)	r	*Babax waddelli*
Silver-eared Mesia	r	*Leiothrix argentauris*
Red-billed Leiothrix	r	*Leiothrix lutea*
Cutia		
(Nepal Cutia)	r	*Cutia nipalensis*
Black-headed Shrike Babbler		
(Rufous-bellied Shrike Babbler)	r	*Pteruthius rufiventer*
White-browed Shrike Babbler		
(Red-winged Shrike Babbler)	r	*Pteruthius flaviscapis*
Green Shrike Babbler	r	*Pteruthius xanthochlorus*
Black-eared Shrike Babbler		

(Chestnut-throated Shrike Babbler)	r	*Pteruthius melanotis*
Chestnut-fronted Shrike Babbler	r	*Pteruthius aenobarbus*
White-hooded Babbler		
(White-headed Shrike Babbler)	r	*Gampsorhynchus rufulus*
Rusty-fronted Barwing		
(Spectacled Barwing)	r	*Actinodura egertoni*
Hoary-throated Barwing		
(Hoary Barwing)	r	*Actinodura nipalensis*
Streak-throated Barwing		
(Austen's Barwing)	r	*Actinodura waldeni*
Blue-winged Minla		
(Blue-winged Siva)	r	*Minla cyanouroptera*
Chestnut-tailed Minla		
(Bar-throated Siva)	r	*Minla strigula*
Red-tailed Minla	r	*Minla ignotincta*
Golden-breasted Fulvetta		
(Golden-breasted Tit Babbler)	r	*Alcippe chrysotis*
Yellow-throated Fulvetta		
(Dusky-green Tit Babbler)	r	*Alcippe cinerea*
Rufous-winged Fulvetta		
(Chestnut-headed Tit Babbler)	r	*Alcippe castaneceps*
White-browed Fulvetta		
(White-browed Tit Babbler)	r	*Alcippe vinipectus*
Streak-throated Fulvetta		
(Brown-headed Tit Babbler)	r	*Alcippe cinereiceps*
Brown-throated Fulvetta		
(Ludlow's Fulvetta)	r	*Alcippe ludlowi*
Rufous-throated Fulvetta		
(Red-throated Tit Babbler)	r	*Alcippe rufogularis*
Rusty-capped Fulvetta		
(Rufous-headed Tit Babbler)	r	*Alcippe dubia*
Brown-cheeked Fulvetta		
(Quaker Babbler)	R	*Alcippe poioicephala*
Nepal Fulvetta		
(Nepal Babbler)	r	*Alcippe nipalensis*
Rufous-backed Sibia		
(Chestnut-backed Sibia)	r	*Heterophasia annectans*
Rufous Sibia		
(Black-capped Sibia)	r	*Heterophasia capistrata*
Grey Sibia	r	*Heterophasia gracilis*
Beautiful Sibia	r	*Heterophasia pulchella*
Long-tailed Sibia	r	*Heterophasia picaoides*
Striated Yuhina		
(White-browed Yuhina)	r	*Yuhina castaniceps*
White-naped Yuhina	r	*Yuhina bakeri*
Whiskered Yuhina		
(Yellow-naped Yuhina)	r	*Yuhina flavicollis*
Stripe-throated Yuhina	r	*Yuhina gularis*
Rufous-vented Yuhina	r	*Yuhina occipitalis*
Black-chinned Yuhina	r	*Yuhina nigrimenta*

White-bellied Yuhina	r	*Yuhina zantholeuca*
Fire-tailed Myzornis	r	*Myzornis pyrrhoura*
Great Parrotbill	r	*Conostoma oemodium*
Brown Parrotbill		
(Brown Suthora)	r	*Paradoxornis unicolor*
Grey-headed Parrotbill	r	*Paradoxornis gularis*
Black-breasted Parrotbill		
(Gould's Parrotbill)	r	*Paradoxornis flavirostris*
Spot-breasted Parrotbill		
(White-throated Parrotbill)	r	*Paradoxornis guttaticollis*
Fulvous Parrotbill		
(Fulvous-fronted Suthora)	r	*Paradoxornis fulvifrons*
Black-throated Parrotbill		
(Orange Suthora)	r	*Paradoxornis nipalensis*
Lesser Rufous-headed Parrotbill		
(Lesser Red-headed Suthora)	r	*Paradoxornis atrosuperciliaris*
Greater Rufous-headed Parrotbill		
(Greater Red-headed Parrotbill)	r	*Paradoxornis ruficeps*

Sylviini

Garden Warbler	V	*Sylvia borin*
Greater Whitethroat		
(Common Whitethroat)	p	*Sylvia communis*
Lesser Whitethroat	W	*Sylvia curruca*
Desert Warbler	w	*Sylvia nana*
Barred Warbler	V	*Sylvia nisoria*
Orphean Warbler	W	*Sylvia hortensis*
Menetries's Warbler	r	*Sylvia mystacea*

Family: Alaudidae

Singing Bushlark	R	*Mirafra cantillans*
Indian Bushlark		
(Red-winged Bushlark)	R	*Mirafra erythroptera*
Rufous-winged Bushlark	R	*Mirafra assamica*
Black-crowned Sparrow Lark		
(Black-crowned Finch Lark)	r	*Eremopterix nigriceps*
Ashy-crowned Sparrow Lark		
(Ashy-crowned Finch Lark)	R	*Eremopterix grisea*
Rufous-tailed Lark		
(Rufous-tailed Finch Lark)	R	*Ammomanes phoenicurus*
Desert Lark (Finch Lark)	r	*Ammomanes deserti*
Greater Hoopoe Lark		
(Bisfasciated Lark)	r	*Alaemon alaudipes*
Bimaculated lark		
(Eastern Calandra Lark)	w	*Melanocorypha bimaculata*
Tibetan Lark		
(Long-billed Calandra Lark)	r	*Melanocorypha maxima*
Greater Short-toed Lark	W	*Calandrella brachydactyla*

Hume's Short-toed Lark	rW	*Calandrella acutirostris*
Asian Short-toed Lark	?	*Calandrella cheleensis*
Sand Lark		
(Indian Short-toed Lark)	R	*Calandrella raytal*
Crested Lark	R	*Galerida cristata*
Malabar Lark	R	*Galerida malabarica*
Sykes's Lark	R	*Galerida deva*
Eurasian Skylark (Skylark)	w	*Alauda arvensis*
Oriental Skylark (Eastern Skylark)	R	*Alauda gulgula*
Horned Lark	r	*Eremophila alpestris*

Family: Nectariniidae

Nectariniinae

Dicaeini

Thick-billed Flowerpecker	R	*Dicaeum agile*
Yellow-vented Flowerpecker	r	*Dicaeum chrysorrheum*
Yellow-bellied Flowerpecker	r	*Dicaeum melanoxanthum*
Legge's Flowerpecker		
(White-throated Flowerpecker)	r	*Dicaeum vincens*
Orange-bellied Flowerpecker	r	*Dicaeum trigonostigma*
Pale-billed Flowerpecker		
(Tickell's Flowerpecker)	R	*Dicaeum erythrorynchos*
Plain Flowerpecker	R	*Dicaeum concolor*
Fire-breasted Flowerpecker	r	*Dicaeum ignipectus*
Scarlet-backed Flowerpecker	r	*Dicaeum cruentatum*

Nectariniini

Ruby-cheeked Sunbird	r	*Anthreptes singalensis*
Purple-rumped Sunbird	R	*Nectarinia zeylonica*
Crimson-backed Sunbird		
(Small Sunbird)	R	*Nectarinia minima*
Purple-throated Sunbird		
(Van Hasselt's Sunbird)	r	*Nectarinia sperata*
Olive-backed Sunbird	r	*Nectarinia jugularis*
Purple Sunbird	R	*Nectarinia asiatica*
Loten's Sunbird	R	*Nectarinia lotenia*
Mrs Gould's Sunbird	?	*Aethopyga gouldiae*
Green-tailed Sunbird		
(Nepal Yellow-backed Sunbird)	r	*Aethopyga nipalensis*
Black-throated Sunbird		
(Black-breasted Sunbird)	r	*Aethopyga saturata*
Crimson Sunbird		
(Yellow-backed Sunbird)	r	*Aethopyga siparaja*
Fire-tailed Sunbird	r	*Aethopyga ignicauda*
Little Spiderhunter	r	*Arachnothera longirostra*

Streaked Spiderhunter	r	*Arachnothera magna*

Family:Passeridae

Passerinae

House Sparrow	R	*Passer domesticus*
Spanish Sparrow	W	*Passer hispaniolensis*
Sind Sparrow	r	*Passer pyrrhonotus*
Russet Sparrow		
(Cinnamon Tree Sparrow)	r	*Passer rutilans*
Eurasian Tree Sparrow	R	*Passer montanus*
Chestnut-shouldered Petronia		
(Yellow-throated Sparrow)	R	*Petronia xanthocollis*
White-winged Snowfinch (Snowfinch)	?	*Montifringilla nivalis*
Tibetan Snowfinch	r	*Montifringilla adamsi*
White-rumped Snowfinch		
(Mandelli's Snowfinch)	V	*Pyrgilauda taczanowskii*
Rufous-necked Snowfinch		
(Red-necked Snowfinch)	w	*Pyrgilauda ruficollis*
Plain-backed Snowfinch		
(Blandford's Snowfinch)	w	*Pyrgilauda blanfordi*

Motacillinae

Forest Wagtail	rW	*Dendronanthus indicus*
White Wagtail (Pied Wagtail)	rW	*Motacilla alba*
White-browed Wagtail		
(Large Pied Wagtail)	R	*Motacilla maderaspatensis*
Citrine Wagtail		
(Yellow-headed Wagtail)	rW	*Motacilla citreola*
Yellow Wagtail	W	*Motacilla flava*
Grey Wagtail	rW	*Motacilla cinerea*
Richard's Pipit	W	*Anthus richardi*
Paddyfield Pipit	R	*Anthus rufulus*
Tawny Pipit	W	*Anthus campestris*
Blyth's Pipit	W	*Anthus godlewskii*
Long-billed Pipit		
(Brown Rock pipit)	R	*Anthus similis*
Tree Pipit	rW	*Anthus trivialis*
Olive-backed Pipit		
(Indian Tree Pipit)	RW	*Anthus hodgsoni*
Meadow Pipit	V	*Anthus pratensis*
Red-throated Pipit	p	*Anthus cervinus*
Rosy Pipit		
(Vinaceous-breasted Pipit)	r	*Anthus roseatus*
Water Pipit	w	*Anthus spinoletta*
Buff-bellied Pipit	w	*Anthus rubescens*
Upland Pipit	r	*Anthus sylvanus*

Nilgiri Pipit	r	*Anthus nilghiriensis*

Prunellinae

Alpine Accentor	R	*Prunella collaris*
Altai Accentor	w	*Prunella himalayana*
Robin Accentor	r	*Prunella rubeculoides*
Rufous-breasted Accentor	r	*Prunella strophiata*
Siberian Accentor	V	*Prunella montanella*
Brown Accentor	r	*Prunella fulvescens*
Black-throated Accentor	w	*Prunella atrogularis*
Maroon-backed Accentor	r	*Prunella immaculata*

Ploceinae

Black-breasted Weaver (Black-throated Weaver)	R	*Ploceus benghalensis*
Streaked Weaver	R	*Ploceus manyar*
Baya Weaver	R	*Ploceus philippinus*
Finn's Weaver (Finn's Baya)	r	*Ploceus megarhynchus*

Estrildinae

Red Avadavat (Red Munia)	R	*Amandava amandava*
Green Avadavat (Green Munia)	R	*Amandava formosa*
Indian Silverbill (White-throated Munia)	R	*Lonchura malabarica*
White-rumped Munia (White-backed Munia)	R	*Lonchura striata*
Black-throated Munia (Rufous-bellied Munia)	r	*Lonchura kelaarti*
Scaly-breasted Munia (Spotted Munia)	R	*Lonchura punctulata*
Black-headed Munia	R	*Lonchura malacca*
Java Sparrow	r?I	*Lonchura oryzivora*

Family: Fringillidae

Fringillinae

Fringillini

Chaffinch		*Fringilla coelebs*
Brambling		*Fringilla montifringilla*

Carduelini

Fire-fronted Serin (Gold-fronted Serin)	r	*Serinus pusillus*
Yellow-breasted Greenfinch		

(Himalayan Greenfinch)	r	*Carduelis spinoides*
Black-headed Greenfinch	r?	*Carduelis ambigua*
Eurasian Siskin	V	*Carduelis spinus*
Tibetan Siskin	?	*Carduelis thibetana*
European Goldfinch	r	*Carduelis carduelis*
Twite	r	*Carduelis flavirostris*
Eurasian Linnet	?	*Carduelis cannabina*
Plain Mountain Finch		
(Hodgson's Mountain Finch)	r	*Leucosticte nemoricola*
Brandt's Mountain Finch	r	*Leucosticte brandti*
Spectacled Finch		
(Red-browed Finch)	r	*Callacanthis burtoni*
Crimson-winged Finch	V	*Rhodopechys sanguinea*
Trumpeter Finch	w	*Bucanetes githagineus*
Mongolian Finch		
(Mongolian Trumpeter Bullfinch)	w	*Bucanetes mongolicus*
Blanford's Rosefinch	r	*Carpodacus rubescens*
Dark-breasted Rosefinch		
(Nepal Rosefinch)	r	*Carpodacus nipalensis*
Common Rosefinch	rW	*Carpodacus erythrinus*
Beautiful Rosefinch	r	*Carpodacus pulcherrimus*
Pink-browed Rosefinch	r	*Carpodacus rodochrous*
Vinaceous Rosefinch	r	*Carpodacus vinaceus*
Dark-rumped Rosefinch		
(Large Rosefinch)	r	*Carpodacus edwardsii*
Spot-winged Rosefinch	r	*Carpodacus rodopeplus*
White-browed Rosefinch	r	*Carpodacus thura*
Red-mantled Rosefinch	r	*Carpodacus rhodochlamys*
Streaked Rosefinch		
(Eastern Great Rosefinch)	r	*Carpodacus rubicilloides*
Great Rosefinch	r	*Carpodacus rubicilla*
Red-fronted Rosefinch		
(Red-breasted Rosefinch)	r	*Carpodacus puniceus*
Crimson-browed Finch		
(Red-headed Rosefinch)	r	*Propyrrhula subhimachala*
Scarlet Finch	r	*Haematospiza sipahi*
Red Crossbill (Crossbill)	r	*Loxia curvirostra*
Brown Bullfinch	r	*Pyrrhula nipalensis*
Orange Bullfinch	r	*Pyrrhula aurantiaca*
Red-headed Bullfinch	r	*Pyrrhula erythrocephala*
Grey-headed Bullfinch		
(Beavan's Bullfinch)	r	*Pyrrhula erythaca*
Hawfinch	w	*Coccothraustes coccothraustes*
Japanese Grosbeak	?	*Eophona personata*
Black-and-yellow Grosbeak	r	*Mycerobas icterioides*
Collared Grosbeak		
(Allied Grosbeak)	r	*Mycerobas affinis*
Spot-winged Grosbeak	r	*Mycerobas melanozanthos*

White-winged Grosbeak	r	*Mycerobas carnipes*
Gold-naped Finch		
(Gold-headed Black Finch)	r	*Pyrrhoplectes epauletta*

Emberizinae

Crested Bunting	R	*Melophus lathami*
Yellowhammer	V	*Emberiza citrinella*
Pine Bunting	w	*Emberiza leucocephalos*
Rock Bunting	r	*Emberiza cia*
Godlewski's Bunting	w?	*Emberiza godlewskii*
Grey-necked Bunting	w	*Emberiza buchanani*
Ortolan Bunting	V	*Emberiza hortulana*
White-capped Bunting		
(Chestnut-breasted Bunting)	rW	*Emberiza stewarti*
House Bunting		
(Striolated Bunting)	r	*Emberiza striolata*
Chestnut-eared Bunting		
(Grey-headed Bunting)	rw	*Emberiza fucata*
Little Bunting	w	*Emberiza pusilla*
Yellow-breasted Bunting	W	*Emberiza aureola*
Chestnut Bunting	w	*Emberiza rutila*
Black-headed Bunting	W	*Emberiza melanocephala*
Red-headed Bunting	W	*Emberiza bruniceps*
Black-faced Bunting	w	*Emberiza spodocephala*
Reed Bunting	rw	*Emberiza schoeniclus*
Corn Bunting	?	*Miliaria calandra*

The above checklist has been derived from AN ANNOTATED CHECKLIST OF THE BIRDS OF THE ORIENTAL REGION published by the Oriental Bird Club. Where major changes in names have taken place, the old names have been put in brackets. Changes in Latin names have not been indicated. The status reports have been incorporated by BIRDLINK, who will be interested to hear from readers on the subject.

Index of Scientific Names

Index of Common Names